SAVE OUR NATION

LESTER M. HADDAD, M. D.

CROSS PUBLICATIONS

SAVE OUR NATION

Library of Congress Catalog Card Number **99-94709**
ISBN **0-9670702-0-1**

You may order this book by phone **912-355-4200**,
    on the internet at www.saveournation.com,
    or write: Cross Publications
                      33 Noble Glen
                      Isle of Hope
                      Savannah, Georgia 31406

Cross Publications, in the interest of Christian unity, has included Bible passages from both Catholic and Protestant sources.

The primary sources of Scripture quotations from the Holy Bible are a family Catholic Douay-Rheims Bible, originally published in 1609, and the Authorized or King James Version of the Holy Bible, originally published in 1611.

Permission to publish Scripture quotations from the Revised Standard Version of the Holy Bible (copyright 1946, 1952, and 1971), including the Book of Revelation, has been granted by the Division of Christian Education of the National Council of the Churches of Christ. Used by permission. All rights reserved.

Scripture from The New Jerusalem Bible, copyright 1985 by Darton, Longman & Todd, Ltd, and Doubleday/Random House, is reprinted by permission.

Scripture quotations from the Catholic New American Bible with Revised New Testament and Psalms Copyright 1991, 1986, 1970 by the Confraternity of Christian Doctrine, 3211 Fourth St., N. E., Washington, D. C. 20017 are used by license of the copyright owner. All rights reserved. No part of the New American Bible may be reproduced in any form without permission from the copyright owner.

Cross Publications is an independent entity.

The views herein expressed are strictly those of the author.

DEDICATION

This book is dedicated to our sons, Matthew, Joseph, and Daniel Haddad; our late son Stephen; and our daughters Jeanne Robinson, Charlene Dimond, Elizabeth Anne and Madeleine Mary Haddad.

ACKNOWLEDGMENTS

The author expresses his gratitude to all who have helped him on this book: especially Father Douglas K. Clark, STL, Theologian to the Bishop of the Catholic Diocese of Savannah, Georgia, for his perceptive commentary, guidance, and review; Fr. Robert Mattingly, Pastor of St. Maximilian Kolbe Catholic Church in Port Charlotte, Florida; Matthew Haddad for his help on Chapter 4, The Bible; Dr. Stephen Miletic and Dr. Andrew Minto of the Department of Theology, Franciscan University in Steubenville, Ohio; Father Paul Walsh of St. Anthony Children's Home in Kingston, Jamaica; Carroll Cann, publisher of our Emergency Medicine textbook on Toxicology; Sister Mary Clarice of St. Joseph's Hospital and Daniel Haddad for their review; Elizabeth Anne Haddad for her secretarial support; Mary Whiteford Morgan for the graphic design of the dust jacket; Mary Tana for the photograph of Mary in Medjugorje; Mary Elizabeth Sperry for her attention to detail; our printers Tommy Lewis, Mark Saunders, and Chris Simmons; Roland Baldwin, Joseph Corcoran, Chuck Prouty, and all who help with distribution; my mother Sara Haddad; and Marilyn, Papa, and all of our family and friends for their enthusiasm and support.

TABLE OF CONTENTS

Introduction

Chapter 1	**1963**	**1**
Chapter 2	**Life in America**	**42**
Chapter 3	**An Emergency Physician's Viewpoint** **on Near-Death Experiences**	**74**
Chapter 4	**The Bible**	**96**
Chapter 5	**The Rosary and The Apparitions of Mary**	**136**
Chapter 6	**The Culture of Life**	**176**
Chapter 7	**SAVE OUR NATION**	**201**

Appendix   **A -1**
    References
    God Bless America

CHAPTER 1
1963

The 1950s were a wonderful time to grow up.   Anything that the United States wanted to do during this incredible decade turned out with a happy ending.   It was a time of peace. American ingenuity could solve any problem. We lived in the idyllic 1950s, living the American dream: the happy American family, husband, wife, and family enjoying life together.

When I was very young, all I remember is being at home with my mother, because Dad travelled a lot on his government job. We lived in a one-bedroom apartment, apartment 3, on the first floor, next door to Blessed Sacrament Grade School in Washington, D. C.   Mom and I loved each other very much. She was very sweet - when I was punished, she used to make me sit in the corner, but then she would stay with me and talk to me until punishment time was over. Mom used to wash the dishes, and I dried them. We used to say grace before dinner, and at bedtime we would say the prayer to our guardian angel. I asked her to stay with me until I fell asleep because I was afraid of the doorknob on the closet door. It was made of glass and looked like a big eye!

Early memories of childhood revolved around Christmas. My eyes lit up with joy when Santa Claus gave me a Lionel train when I was five years old. Every Christmas Santa would bring a new car or train switch for my growing railroad. Much of my early childhood was spent playing with the train, and listening to classical music with Mom.

The Christmas Eve when I was seven years old, I woke up in the middle of the night. I thought I heard Dad in the living room with my uncle. I looked over to Mom and Dad's bed, and Dad wasn't there. I thought I heard them playing with the train. I rolled over and went back to sleep. I remember thinking that I wished my uncle would go home, and Dad would go to bed, because Santa Claus doesn't come until everybody is asleep!

Being born and raised in Washington, D. C., part of my childhood was spent attending sporting events. Dad used to take me to the Washington Redskins football games. They weren't very good in the 1950s, but going to games was a lot of fun - there's nothing like a hot dog at a stadium! My neighborhood friends, Jackie and Packie Gaines, and I used to take the bus down to Griffith Stadium to see the Washington Senators baseball team sometimes on Saturdays. We had to pay a dollar to get in for a double-header, but you could get that much selling lemonade on Chevy Chase circle during the week.

On Sundays, Mom, Dad, and I would visit my mother's parents, Mama and Papa, after Church. Papa was very serious and quiet, but he was a kind man. He used to try to teach me different things. He always said I had to take my time eating meals because my stomach was only as big as my fist. Mama was funny and energetic, and we played cards together.

All we had in our home in the early 1950s was the radio. In addition to music, we listened to the evening radio shows such as "The Lone Ranger," "The Shadow Knows," "Amos 'n' Andy," and "The Jack Benny Show." "The Lone Ranger" was my favorite. After The Lone Ranger would say "Hi-yo, Silver away," you could hear his trusty sidekick Tonto cry out, "Get 'em up, Scout," before the stirring William Tell Overture began . I used to wonder how they could mix in the hoofbeats with the Overture so well. Tonto would always give wise Indian advice to "Kemo sabe," the lone and independent ranger who fought for law and order with his silver bullets, against all odds.

In 1953, when I was eleven years old, Dad brought home our first television set. I could finally see my childhood hero, The Lone Ranger, on ABC television. Clayton Moore played "The Lone Ranger", and Jay Silverheels played Tonto. We used to huddle around the television set as a family, watching our favorite shows, such as Ozzie and Harriet Nelson, David and Ricky on "The Adventures of Ozzie and Harriet;" "Abbott and Costello;" Jackie Gleason in "The Honeymooners;" and Lucille Ball in "I Love Lucy." In 1953 a new show started on ABC with Danny Thomas in "Make Room for Daddy." We never missed watching this show - Dad and I thought Uncle Tanoose was too funny for words.

On Tuesday night we all watched Bishop Fulton J. Sheen, and he reminded us "the family that prays together stays together." We used to say the rosary together. It only lasted 15 minutes, but it did give us a sense of family. We used to eat dinner together, but there were four of us at the table: Mom, Dad and I, and the TV set. With the rosary, the three of us relaxed together.

Living next door to Blessed Sacrament on Chevy Chase Circle was fun, because I could go home at lunch and work on my garden. Sometimes I would stay home until the school bell rang, and then run to the playground and get in line just in time for class. In the morning, we would line up on the playground, and Sister Annella and Sister Paul Marie, after having us say the Pledge of Allegiance to the Flag, would lead us in singing "God Bless America." It was mostly the girls that would do the singing, but it was beautiful.

At recess, we played a game called "bean-on-ball." Everybody would chase the guy that had the ball, and when he got caught, he would either lateral the ball or we would all pile on. When everybody got off, he threw the ball in the air, and then we would chase the guy who caught the ball. I used to love getting the ball, and would run through crowds so they had trouble catching me.

In 1955, when I turned thirteen, rock'n' roll exploded on the American scene with Bill Haley's "Rock Around the Clock." Elvis Presley followed with "Heartbreak Hotel" in 1956, and then "Don't Be Cruel," which was probably the only song ever to be number one on the popular, soul, and country charts at the same time. His rendition of "Hound Dog" on the Sunday night "Ed Sullivan Show" left parents appalled, but rock 'n' roll was here to stay. With the possible exception of "I was the One", a ballad on the flip side of "Heartbreak Hotel," and some of his later gospel music, Elvis was considered too wild for most parents.

The girl next door, Mary Fran, was wild about Ricky Nelson, and she liked him even more when he started singing songs like "Stood Up" (1957), "Poor Little Fool," (1958) and "It's Late (1959)." Ricky Nelson was from America's favorite TV family, and he was considered okay with America's parents.

Personally I had many favorite songs. I loved rhythm and blues, like the Penguins' "Earth Angel" (1955), the Five Satins' "In the Still of the Night" (1956), and the Clovers' "Devil or Angel" (1956). One of my all-time favorites was the song that was out for a year before it made it all the way to number one in 1958, Conway Twitty's "It's Only Make Believe." Paul Anka had "Diana" and "Don't Gamble With Love" (1957), and "Put Your Head on my Shoulder" (1959). Country music became popular with the Everly Brothers, "Bye, Bye, Love" (1957). I will never forget the 1959 two-sided hit by Ritchie Valens, "Donna" and "La Bamba." And every Friday night dance ended with Jesse Belvin's "Goodnight My Love" (1956).

Family vacations were a fun tradition. We used to drive from our home in Washington, D. C. to visit my father's parents every summer in Jacksonville, Florida. That was always a fun time, and lasted from when I was five (1947) to thirteen (1955).

My grandfather "Judoo" was my favorite. Every day he would take me to the ocean at Jacksonville Beach. My parents were always very nervous because Judoo was a terrible driver. One day he backed out of the driveway so fast we ran into the light pole on the other side of the street, and put a dent in his back bumper. Judoo got mad at the light pole and said the city should have put the light pole somewhere else. Somehow we always made it to Jacksonville Beach, and he would always buy me an ice cream cone.

Judoo was very wise, and on the way to the beach told me Jacksonville one day would be built up all the way to the beach. He used to tell me never to spend more than I make, and then I would always be free.

Judoo had a strong sense of right and wrong, and used to get mad at the bad guys in the westerns on Footlight theatre which was on TV from 5 to 6 in the evening. When he played cards and backgammon with his friends, he would always put a chair for me to sit next to him. Judoo never got mad at me. His eyes would light up and he would smile whenever I came around.

The summer of 1958, when I was 15, my cousin Pat got my friend Frank and I a job with the *Army Times*. They wanted to increase subscriptions, and agreed to pay us 1 and 1/4 cents for every name we could give them to increase their mailing list. We went down to the Library of Congress and started going through City Directories. The first week we only came up with about 100 names. What a waste - $1.25 for one week's work! The next week for some reason I picked out Groton, Connecticut, and nearly every name had USN after it. We picked names like Jones, Smith, Johnson, and Williams and began using ditto marks, and collected a whole bunch of names. We finally figured out to pick towns with a large military population. The next city we did was Newport News. The second week we made almost $100.00! The summer of 1958 was a real bonanza to Frank and me! The next summer, the Army Times decided they were better off to put me on salary and stuck me in the mail room for $1.00 an hour, but that was okay. When I turned 17 on September 7th, 1959, I had saved enough money and bought my own car, a '53 Chevy, and was I proud! Mary Fran loved my new car. I guess that's when I realized that Mary Fran liked me. I always thought of her as my kid sister, the one I never had. I never would have considered taking her out. She was more of a friend, well, the girl next door.

The quiet 1950s were a great time. A simple, fun time, when everything worked out. Growing up in the 1950s was life in a trouble-free society. Maybe it was because of all the turmoil of World War II, and the Nation wanted a quiet and trouble-free era. Maybe it was because America had great confidence in its ability to solve any problem that came our way. Or it was because we all had a great faith in God, and America was a very family-oriented society, reflected in the wholesomeness of the television shows. But for whatever reason, it was a wonderful time to grow up.

In September of 1960, I began my first year at Holy Cross College in Massachusetts. We were all very excited with the elections that year, because John F. Kennedy was running for President. He was young, bright, energetic, and captured the imagination of the young.

During World War II Jack Kennedy became a war hero. He was commander of a Navy Patrol boat PT-109 in the South Pacific. During a night attack on August 2, 1943, a Japanese destroyer rammed PT-109 and split her in two, instantly killing two of the crew. One of his crew, Patrick McMahon, was wounded, and Jack, in spite of a back injury, swam four hours pulling the man on his back, held in place by gripping a strap of the man's life jacket held between his teeth. Jack, the wounded man, and nine others held on to wreckage and had to swim three miles before they reached the nearest island. After no one came, Jack led a small party and swam to two other islands, and finally found natives who happened to be in the employ of an Australian Navy coastwatcher. They were finally rescued on August 7th. For his heroism and leadership, he received the Navy and Marine Corps Medal.

When his brother Joe was shot down and died in a flying mission on August 12, 1944, Jack was called on to fulfill his father's political aspirations. He reluctantly ran and won a Massachusetts House seat in 1946, and upset Republican Henry Cabot Lodge Jr. in 1952 to become U. S. Senator from Massachusetts. While a Senator recovering from back surgery in 1955, he wrote a book called *Profiles in Courage,* describing men in political life who stood up for what was right in the face of the majority, men such as John Quincy Adams, Daniel Webster, and Robert A. Taft.

It was the Kennedy-Nixon television debates that won him the uphill battle for the election. Kennedy came across with charisma, decisiveness, an excellent delivery, and portrayed the sense he would move the country forward with his "New Frontier." These 4 debates were the first television debates, and there was a true debate of the issues.

November 8, 1960 was election night, and it was one of the most exciting elections ever. We stayed up all night!

Both Kennedy and Nixon went to bed at 3 in the morning. At 3:17 a. m. Mr. Nixon stated "I did the best I can." Kennedy was barely ahead with only a few hundred thousand of the popular vote, but not yet having enough electoral votes to win. It was not until 8 a. m. the following morning when he seemed safely ahead in California that he was proclaimed the President-elect.

John F. Kennedy became the 35th President of the United States. His inaugural address on January 20, 1961 showed his energy, his eloquence, his idealism and his leadership, in a speech which became instantly famous, the beginning of a New Frontier:

"We observe today not a victory of a party but a celebration of freedom - symbolizing an end as well as a beginning - signifying renewal as well as change. For I have sworn before you and Almighty God the same solemn oath our forebears prescribed nearly a century and three quarters ago.

The world is very different now. For man holds in his mortal hands the power to abolish all forms of human poverty and all forms of human life.

And yet the same revolutionary beliefs for which our forebears fought are still at issue around the globe - the belief that the rights of man come not from the generosity of the state but from the hand of God.

We dare not forget today that we are the heirs of that first revolution. **Let the word go forth from this time and place, to friend and foe alike, that the torch has been passed to a new generation of Americans - born in this century, tempered by war, disciplined by a hard and bitter peace, proud of our ancient heritage - and unwilling to witness or permit the slow undoing of those human rights to which this Nation has always been committed, and to which we are committed today at home and around the world.**

Let every nation know, whether it wishes us well or ill, that we shall pay any price, bear any burden, meet any hardship, support any friend, oppose any foe to assure the survival and success of liberty.

This much we pledge - and more. To those old allies whose cultural and spiritual origins we share, we pledge the loyalty of faithful friends. United, there is little we cannot do in a host of cooperative ventures. Divided, there is little we can do - for we dare not meet a powerful challenge at odds and split asunder.

To those new states whom we welcome to the ranks of the free, we pledge our word that one form of colonial control shall not have passed away merely to be replaced by a far more iron tyranny. We shall not always expect to find them supporting our view. But we shall always hope to find them strongly supporting their own freedom - and to remember that, in the past, those who foolishly sought power by riding the back of the tiger ended up inside.

To those people in the huts and villages of half the globe struggling to break the bonds of mass misery, we pledge our best efforts to help them help themselves, for whatever period is required - not because the Communists may be doing it, not because we seek their votes, but because it is right. If a free society cannot help the many who are poor, it cannot save the few who are rich.

To our sister republics south of our border, we offer a special pledge - to convert our good words into good deeds - in a new alliance for progress -to assist free men and free governments in casting off the chains of poverty.

But this peaceful revolution of hope cannot become the prey of hostile powers. Let all our neighbors know that we shall join with them to oppose aggression or subversion anywhere in the Americas. And let every other power know that this hemisphere intends to remain the master of its own house.

To that world assembly of sovereign states, the United Nations, our last best hope in an age where the instruments of war have far outpaced the instruments of peace, we renew our pledge of support - to prevent it from becoming merely a forum for invective - to strengthen its shield of the new and the weak - and to enlarge the area in which its writ may run.

Finally, to those nations who would make themselves our adversary, we offer not a pledge but a request: that both sides begin anew the quest for peace, before the dark powers of destruction unleashed by science engulf all humanity in planned or accidental self-destruction.

We dare not tempt them with weakness. For only when our arms are sufficient beyond doubt can we be certain beyond doubt that they will never be deployed.

But neither can two great and powerful groups of nations take comfort from our present course - both sides overburdened by the cost of modern weapons, both rightly alarmed by the steady spread of the deadly atom, yet both racing to alter that uncertain balance of terror that stays the hand of mankind's final war.

So let us begin anew - remembering on both sides that civility is not a sign of weakness, and sincerity is always subject to proof. Let us never negotiate out of fear. But let us never fear to negotiate.

Let both sides explore what problems unite us instead of belaboring those problems which divide us. Let both sides, for the first time, formulate serious and precise proposals for the inspection and control of arms - and bring the absolute power to destroy other nations under the absolute control of all nations.

Let both sides seek to invoke the wonders of science instead of its terrors. Together let us explore the stars, conquer the deserts, eradicate disease, tap the ocean depths, and encourage the arts and commerce.

Let both sides unite to heed in all corners of the earth the command of Isaiah [58:7]- to "undo the heavy burdens ... and let the oppressed go free."

And if a beach-head of cooperation may push back the jungle of suspicion, let both sides join in a new endeavor: creating not a new balance of power, but a new world of law, where the strong are just and the weak secure and the peace preserved.

All this will not be finished in the first one hundred days. Nor will it be finished in the first one thousand days, nor in the life of this Administration, nor even perhaps in our lifetime on this planet. But let us begin.

In your hands, my fellow citizens, more than mine, will rest the final success or failure of our course. Since this country was founded, each generation of Americans has been summoned to give testimony to its national loyalty. The graves of young Americans who answered the call to service surround the globe.

Now the trumpet summons us again - not as a call to bear arms, though arms we need - not as a call to battle, though embattled we are - but a call to bear the long twilight struggle, year in and year out, "rejoicing in hope, patient in tribulation" - a struggle against the common enemies of man: tyranny, poverty, disease and war itself.

Can we forge against these enemies a grand and global alliance, North and South, East and West, that can assure a more fruitful life for all mankind?

Will you join in that historic effort?

In the long history of the world, only a few generations have been granted the role of defending freedom in its hour of maximum danger. I do not shrink from this responsibility - I welcome it. I do not believe that any of us would exchange places with any other people or any other generation.

The energy, the faith, the devotion which we bring in this endeavor will light our country and all who serve it - and the glow from that fire can truly light the world.

And so, my fellow Americans: Ask not what your country can do for you - ask what you can do for your country.

My fellow citizens of the world: Ask not what America will do for you, but what together we can do for the freedom of man.

Finally, whether you are citizens of America or citizens of the world, ask of us here the same high standards of strength and sacrifice which we ask of you. With a good conscience our only sure reward, with history the final judge of our deeds, let us go forth to lead the land we love, asking His blessing and His help, but knowing that here on earth God's work must truly be our own."

His first major action as President was starting the Peace Corps in March of 1961. This was met with great enthusiasm and many young people agreed to serve. Perhaps because he was the first President to come from a minority, he was open and accepting of people from all races. The first year of his presidency was an exciting year.

Russia had orbited the first satellite Sputnik in 1958 and the Russian Yuri Gagarin became the first man in space in the Sputnik Vostok on April 12, 1961. The first American in space was Alan Shepard on May 23, 1961. President Kennedy called for placing a man on the moon by the end of the decade.

On April 17, 1961, CIA-organized anti-Castro Cubans invaded Cuba, and met with disastrous defeat. When Fidel Castro became Premier of Cuba in 1959,

President Eisenhower was faced with thousands of Cuban refugees. Several began forming small groups in Miami to plan to recover their homeland. In 1960, President Eisenhower, in his last year of office, placed Vice-President Nixon in charge of a CIA covert action committee to oversee the effort to organize these groups by CIA leaders. Even though the planning was prior to his term of office, President Kennedy assumed responsibility for the fiasco.

Russian leader Nikita Khrushchev met with President Kennedy in the spring of 1961, and apparently was not impressed with our young President. Khrushchev shortly thereafter erected the Berlin Wall almost overnight. But President Kennedy insisted on free access to Berlin from West Germany, a free Berlin, and the presence of Allied troops in Berlin. He backed his words with action by sending an armored troop division from West Germany across the Autobahn in serials of 60 trucks each right into Berlin. This heightened world tension and produced international headlines, but the troops made it to West Berlin without a shot being fired. This action recovered Kennedy's confidence. He was elected Time's Man of the Year in 1961.

Martin Luther King came to lecture at Holy Cross College the spring of 1961. Dr. King was a black Baptist minister who received attention when he was asked to lead a Negro boycott of the Montgomery, Alabama segregated bus system in 1955. That year Rosa Parks was arrested because she disobeyed a city law and the custom of the times by refusing to move to the back of the bus to give her seat to a white person. This event triggered the boycott, and Martin Luther King gave his first speech, in which he called the "great glory of American democracy is the right to protest for right." The boycott continued until 1956, when the Supreme Court ordered Montgomery, Alabama to have equal and integrated seating on city buses.

There was great tension the night that Martin Luther King spoke. The faculty and administration were worried about the impact of his lecture, and the student body did not know what to expect. Was he going to chastise us for our prejudice? Was he going to be angry and verbally assault us? I was very inter-ested in what he had to say. I got there early and was in the second row. While he had not yet achieved national fame at that point, he was somebody that everyone was just beginning to hear about.

We grew up with prejudice. While we conceptually believed that black people should have the same life as us, we were very uncomfortable with the practice. Prejudice was very much alive in my childhood.

There was a sense of relief and pleasant surprise after his speech on racial equality. We were all very deeply moved. Martin Luther King had a real presence about him. He conveyed a feeling of caring and a strong sense of right and wrong and he did it in an intellectual and gentlemanly way. He spoke from our Christian beliefs, and from our national heritage. After the speech I was privileged enough to meet him and always maintained a deep respect for him.

The popular music of 1961 reflected the energy and the enthusiasm of the times, such as Del Shannon's "Runaway", the Marcels' "Blue Moon", and Dion and the Belmonts' "Runaround Sue". Everyone had a laugh with Ernie K. Doe's "Mother-in-law". And then there was the beautiful ballad by the Shirelles, "Will You Still Love Me Tomorrow".

October 22, 1962 was a frightening day. President Kennedy faced the Cuban Missile Crisis and for nine days the world stood on the brink of nuclear war. In a series of outstanding decisions, President Kennedy showed the man he was and literally saved our country, all without a shot being fired. Nikita Khrushchev underestimated the character of our youthful President and had secretly undertaken a Soviet military buildup on the island of Cuba. A series of offensive missile sites with nuclear strike capability against our country were in preparation on the island. Here are key parts of the text from President Kennedy's White House speech of October 22, 1962 to the nation on the Cuban Missile Crisis:

> "This Government, as promised, has maintained the closest surveillance of the Soviet military buildup on the island of Cuba. Within the past week, unmistakable evidence has established the fact that a series of offensive missile sites is now in preparation on that imprisoned island. The purpose of these bases can be none other than to provide a nuclear strike capability against the Western hemisphere.

President Kennedy then presented his plan of action:

> "Acting, therefore, in the defense of our own security and of the entire Western Hemisphere, and under the authority entrusted to me by the Constitution as endorsed by the resolution of the Congress, I have directed that the following initial steps be taken immediately:

*First: To halt this offensive buildup, a strict quarantine on all offensive military equipment under shipment to Cuba is being initiated. All ships of any kind bound for Cuba from whatever nation or port will, if found to contain cargoes of offensive weapons, be turned back. This quarantine will be extended, if needed, to other types of cargo and carriers. We are not at this time, however, denying the necessities of life as the Soviets attempted to do in their Berlin blockade of 1948.

*Second: I have directed the continued and increased close sur-veillance of Cuba and its military buildup. The foreign ministers of the OAS, in their communique of October 6th, rejected secrecy on such matters in this hemisphere. Should these offensive military preparations continue, thus increasing the threat to the hemi-sphere, further action will be justified. I have directed the Armed Forces to be prepared for any eventualities; and I trust that in the interest of both the Cuban people and the Soviet technicians at the sites, the hazards ...of continuing this threat will be recognized.

*Third: It shall be the policy of this Nation to regard any nuclear missile launched from Cuba against any nation in the Western Hemisphere as an attack by the Soviet Union on the United States, requiring a full retaliatory response upon the Soviet Union..."

When President Kennedy said "any nuclear missile launched from Cuba...," many nervously laughed at his accent as he pronounced it "Cuber." Nobody said a word when he finished the sentence, "requiring a full retaliatory response upon the Soviet Union." Everyone knew this could be the big one.

Fearing a nuclear war, we asked our loved ones to come up to Holy Cross early for the upcoming Homecoming weekend. But we all supported our President, and we had complete trust in him.   We knew he would do what was right.

And sure enough President Kennedy came through. The missiles were removed ensuring the safety of our country and the American way. Nikita Khrushchev saved face by achieving removal of our Jupiter missiles in Turkey.

And, once again, America won. America was successful by facing the truth, seeing right from wrong, and meeting the crisis head on. I believe this was what made America great. Unfortunately, the Cuban Missile Crisis was probably the last time America responded in a noble and courageous fashion.

I will never forget **1963**.

1963 was a year of powerful events.

Our nation and our world changed in 1963. I personally find this a pivotal year in the history of the United States. We would never be the same after 1963. Our ability and confidence as leaders of the free world, our faith and trust in our Federal government, our morals and our ability to distinguish right from wrong began to end in 1963.

1963 was a year of powerful speeches.

These speeches address the founding principles of our Nation, namely that each individual human being has certain unalienable rights, and that all men are created equal.

The men that gave these speeches, John Fitzgerald Kennedy and Martin Luther King, were each gunned down in separate and tragic events. They gave us racial equality. They died for our freedom.

I urge you to take the time to read these important speeches.

Our modern society lives in the Information Age, as we struggle daily to keep up with all the latest news. While we are mesmerized if not overwhelmed by the deluge of facts, we have become accustomed to small packets of information at a time. The outcome of this is a markedly diminished attention span, for we have little patience to look in-depth at any given situation. For example, because people become bored, restless, and move on to something else, a key factor in the success of an internet web-site is a loading time of 15-30 seconds or less!

Unfortunately, our fast-forward society allows us little time to think and reflect. We are becoming a society of passive viewers, easily led - and manipulated - by the media. And this is one of the reasons we are in such a tragic state of affairs today.

The United States of America has a clear choice as we enter the new millennium: are we going to respect the God-given rights of the individual, or are we going to become faceless, numbered humans in the godless one-world order of the United Nations, ruled by a powerful few?

The subtle slide to a one-world order can only be prevented by making an effort to remember the Biblical foundation of our nation. We must take the time to reflect, to look back, and to stand up for our rich national heritage, for our founding principles, principles addressed in these wonderful speeches.

The speeches of 1963 impact our lives today.

The Cuban missile crisis signaled the end of the tranquil fifties, and set the stage for the events of 1963.

January 2, 1963 the Viet Cong downed five U. S. helicopters in the Mekong Delta leaving 30 American servicemen dead. Our country knew little about Vietnam up until this time. Following World War II, there was a struggle for power in Vietnam between the Communists in the North, and the French in the South. War broke out, and a peace settlement in 1954 divided Vietnam into Communist North Vietnam and the Nationalist South Vietnam. Over one million Catholic refugees fled Northern Vietnam for the safety of South Vietnam, led by Catholic President Ngo Dinh Diem. In 1957, Communists in South Vietnam, known as the Viet Cong, began resisting the leadership of President Diem, and were supported by Communist North Vietnam. The United States under President Eisenhower began sending military advisors and the Central Intelligence Agency (CIA) to South Vietnam as early as 1957! The Communists' Viet Cong stepped up elusive warfare efforts against Pro-Western governments in Vietnam and Laos in early 1961. In fact, President Kennedy had sent military advisors in the spring of 1961 to help train both the Laotian army (March 21, 1961) and the South Vietnamese army (May 13, 1961). The presence of military advisors in Laos and South Vietnam hardly received attention at home as we were all focused on the space race.

On January 7, 1963 the U. S. Post Office raised the cost of sending a letter to 5 cents. This was a big deal to those of us in college as it represented a 25% increase.

In early 1963, nobody could believe the San Francisco Giants paid $100,000 to sign Willie Mays for the upcoming baseball season. Not to be out-done, the New York Yankees signed on Mickey Mantle for the same figure. Granted, they were the two best baseball players in the country, but imagine paying $100,000 a year for a baseball player!

The Cuban missile crisis was being resolved on the political front. Premier Khrushchev had pulled out all nuclear missiles and bombers from Cuba, and had bulldozed the missile sites, despite Fidel Castro's pleas. Castro feared an attack from the United States even though President Kennedy made assurances to the contrary. On February 18, 1963, Premier Khrushchev promised that several thousand Soviet troops would be withdrawn by March 15, 1963.

However, an undercurrent of resistance fueled by anti-Castro Cubans, supported by the Miami office of the CIA, impeded the pullout of Soviet troops.

The CIA had continued covert operations against Fidel Castro, and had been training anti-Castro Cubans in Agency training camps in Florida's No-Name Key and Lake Pontchartrain, Louisiana. President Kennedy, as Presidents Truman and Eisenhower before him, gradually became aware of the alarming power of CIA covert military action, and planned to reign in the CIA.

Reacting to an anti-Castro Cuban attack on the Soviet ship *L'Gov* in Cuba, President Kennedy, on March 21, 1963, criticized recent attacks on Cuba by Cuban "exiles," saying that the raids only "strengthened the Russian position in Cuba."

In spite of President Kennedy's statement, on March 26, 1963, an anti-Castro group L-66 proceeded to attack and sink the Soviet ship *Baku* as it loaded Cuban sugar at the harbor of Caibarien, Cuba. The assault on the *Baku* led Khrushchev to accept Castro's plea to leave some Soviet military troops in Cuba.

Betty Friedan published a book in 1963 entitled *The Feminine Mystique*. She later became founder of the National Organization of Women, a vocal group for women's rights, and is considered a pioneer in the women's liberation movement.

Discord over the civil rights movement came to the forefront in 1963. Of all the issues of his Presidency, none was more bitterly resisted by the public than President Kennedy's efforts for civil rights. Theodore "Ted" Sorensen, who served as Special Counsel to the President, wrote in his 1965 book *Kennedy:* "In 1963 the Negro revolution in America rose more rapidly than ever before. John Kennedy did not start that revolution and nothing he could have done could have stopped it... But he was deeply and fervently committed to the cause of human rights as a moral necessity."

Racial tension had been building in the South, and intensified in Mississippi in September of 1962, when the negro James Meredith tried to gain entrance into the University of Mississippi. Governor Ross Barnett of Mississippi, initially defiant of Federal law, capitulated and allowed entrance of James Meredith into the all-white, segregated University of Mississippi. But the incident brought domestic violence, and the Mississippi National Guard had to be employed to ensure Meredith's entrance and his attendance of college classes.

The events in Mississippi only served to heighten racial tension in 1963. Those of us at Holy Cross were shocked when the Reverend Martin Luther King was arrested in Birmingham, Alabama on April 12, 1963, following a peace march with Reverend Ralph Abernathy in the streets of Birmingham.   In his famous letter from a Birmingham jail addressed to his fellow ministers on April 16, 1963, he stated, "We will reach the goal of freedom in Birmingham, and all over the nation, because the goal of America is freedom...If the inexpressible cruelties of slavery could not stop us, the opposition we now face will surely fail...We will win our freedom because of the sacred heritage of our Nation and the eternal will of God are echoed in our echoing demands."

The issue of school segregation began to divide our country and the focal point was the state of Alabama. Governor George Wallace, a white supremacist, refused to allow segregation in defiance of Federal integration laws. The strident figure for the blacks was Malcolm X. Our age group felt that both George Wallace and Malcolm X, who were diametrically opposed to each other, were extremists.   Martin Luther King called for peaceful, non-violent demonstrations and President Kennedy reminded us that all men are created equal and that Negroes should have the opportunity to attend good schools and colleges like everybody else. Once again Martin Luther King and John F. Kennedy were the voices of fairness and moderation.

President Kennedy sent his brother Attorney General Robert Kennedy to Birmingham to meet with Alabama Governor George Wallace on April 25, 1963. Governor Wallace remained in defiance of United States laws and refused to allow integration in Alabama schools. Robert Kennedy left frustrated, and was quoted, "It's like a foreign country. There's no communication."

On May 2, 1963 about 500 Negroes, many of them students and children marched in peaceful demonstration, and were hauled off to jail. The next day more students marched, and white bystanders threw bricks and bottles. The Birmingham police turned fire hoses on the marchers, and Birmingham Police Chief Eugene "Bull" Connor released police dogs on the marchers, many of them children. Newspapers throughout the United States and around the world re-leased a shocking photograph of a police dog lunging at a Negro woman.

The situation became so bad in Alabama that for the first time since the Civil War President Kennedy had to send federal troops to Alabama on May 18, 1963. Civil unrest spread throughout the South.   On May 21, 1963 a Federal judge ruled the University of Alabama must admit two Negroes to its summer session in June.

June of 1963 was a pivotal month for President Kennedy and for our Nation. The President gave two historic speeches within 24 hours, one on world peace on June 10, 1963, and one on civil rights on June 11, 1963. And the Supreme Court made its controversial decision on school prayer on June 17, 1963.

The Cuban missile crisis had a *profound* effect on the world. The sudden threat of nuclear war and the possibility of nuclear holocaust made all the leaders of the world pause and realize how fragile our world had become, especially the leaders of the two great world powers. Russian Chairman Nikita Khrushchev had retreated from Cuba and from his quest for world domination. And President Kennedy saw the need to restore communication with Khrushchev, in the hopes of reaching detente with Russia and hopefully beginning an initiative for world peace. He presented the first of three speeches on world peace at the Commencement Address at American University in Washington, D. C. on June 10, 1963, an historic speech in which he extended his hand in a gesture of peace to Russia. President Kennedy opened his speech calling "world peace the rational end of rational men." He then was gracious to Russia:

> *No government or social system is so evil that its people must be considered as lacking in virtue.* As Americans, we find communism profoundly repugnant as a negation of personal freedom and dignity. But we can still hail the Russian people for their many achievements - in science and space, in economic and industrial growth, in culture and in acts of courage.
>
> Among the many traits the peoples of our two countries have in common, none is stronger than our mutual abhorrence of war. Almost unique among the major world powers, we have never been at war with each other. And no nation in the history of battle ever suffered more than the Soviet Union suffered in the course of the Second World War. At least 20 million lost their lives. Countless millions of home and farms were burned or sacked. A third of the nation's territory, including nearly two thirds of its industrial base, was turned into a wasteland - a loss equivalent to the devastation of this country east of Chicago.
>
> Today, should total war ever break out again - no matter how - our two countries would become the primary targets.

It is an ironic but accurate fact that the two strongest powers are the two in the most danger of devastation. All we have built, all we have worked for, would be destroyed in the first 24 hours. And even in the cold war, which brings burdens and dangers to so many nations, including this Nation's closest allies - our two countries bear the heaviest burdens. For we are both devoting massive sums of money to weapons that could be better devoted to combating ignorance, poverty, and disease. We are both caught up in a vicious and dangerous cycle in which suspicion on one side breeds suspicion on the other, and new weapons beget counterweapons.

In short, both the United States and its allies, and the Soviet Union and its allies, have a mutually deep interest in a just and genuine peace and in halting the arms race. Agreements to this end are in the interests of the Soviet Union as well as ours - and even the most hostile nations can be relied upon to accept and keep those treaty obligations, and only those treaty obligations, which are in their own interest.

So, let us not be blind to our differences - but let us also direct attention to our common interests and to the means by which those differences can be resolved. And if we cannot end now our differences, at least we can help make the world safe for diversity.

For, in the final analysis, our most basic common link is that we all inhabit this small planet. We all breathe the same air. We all cherish our children's future. And we are all mortal.

Third: let us reexamine our attitude toward the cold war, remembering that we are not engaged in a debate, seeking to pile up debating points. We are not here distributing blame or pointing the finger of judgement. **We must deal with the world as it is,** and not as it might have been had the history of the last 18 years been different.

The President then announced a plan for a nuclear test ban treaty.

First: Chairman Khrushchev, Prime Minister MacMillan, and I have agreed that high-level discussions will shortly begin in Moscow looking toward early agreement on a comprehensive test ban treaty. Our hopes must be tempered with the caution of history - but with our hopes go the hopes of all mankind.

Second: to make clear our good faith and solemn convictions on the matter, I now declare that the United States does not propose to conduct nuclear tests in the atmosphere so long as other states do not do so. We will not be the first to resume. Such a declaration is no substitute for a formal binding treaty, but I hope it will help us achieve it.

Finally, my fellow Americans, let us examine our attitude toward peace and freedom here at home. The quality and spirit of our own society must justify and support our efforts abroad. We must show it in the dedication of our own lives - as many of you who are graduating today will have a unique opportunity to do, by serving without pay in the Peace Corps abroad or in the proposed National Service Corps here at home.

But wherever we are, we must all, in our daily lives, live up to the age-old faith that peace and freedom walk together. In too many of our cities today, the peace is not secure because the freedom is incomplete.

It is the responsibility of the executive branch at all levels of government - local, State, and National - to provide and protect that freedom for all of our citizens by all means within their authority. It is the responsibility of the legislative branch at all levels, wherever that authority is not now adequate, to make it adequate. And it is the responsibility of all citizens in all sections of this country to respect the rights of all others and to respect the law of the land.

All this is not unrelated to world peace. 'When a man's way pleases the Lord,' the Scripture [Proverbs 16:7] tells us, 'he maketh even his enemies to be at peace with him.' And is not peace, in the last analysis, basically a matter of human rights - the right to live out our lives without fear of devastation - the right to breathe air as nature provided it - the right of future generations to a healthy existence?

While we proceed to safeguard our national interests, let us also safeguard human interests. And the elimination of war and arms is clearly in the interest of both. No treaty, however much it may be to the advantage of all, however tightly it may be worded, can provide absolute security against the risks of deception and evasion. But it can - if it is sufficiently effective in its enforcement and if it is sufficiently in the interests of its signers - offer far more security and far fewer risks than an...unpredictable arms race.

The United States, as the world knows, will never start a war. We do not want a war. We do not now expect a war. This generation of Americans has already had enough - more than enough - of war and hate and oppression. We shall be prepared if others wish it. We shall be alert to try to stop it. But we shall also do our part to build a world of peace where the weak are safe and the strong are just. We are not helpless before that task or hopeless of its success. Confident and unafraid, we labor on - not toward a strategy of annihilation but toward a strategy of peace."

Chairman Khrushchev of Russia was deeply moved by the American University speech, and, according to Arthur Schlesinger in his 1965 book *A Thousand Days,* told American envoy Averell Harriman "with evident feeling that it was 'the greatest speech by any American president since Roosevelt.'" A nuclear test-ban treaty, which had been resisted for years , was reached within 6 weeks between the United States and Russia!   President Kennedy announced this treaty in his second speech on peace in a television address to the American people on July 26, 1963, in which he stated, "...now, for the first time in many years, the path of peace may be open."

On June 11, 1963, the day following the American University speech on peace, Governor George Wallace personally blocked the entry of Negro students and federal marshals into the administration building of the University of Alabama in Tuscaloosa. President Kennedy immediately commandeered the Alabama National Guard and sent troops onto campus, and Governor Wallace backed down. Finally after months of defiance, two Negroes, Vivian Malone and James Hood, entered the University of Alabama in Tuscaloosa.

The evening of June 11, 1963, President Kennedy gave a television address to the Nation and expressed the hope that every American would examine his conscience, and announced he would submit his historic Civil Rights legislation the following week to Congress, his historic *Civil Rights Speech,* presented here in its entirety (see page 22):

EVENTS OF 1963

January 2	Vietnam Viet Cong down 5 helicopters, 30 US men dead.
April 12	Martin Luther King arrested in Birmingham after peace march.
May 13	US Military advisors sent to Vietnam.
June 10	President Kennedy gave first speech on peace in Washington.
June 11	George Wallace blocked entry of black students in Alabama.
June 11	President Kennedy gave historic civil rights speech.
June 17	200 years of public school prayer and Bible readings end.
July 26	Second Kennedy peace speech on Nuclear test ban treaty
July 30	60,000 Buddhists march in protest of Diem government.
August 28	Martin Luther King gave historic "I have a dream" speech.
September 3	President Kennedy expressed concerns about Vietnam.
September 20	President Kennedy gave third speech on world peace.
October 11	President Kennedy directive to remove US military in Vietnam.
November 1	Assassination of President Diem of Vietnam.
November 22	President Kennedy is shot dead in Dealey Plaza in Dallas.
November 23	The country and the whole world mourn our President's death.
November 24	The President is laid in state in the Capitol Rotunda.
November 25	John Kennedy Jr., age 3, salutes his father in funeral parade.
November 26	Lyndon Johnson directive to expand US military in Vietnam.

"Good evening, my fellow citizens:

This afternoon, following a series of threats and defiant statements, the presence of Alabama National Guardsmen was required on the University of Alabama campus to carry out the final and unequivocal order of the United States District Court of the Northern District of Alabama. That order called for the admission of two clearly qualified young Alabama residents who happened to have been born Negro.

That they were admitted peacefully on the campus is due in good measure to the conduct of the students of the University of Alabama, who met their responsibilities in a constructive way.

I hope that every American, regardless of where he lives, will stop and examine his conscience about this and other related incidents. This Nation was founded by men of many nations and backgrounds.

It was founded on the principle that all men are created equal, and that the rights of every man are diminished when the rights of one man are threatened.

Today we are committed to a worldwide struggle to promote and protect the rights of all who wish to be free. And when Americans are sent to Viet-Nam or West Berlin, we do not ask for whites only. It ought to be possible, therefore, for American students of any color to attend any public institution they select without having to be backed up by troops.

It ought to be possible for American consumers of any color to receive equal service in places of public accommodation, such as hotels and restaurants and theaters and retail stores, without being forced to resort to demonstrations in the street, and it ought to be possible for American citizens of any color to register and to vote in a free election without interference or fear of reprisal.

It ought to be possible, in short, for every American to enjoy the privileges of being American without regard to his race or his color. In short, every American ought to have the right to be treated as he would wish to be treated, as one would wish his children to be treated.

But this is not the case.

The Negro baby born in America today, regardless of the section of the Nation in which he is born, has about one-half as much chance of completing a high school as a white baby born in the same place on the same day, one-third as much chance of completing college, one-third as much chance of becoming a professional man, twice as much chance of becoming unemployed, about one-seventh as much chance of earning $10,000 a year, a life expectancy which is 7 years shorter, and the prospects of earning only half as much.

This is not a sectional issue. Difficulties over segregation and discrimination exist in every city, in every State of the Union, producing in many cities a rising tide of discontent that threatens the public safety. Nor is this a partisan issue. In a time of domestic crisis men of good will and generosity should be able to unite regardless of party or politics. This is not even a legal or legislative issue alone. It is better to settle these matters in the courts than on the streets, and new laws are needed at every level, but law alone cannot make men see right.

We are confronted primarily with a moral issue. It is as old as the Scriptures and is as clear as the American Constitution.

The heart of the question is whether all Americans are to be afforded equal rights and equal opportunities, whether we are going to treat our fellow Americans as we want to be treated. If an American, because his skin is dark, cannot eat lunch in a restaurant open to the public, if he cannot send his children to the best public school available, if he cannot vote for the public officials who represent him, if, in short, he cannot enjoy the full and free life which all of us want, then who among us would be content to have the color of his skin changed and stand in his place? Who among us would then be content with the counsels of patience and delay?

One hundred years of delay have passed since President Lincoln freed the slaves, yet their heirs, their grandsons, are not fully free. They are not yet fully freed from social and economic oppression. And this Nation, for all its hopes and all its boasts, will not be fully free untill all its citizens are free.

We preach freedom around the world, and we mean it, and we cherish our freedom here at home, but are we to say to the world, and much more importantly, to each other that this is a land of the free except for the Negroes; that we have no second-class citizens except Negroes; that we have no class or caste system, no ghettoes, no master race except with respect to Negroes?

Now the time has come for this Nation to fulfill its promise. The events in Birmingham and elsewhere have so increased the cries for equality that no city or State or legislative body can prudently choose to ignore them.

The fires of frustration and discord are burning in every city, North and South, where legal remedies are not at hand. Redress is sought in the streets, in demonstrations, parades, and protests which create tensions and threaten violence and threaten lives. We face, therefore, a moral crisis as a country and as a people. It cannot be met by a repressive police action. It cannot be left to increased demonstrations in the streets. It cannot be quieted by token moves or talk. It is a time to act in the Congress, in your State and local legislative body and, above all, in all of our daily lives.

It is not enough to pin the blame on others, to say this is a problem of one section of the country or another, or deplore the facts that we face. A great change is at hand, and our task, our obligation, is to make that revolution, that change, peaceful and constructive for all.

Those who do nothing are inviting shame as well as violence. Those who act boldly are recognizing right as well as reality.

Next week I shall ask the Congress of the United States to act, to make a commitment it has not fully made in this century to the proposition that **race has no place in American life or law.** The Federal judiciary has upheld that proposition in a series of forthright cases. The executive branch has adopted that proposition in the conduct of its affairs, including the employment of Federal personnel, the use of Federal facilities, and the sale of federally financed housing.

But there are other necessary measures which only the

Congress can provide, and they must be provided at this session. The old code of equity law under which we live commands for every wrong a remedy, but in too many communities, in too many parts of the country, wrongs are inflicted on Negro citizens and there are no remedies at law. Unless Congress acts, their only remedy is in the street.

I am, therefore, asking the Congress to enact legislation giving all Americans the right to be served in facilities which are open to the public - hotels, restaurants, theaters, retail stores, and similar establishments.

This seems to me to be an elementary right. Its denial is an arbitrary indignity that no American in 1963 should have to endure, but many do.

I have recently met with scores of business leaders urging them to take voluntary action to end this discrimination and I have been encouraged by their response, and in the last two weeks over 75 cities have seen progress made in desegregating these kinds of facilities. But many are unwilling to act alone, and for this reason, nationwide legislation is needed if we are to move this problem from the streets to the courts.

I am also asking Congress to authorize the Federal government to participate more fully in lawsuits designed to end segregation in public education. We have succeeded in persuading many districts to desegregate voluntarily. Dozens have admitted Negroes without violence.

Today a Negro is attending a State-supported institution in every one of our 50 States, but the pace is very slow.

Too many Negro children entering segregated grade schools at the time of the Supreme Court's decision nine years ago will enter segregated high schools this fall, having suffered a loss which can never be restored. The lack of an adequate education denies the Negro a chance to get a decent job.

The orderly implementation of the Supreme Court's decision, therefore, cannot be left solely to those who may not have the economic resources to carry the legal action or who may be subject to harassment.

Other features will be also requested, including greater protection for the right to vote. But legislation, I repeat, cannot solve this problem alone. It must be solved in the homes of every American in every community across our country.

In this respect, I want to pay tribute to those citizens North and South who have been working in their communities to make life better for all. They are acting not out of a sense of legal duty but out of a sense of human decency.

Like our soldiers and sailors in all parts of the world they are meeting freedom's challenge on the firing line, and I salute them for their honor and their courage.

My fellow Americans, this is a problem which faces us all - in every city of the North as well as the South. Today there are Negroes unemployed, two or three times as many compared to whites, inadequate in education, moving into the large cities, unable to find work, young people particularly out of work without hope, denied equal rights, denied the opportunity to eat at a restaurant or lunch counter or go to a movie theater, denied the right to a decent education, denied almost today the right to attend a State university even though qualified. It seems to me that these are matters which concern us all, not merely President or Congressmen or Governors, but every citizen of the United States.

This is one country. It has become one country because all of us and all the people who came here had an equal chance to develop their talents.

We cannot say to ten percent of the population that you can't have that right; that your children can't have the chance to develop whatever talents they have; that the only way that they are going to get their rights is to go into the streets and demonstrate. I think we owe them and owe ourselves a better country than that.

Therefore, I am asking for your help in making it easier for us to move ahead and to provide the kind of equality of treatment which we would want ourselves; to give a chance for every child to be educated to the limit of his talents.

As I have said before, not every child has an equal talent or an equal ability or an equal motivation, but they should have the equal right to develop their talent and their ability and their motivation, to make something of themselves.

We have a right to expect that the Negro community will be responsible, will uphold the law, but they have a right to expect that the law will be fair, that the Constitution will be color blind, as Justice Harlan said at the turn of the century.

This is what we are talking about and this is a matter which concerns this country and what it stands for, and in meeting it I ask the support of all our citizens. Thank you very much."

The President's speech was a difficult one, and it only added to the discomfiture of the white establishment. But sensible Americans and those of us in college realized his recommendations were necessary if the country was going to maintain any semblance of unity, decency, and law and order.

The night of the President's speech, Medger Evers, the President of the National Association for the Advancement of Colored People, was shot dead in an ambush by a white man in front of his home in Jackson, Mississippi.

Probably the most important event to change the course of American history passed virtually unnoticed in the American conscience: on June 17, 1963 the United States Supreme Court reversed over 80 previous court decisions and forbade the Lord's prayer and daily Bible readings in public schools, in *Abington School District v. Schempp* (374 U.S. 203) (and in an earlier decision *Engel v. Vitale* (370 U.S. 421) June 25, 1962).

The arguments in both *Engel v. Vitale* (370 US 421, 1962) and *School District of Abington Township v. Schempp* (374 US 203, June 17, 1963) are similar. Citing the importance of the separation of Church and State, the Supreme Court ruled against establishment of an official state religion. They referred to the oppression caused by the Church of England and the Book of Common Prayer approved by the British Parliament in 1548.

The Supreme Court referred to Thomas Jefferson and James Madison, who wanted to allow freedom of religion, but not have religion dictated for the American public by an authoritarian government. Thomas Jefferson and James Madison were faced with the growing number of minority Christian groups, such as the Presbyterians, Baptists, Lutherans, and Quakers, that wanted freedom to practice their beliefs, instead of the dominant Episcopal Church.

Justice Potter Stewart dissented in both cases, and pointed out the First Amendment states that "**Congress shall make no law respecting an establishment of religion or prohibiting the free exercise thereof.**"

In *Engel v. Vitale,* Justice Stewart states, "With all respect, I think the Court has misapplied a great constitutional principle. I cannot see how an 'official religion' is established by letting those who want to say a prayer say it. On the contrary, I think that to deny the wish of these school children to join in reciting this prayer is to deny them the opportunity of sharing in the spiritual heritage of our Nation."

Justice Stewart questioned the relevance of discussion of 16th century England or 18th century America. "What *is* relevant to the issue here is not the history of an established church in sixteenth century England or in eighteenth century America, but the history of the religious traditions of our people, reflected in countless practices of the institutions and officials of our government."

He pointed out that each day's session of the Supreme Court begins with the prayer, "God save the United States and this Honorable Court. Each President, from George Washington to John F. Kennedy, has, upon assuming office, asked the protection and help of God. Each of our coins is stamped with the imprint "In God We Trust." Our Pledge of Allegiance to the Flag states, "One Nation under God, indivisible, with liberty and justice for all." Our National Anthem, the Star-Spangled Banner, includes the phrase, "In God is Our Trust."

Justice Stewart further points out, in *Abington v. Schempp,* that "For a compulsory state educational system so structures a child's life that, if religious exercises are held to be an impermissible activity in schools, *religion is placed at an artificial and state-created disadvantage.* Viewed in this light, permission of such exercises for those who want them is necessary if the schools are truly to be neutral in the matter of religion. And a refusal to permit religious exercises thus is seen not as the realization of state neutrality, but rather as the establishment of a religion of secularism, or, at the least, as government support of the beliefs of those who think that religious exercises should be conducted only in private."

There is also a major difference between the establishment of a state religion, and allowing children to pray in public schools! While Thomas Jefferson and James Madison were opposed to a dictatorial government forcing what religious thoughts individuals were allowed to think and what prayers they were allowed to say, they obviously allowed children to say prayers in school! Thomas

Jefferson and James Madison allowed free religious expression in public schools!

It is important to believe in God. Because God the Creator made you, you are special and have self-worth as an individual. America was founded on the freedom and independence of the individual. And children have been praying in public schools, learning the Ten Commandments, and reading the Bible for 200 years! Children learned respect for Our Creator, children learned respect for parents and authority, children learned respect for their neighbor, and learned respect for themselves!

The foundation of Western civilization is the Biblical ethic, as noted for example in our Declaration of Independence, which speaks of God our Creator and the natural law. Our public schools taught our society to live in harmony with our Creator and follow His laws, to respect life, and to treat all members of the human race with dignity and respect. Our 200-year Christian heritage and free religious expression as guaranteed by the First Amendment of the Constitution of the United States ended in public education in 1963.

The turmoil of 1963 that shattered the peaceful "fifties" here at home continued on a world-wide front. On June 6, 1963, the Ayatullah Khomeini was arrested in Iran for inciting the Shiite Muslims to riot against the regime of Shah Mohammed Reza Pahlevi. The Ayatullah was exiled to France, but returned in triumph in 1979 when the Shah was overthrown.

President Ngo Dinh Diem of Vietnam set forth a decree prohibiting the celebration of Wesak, the most important Buddhist national holiday. On June 13, 1963 a Buddhist monk set himself on fire and incited widespread Buddhist riots. On July 30, 60,000 Buddhists marched in protest of the Diem government. On August 21, 1963 the Diem army arrested over 100 Buddhist monks while they were praying in the temple!

These events made President Kennedy wary of Vietnam. As noted in both Arthur Schlesinger's 1965 book *A Thousand Days,* and Theodore Sorensen's 1965 book *Kennedy,* the President was very direct in a televised interview on September 3, 1963: "I don't think that the war can be won unless the people support the effort and, in my opinion, in the last two months, the government has gotten out of touch with the people. In the final anaysis, it is their war. They are the ones who have to win it or lose it. We can help them, we can give them equipment, we can send our men out there as advisers, but **they** have to win it, the people of Vietnam." These events led to intolerable civil strife until finally the regime of President Diem ended when he and Madame Nhu were murdered in a military coup on November 1, 1963.

Folk music became popular and reflected the traumatic upheaval in our society. Peter, Paul and Mary recorded on the first album a song written by Lee Hays and Pete Seeger called "If I Had a Hammer." In May of 1963 Bob Dylan wrote "Blowing in the Wind," which was recorded by Peter, Paul and Mary and became one of the most popular songs of that summer.   The folk singer Odetta (Holmes) from Alabama sang a beautiful ballad written by Peter, Paul and Mary called "All My Trials, Lord , Will Soon Be Over." Bob Dylan's following album was appropriately called "The Times They Are A-Changing."

President Kennedy went to Berlin, and on June 28, 1963 gave a stirring speech on freedom at the Berlin Wall:

> "Freedom has many difficulties and democracy is not perfect, but we have never had to put a wall up to keep our people in, to prevent them from leaving us...While the wall is the most obvious example and vivid demonstration of the failures of the Communist system, for all the world to see, we take no satisfaction in it, for it is an offense not only against history but an offense against humanity, separating families, dividing husbands and wives and brothers and sisters, and dividing a people who wish to be joined together.
>
> What is true of this city is true of Germany - real lasting peace in Europe can never be assured as long as one German out of four is denied **the elementary right of free men, which is to make a free choice**."

President Kennedy continued:
 " **Freedom is indivisible, and when one man is enslaved, all are not free**."

Much to the joy and satisfaction of the people of Berlin, he ended his speech with
"Ich bin ein Berliner!"

The Summer of 1963 gave us all some relief from the civil unrest and turmoil of the preceding few months, but was also marked by sadness. One of our most popular Popes, John XXIII, died in Rome and he was succeeded by the serious Pope Paul VI. The U. S. Post Office started the zip code system July 1, 1963. Jackie Kennedy gave premature birth to Patrick Bouvier Kennedy, and he weighed only 4 pounds, 8 ounces. Joy turned to sadness when he died August 8, 1963, the day following his birth, of hyaline membrane disease.

The United States was just beginning to hear about a new English phenomenon known as the Beatles. Paul McCartney, George Harrison, John Lennon, and Ringo Starr recorded their first album "Please Please Me" in early 1963, which shot to number one in England for 29 weeks. The "British Invasion" began with two singles released in the States late in 1963, "She Loves You" and "I Want to Hold Your Hand."

The big event in the Summer of 1963 was the upcoming speech by Martin Luther King on August 28, 1963 in Washington, D.C. Fears of demonstrations, riots, and countermarches by both the American Nazi party and the Black Muslims, who were both in opposition, failed to materialize. An appeal for a peaceful assembly by march leader A. Philip Randolph was respected.

It was a beautiful summer day, and a festive occasion. And it was the biggest crowd to ever assemble on the Washington Mall - people came from all over the country. The presence of artists such as Peter, Paul and Mary, and Odetta (Holmes) generated enthusiasm and spirit for the event. Odetta sang "All My Trials, Lord" and Peter, Paul and Mary sang "If I Had a Hammer" and their summer hit, "Blowing in the Wind" from the steps of the Lincoln Memorial.

Martin Luther King delivered his famous "I Have a Dream" speech on a sunny afternoon, on the steps of the Lincoln Memorial, with the statue of President Lincoln behind him, and the crowd stretching out on the mall to the Washington monument.

"Five score years ago, a great American, in whose symbolic shadow we stand signed the Emancipation Proclamation. This momentous decree came as a great beacon of light of hope to millions of Negro slaves who had been seared in the flames of withering injustice. It came as a joyous daybreak to end the long night of captivity.

But one hundred years later, we must face the tragic fact that the Negro is still not free. One hundred years later, the life of the Negro is still sadly crippled by the manacles of segregation and the chains of discrimination. One hundred years later, the Negro lives on a lonely island of poverty in the midst of a vast ocean of material prosperity. One hundred years later, the Negro is still languishing in the corners of American society and finds himself an exile in his own land. So we have come here today to dramatize an appalling condition.

In a sense we have come to our nation's capital to cash a check. When the architects of our republic wrote the magnificent words of the Constitution and the Declaration of Independence, they were signing a promissory note to which every American was to fall heir. This note was a promise that all men would be guaranteed the inalienable rights of life, liberty, and the pursuit of happiness.

It is obvious today that America has defaulted on this promissory note insofar as her citizens of color are concerned. Instead of honoring this sacred obligation, America has given the Negro people a bad check which has come back marked 'insufficient funds.' But we refuse to believe that the bank of justice is bankrupt. We refuse to believe that there are insufficient funds in the great vaults of opportunity of this nation. So we have come to cash this check - a check that will give us upon demand the riches of freedom and the security of justice. We have also come to this hallowed spot to remind America of the fierce urgency of now. This is no time to engage in the luxury of cooling off or to take the tranquilizing drug of gradualism. Now is the time to rise from the dark and desolate valley of segregation to the sunlit path of racial justice. Now is the time to open the doors of opportunity to all of God's children. Now is the time to lift our nation from the quicksands of racial injustice to the solid rock of brotherhood.

It would be fatal for the nation to overlook the urgency of the moment and to underestimate the determination of the Negro. This sweltering summer of the Nation's discontent will not pass until there is an invigorating autumn of freedom and equality. 1963 is not an end, but a beginning. Those who hope that the Negro needed to blow off steam and will now be content will have a rude awakening if the nation returns to business as usual. There will never be rest or tranquillity in America until the Negro is granted his citizenship rights. The whirlwinds of revolt will continue to shake the foundations of our nation until the bright day of justice emerges.

But there is something I must say to my people who stand on the warm threshold which leads into the palace of justice. *In the process we must not be guilty of wrongful deeds. Let us not seek to satisfy our thirst for freedom by drinking from the cup of bitterness and hatred.*

We must forever conduct our struggle on the high plane of dignity and discipline. ***We must not allow our creative protest to degenerate into physical violence.*** Again and again we must rise to the majestic heights of meeting physical force with soul force. The marvelous new militancy which has engulfed the Negro community must not lead us to distrust all white people, for many of our white brothers, as evidenced by their presence here today, have come to realize that their destiny is tied up with our destiny and their freedom is inexorably bound to our freedom. We cannot walk alone. And as we walk, we must make the pledge that we shall march ahead.

We cannot turn back. There are those who are asking the devotees of civil rights, 'when will you be satisfied?' We can never be satisfied as long as our bodies, heavy with the fatigue of travel, cannot gain lodging in the motels of the highways and the hotels of our cities. We cannot be satisfied as long as the Negro's basic mobility is from a smaller ghetto to a larger one. We can never be satisfied as long as a Negro in Mississippi cannot vote and a Negro in New York believes he has nothing for which to vote. No, no, we are not satisfied, and we will not be satisfied until justice rolls down like waters and righteousness like a mighty stream.

I am not unmindful that some of you have come here out of great trials and tribulations. Some of you have come fresh from narrow cells. Some of you have come from areas where your quest for freedom left you battered by the storms of persecution and staggered by the winds of police brutality. You have been the veterans of creative suffering. Continue to work with the faith that unearned suffering is redemptive.

Go back to Mississippi, go back to Alabama, go back to

Georgia, go back to Louisiana, go back to the slums and ghettos of our northern cities, knowing that somehow this situation can and will be changed. Let us not wallow in the valley of despair.

"I say to you today, my friends, so even though we face the difficulties of today and tomorrow, I still have a dream. It is a dream deeply rooted in the American dream.

I have a dream that one day this nation will rise up and live out the true meaning of its creed: "We hold these truths to be self-evident; that all men are created equal." I have a dream that one day on the red hills of Georgia the sons of former slaves and the sons of former slaveowners will be able to sit down at the table of brotherhood.

I have a dream that one day even the state of Mississippi, a desert state, sweltering with the heat of injustice and oppression, will be transformed into an oasis of freedom and justice.

I have a dream that my four little children will one day live in a nation where they will not be judged by the color of their skin but by the content of their character.

I have a dream today.

I have a dream that one day the state of Alabama, whose governor's lip's are presently dripping with the words of interposition and nullification, will be transformed into a situation where little black boys and black girls will be able to join hands with little white boys and white girls and walk today as sisters and brothers.

I have a dream today.

I have a dream that one day every valley shall be exalted, every hill and mountain shall be made low, the rough places will be made plain, and the crooked places will be made straight, and the glory of the Lord shall be revealed, and all flesh shall see it together.

This is our hope. This is the faith that I go back to the South with. With this faith we will be able to hew out of the mountain of despair a stone of hope. With this faith we will be able to transform the jangling discords of our nation into a beautiful symphony of brotherhood.

And this will be the day. This will be the day when all of

God's children will be able to sing with new meaning,
  'My country 'tis of thee, sweet land of liberty, of thee I sing.
  Land where my fathers died, land of the Pilgrims' Pride,
   from every mountainside, let freedom ring.'
  And if America is to become a great nation, this must become true. So let freedom ring from the prodigious hilltops of New Hampshire. Let freedom ring from the mighty mountains of New York. Let freedom ring from the heightening Alleghenies of Pennsylvania! Let freedom ring from the snowcapped Rockies of Colorado! Let freedom ring from the curvaceous slopes of California. But not only that let freedom ring from Stone Mountain of Georgia! Let freedom ring from Lookout Mountain of Tennessee. Let freedom ring from every hill and every molehill of Mississippi. From every mountainside, let freedom ring.
  And when this happens, and when we allow freedom to ring, when we let it ring from every village and every hamlet, from every state and every city, we will be able to speed up that day when all of God's children, black men and white men, Jews and Gentiles, Protestants and Catholics, will be able to join hands and sing in the words of the old Negro spiritual, "Free at last!
  Free at last! Thank God Almighty, we are free at last."

There was a wonderful feeling of happiness and freedom and a new beginning. We all felt that way in downtown Washington. There was a sense of brotherhood and love for our fellow man. True, he forcefully stated his case, but it was with peace and dignity, and in a non-violent fashion, unlike his more radical brethren. And the ending conveyed brotherhood and conciliation.

That evening I went home and watched the speech on television with my parents in our suburban Maryland home - what a lesson in media manipulation! The only paragraph that went on nationwide television was the one paragraph that spoke of "revolt." Not one mention of the Negro waiting one hundred years and asking his just due was ever mentioned. Instead of capturing the spirit of freedom and brotherhood among men, television portrayed the speech as purely a demand for civil rights and made it sound like a Negro uprising. My father was shocked and aghast. It was then I realized the power of the media to influence public opinion. A beautiful moment in American history was conveyed negatively to the nation and we can thank the media for this horrible distortion of the truth.

President Kennedy met with Reverend Martin Luther King and A. Philip Randolph on the evening following the speech. According to Theodore Sorensen, he was "deeply touched" by the event, and marvelled at the peaceful nature and obvious spirit of the occasion.

The reaction nationwide to the speech as expected was mixed and divisive. While the majority of Americans philosophically agreed with the President's concepts on civil rights, the majority also felt that he was "pushing too fast." In fact, throughout the country, the reality of integration was too much for most white people to bear.

At the same time, the peaceful event served to crystallize and unify the civil rights movement, and the August 28, 1963 happening itself became forever imprinted as part of the American experience.

Children returned to schools in the fall, and more civil unrest broke out in Alabama. On September 2, 1963 Governor Wallace called state troopers to Tuskegee High School to stop integration. On September 5 Birmingham shut down all its public schools scheduled for integration.

September 15, 1963 was the first church bombing. A church was bombed in Birmingham killing four little Negro girls. Whereas most of the country was wary of integration, it was television coverage of this event that added to the national backlash and sympathy among many for the Negro movement. Dudley Randall wrote the moving *Ballad of Birmingham* based on this incident.

On September 20, 1963, President Kennedy opened his third speech on world peace before the United Nations: " We meet again in the quest for peace." He announced progress in the search for peace, such as the nuclear test ban treaty. And in a very profound comment, he concluded, "But peace does not rest in charters and covenants alone. *Peace lies in the hearts and minds of all people...Let us strive to build peace, a desire for peace, a willingness to work for peace, in the hearts and minds of all our people."*

Our age group loved and respected President Kennedy. He stood up for what was right in a time of sweeping change, and in the face of almost overwhelming turmoil both at home and abroad. He started the Peace Corps, an effort to serve other countries in a humanitarian fashion. He began the Space effort to reach the moon, culminating in Neil Armstrong's historic Apollo 11 landing on the moon on July 20, 1969. He was for an equal chance for all, and his initiative brought us the equality we have today. He began the initiative for detente with Russia and for world peace. His support of the literature and the arts ultimately gave us the Kennedy Center in Washington, D. C.

In September 1963 I gained early admission to Georgetown University School of Medicine in Washington, D.C. after completing three years of college at Holy Cross. We had 101 in our class--98 men and 3 women. And we all became quite close. Medical school was tough. It seems all I ever had time to do was study. There was no time for socialization or going out like we did in college. About the only people I ever talked to were my fellow classmates. Life became a whirlwind of study, and national events became a blur.

Everyone of age at the time remembers where they were the early afternoon of November 22, 1963. We were just about to start class for the afternoon session when a student, who was always late, came running in and announced that President Kennedy had been shot. Everybody was in a state of shock and disbelief and nobody said anything. The teacher just stood there and time just became suspended and just stood still. Then everybody began talking and aimlessly began to wander about the classroom and into the hall. The teacher just stood there and never said anything. He didn't continue the lecture. He didn't adjourn the class. He was as deeply moved as all of us. Everybody started to leave the classroom to find out more news about what had happened in Dallas, Texas.

President and Jackie Kennedy had arrived at Love Field in Dallas, Texas at 11:37 a. m., the day of November 22, 1963. He was to speak at the Dallas Trade Mart at a luncheon. Mrs. Elizabeth Cabell, wife of the Mayor of Dallas, Earle Cabell, gave Mrs. Kennedy a bouquet of red roses; she then gave Ladybird Johnson and the other ladies present the traditional yellow roses of Texas.

The motorcade left from the airport. The first car contained Dallas police and Secret Servicemen. The President's car was second in the motorcade, followed by a car of Secret Service agents, and then the fourth a limousine with Vice President and Mrs. Lyndon Johnson. The President sat in the right rear of an open limousine, Jackie was on the left. Governor John Connally was in a jump seat in front of the President, Mrs. Connally was on her husband's left. The motorcade drove through downtown Dallas, the crowd cheering the open limousine with President Kennedy.

There was a huge crowd on Main Street, as well as Houston Street. The motorcade then had to slow to 11 miles per hour to make the sharp, 120 - degree turn from Houston to Elm street into Dealey Plaza, past the Texas School Book Depository. The motorcade started the gradual descent down Elm Street to a triple railroad underpass en route to Stemmons Freeway. A grassy knoll was on the right; at the top of the grassy knoll are two small arbors or pergolas, then a cement wall, and then a wooden picket stockade fence, behind which is the railroad yard and a parking lot.

There were very few spectators on Elm Street. One of the spectators on the right was Abraham Zapruder with his secretary, filming the motorcade perched on the steps of the pergola leading to the grassy knoll. **At 12:30 p. m., exactly 53 minutes after he landed in Dallas, President Kennedy was shot.** While the Texas Book Depository was *behind* the President, the President, slumped *backwards ,* indicating the bullet(s) that struck him were in front of him, from the grassy knoll. When he slumped over, Jackie Kennedy cradled her fallen husband in her arms, and cried, "Oh, no! Oh, no! I love you, Jack."

The driver rushed to Parkland Memorial Hospital, 4 miles from the scene, on Henry Hines Boulevard. The President never regained consciousness, and efforts by the Parkland medical staff were to no avail. Father Oscar Huber, a Catholic priest, arrived. He drew back a sheet covering the President and anointed his forehead with oil, giving him the Last Rites and conditional absolution. Jacqueline Kennedy stood next to the President's body, and prayed with the priest and the others the Our Father and Hail Mary for her husband. She took off her wedding band and slipped it on his finger. There in the Emergency Room at 1 p. m., central standard time, Friday, November 22, 1963, President John Fitzgerald Kennedy was pronounced dead.

While the first reports spoke only of his being shot, I did not learn of President Kennedy's death until I got back home. I saw Mary Fran on the porch across the street babysitting. She was crying as she ran up to me and I held her. We then watched television together on the porch and she continued to cry. I heard someone say that the President's body was being flown to Bethesda Navy Hospital. We lived less than a mile from there and I wanted to go see and so I drove over there. Since my father was in the government, we had privileges at Bethesda Navy Hospital. One of the security guards let me accompany him to the entrance where President Kennedy was to be brought, and let me stand right at the very front of the entrance.

The limousine drove up right to where I was standing. Jacqueline Kennedy stepped out right in front of me. She left an indelible impression that has always stayed with me. She was the most beautiful woman I had ever seen. Her face, her eyes were filled with sadness and anger, and she wore the same dress that she wore in the parade on Dealey Plaza in Dallas, Texas. Her dress was covered with blood.

All of us who lived during those few days will remember them as the saddest in American history. President Kennedy was one of the most loved Presidents of all time, especially by the young, and he was taken from us. There are those who call this tragic event *the* pivotal event of our century, one that irrevocably altered the course of American history.

It was the first national tragedy to be watched by everyone on television. On Saturday, November 23, 1963, his flag-draped casket lay in the East Room of the White House, where former Presidents Eisenhower and Truman, and national leaders paid their respects to our fallen leader.

On Sunday, November 24, a flag-draped caisson, drawn by six gray horses and followed by a riderless horse, carried the President to the Capitol Rotunda, where he laid in state in a closed casket. The procession from the White House was watched by the crowd and millions on television in stunned silence. Mrs. Kennedy was accompanied by their daughter Caroline, age 5, and John-John, whose birthday was that very day. They were escorted by his brother, the attorney general, Robert Kennedy.

Senator Mike Mansfield of Montana, the Majority Leader, gave the most moving speech:

"There was a sound of laughter; in a moment, it was no more. And so, she took a ring from her finger and placed it in his hands.

There was a wit in a man neither young nor old, but a wit full of an old man's wisdom and of a child's wisdom, and, then, in a moment, it was no more. And so she took a ring from her finger and placed it in his hands.

There was a man marked with the scars of his love of country, a body active with the surge of a life far, far from spent and, in a moment, it was no more. And so she took a ring from her finger and placed it in his hands.

There was a father with a little boy, a little girl and a joy of each in the other. In a moment it was no more, and so she took a ring from her finger and placed it in his hands.

There was a husband who asked much and gave much, and, out of the giving and the asking, wove with a woman what could not be broken in life, and, in a moment, it was no more. And so she took a ring from her finger and placed it in his hands, and kissed him and closed the lid of a coffin.

A piece of each of us died at that moment. Yet, in death he gave of himself to us. He gave us a good heart from which the laughter came. He gave us of a profound wit, from which a great leadership emerged. He gave us of a kindness and a strength fused into human courage to seek peace without fear.

He gave us of his love that we, too, in turn, might give. He gave that we might give of ourselves, that we might give to one another until there would be no room, no room at all, for the bigotry, the hatred, prejudice and the arrogance which converged in that moment of horror to strike him down.

In leaving us - these gifts, John Fitzgerald Kennedy, President of the United States, leaves with us. Will we take them, Mr. President? Will we have, now, the sense and the responsibility and the courage to take them?

I pray to God that we shall, and under God we will."

Thousands of persons went to the Capitol to pay their last respects to our President. People visited from all over the country well into the night. At one point, the line was 30 blocks from the Capitol. The Capitol rotunda remained open throughout the night.

Monday, November 25, 1963 was the day of the funeral Mass at St. Matthew's Cathedral, and the burial at Arlington Cemetery. It was a national day of mourning. Representatives from 53 countries were there to attend the funeral. The funeral procession went from the Capitol Rotunda to the White House, and then to St. Matthew's Cathedral.

Cardinal Cushing began the service at the door of the Church by sprinkling the coffin with holy water. At the funeral, there was Luigi Vena of Boston, singing *Ave Maria* just as he had sung it 10 years before at the wedding of John Kennedy and Jacqueline Bouvier.

Then the three-mile funeral procession, leaving Washington and Capitol

Hill behind, made its way across the Potomac for the burial at Arlington Cemetery. As they lowered the casket, taps was played in the background. French President Charles DeGaulle and others stood at attention and saluted the President. The eternal flame still burns today over the gravesite of President John F. Kennedy. At night you can see the eternal flame over his gravesite beneath the Lee Mansion for miles away.

But the most moving moment of all was not all the dignitaries, not the pomp and circumstance, not the processions, none of it.

We will always remember little John-John Kennedy, age 3, when he saluted his father as he passed by in the funeral procession.

CHAPTER 2
LIFE IN AMERICA

Growing up in a time which taught independence, standing up for the right against all odds, and family values, our hope was to live the American dream. Marilyn Southall of Richmond, Virginia and I married in 1966. I graduated from Georgetown Medical School in Washington, D. C. in 1967.

This chapter presents some patient experiences in Emergency Medicine, and a brief picture of our family life, during a turbulent period in American society, a time in which America lost its sense of values and direction. Names and circumstances often have been changed to ensure patient privacy.

This was a time when the American people began to lose trust in the Federal Government to lead our country. The American individual and the American family became frustrated and felt helpless in providing direction to our society and finding solutions to our nation's problems through the democratic process. The attitude became - I can't solve everybody else's problems, I'll just have to look out for my family and myself.

This lack of trust began almost immediately after the assassination of **President Kennedy** with the Warren Commission. The Warren Commission claimed that President Kennedy was killed and Governor Connally injured by a lone gunman, Lee Harvey Oswald, with a single bullet. Obviously, no one I know in my age group believes for a second Lee Harvey Oswald acted alone, or that a single bullet killed our beloved President. Let the reader answer one simple question: if Lee Harvey Oswald acted completely alone, assuming he could arrange all by himself the complete lack of security precautions, how could one single bullet that was found completely intact cause the many wounds in both President Kennedy and Governor Connally?!

The single bullet theory is not only absurd, it is an impossibility. Dr. Malcolm Perry and Dr. Robert McClelland, who attended the President in Parkland ER, described the President to have a small throat wound that was an **entrance** wound. Dr. Kemp Clark, who attended the President in the ER at Parkland Hospital and pronounced the President at 1 p. m., stated to the New York Times (November 27, 1963) one bullet struck him at the necktie knot and 'it ranged downward in his chest and did not exit.' This means that this bullet that struck the President had to come from the grassy knoll, in front of the President, causing him to fall backwards, as documented on film. This means it was impossible for that bullet to come from the Texas Book Depository. Dr. Kemp Clark also described a second tangential wound, caused by a second bullet that struck the 'right back of his head.' A third wound in the President's back was also noted.

Too many facts kept coming to the surface disputing the conclusions of the Warren Commission. Early newspaper reports, eyewitness statements and spectator photographs, before Herbert Hoover, the FBI, and the Warren Commission could put the government spin on the President's death, revealed the President to be shot in a crossfire, from both the Texas Book Depository and the grassy knoll.

Abraham Zapruder was a Dallas clothing manufacturer who was in front of the motorcade route to see President Kennedy, and filmed the entire scene with his new Bell and Howell 8 mm movie camera. He had perched himself on a concrete block on the steps leading to the pergola on the grassy knoll. The camera shot 18.3 films per second, and his film is one of the most scrutinized films in history.

There were multiple witnesses that heard the shots fired from the grassy knoll, such as Abraham Zapruder, who thought the shots came from behind him, the Newman family, and Jesse Price. Immediately after the shots fired in Dealey Plaza, Dallas police and a large crowd of onlookers reacted to where shots had been fired and ran up the grassy knoll. But witnesses such as Jean Hill and others in the crowd who ran up the knoll were turned back from the cement retaining wall and the railroad yard beyond the knoll by a group of men flashing Secret Service badges.

In fact, several photographs, such as the one by Mary Moorman, have documented a man behind the cement retaining wall, who ran and jumped over the stockade fence after the shooting, leaving only a Coke bottle behind. A deaf man Ed Hoffman saw a man with a rifle run to the picket stockade fence and throw the rifle to another man. Lee Bowers was in the railroad tower behind the grassy knoll and also saw two unidentified men in the railroad yard. Later an unauthorized train began to pull out, which he stopped. Ed Hoffman and Lee Bowers' testimony was discounted by the FBI.

The Dallas police department first stated the weapon found in the Texas School Book Depository was a 7.65 German Mauser, as signed in an affidavit by Dallas Deputy Sheriff Weitzman. Later, the official murder weapon was changed to a 6.5 Mannlicher-Carcano Italian rifle, the same rifle Oswald obtained by mail-order. It is on record that Lee Harvey Oswald had a negative nitrate cheek test for gunpowder, which indicates he did not fire a rifle.

Hundreds of publications have been written about the death of President Kennedy, but it was Mark Lane in his 1966 best-seller *Rush to Judgement* that disputed the Warren Commission and blew the case wide open.

How does one explain the scores of people associated with this incident who have mysteriously died, often under the most violent and grisly of circumstances?

New Orleans District Attorney Jim Garrison originally began his investigation against David Ferrie, and brought him in for questioning on November 25, 1963. He had heard that David Ferrie knew Lee Harvey Oswald and Jack Ruby and had gone to Dallas the day of the assassination. He turned David Ferrie over to the FBI, who promptly released him.

We are familiar with the violent death of Lee Harvey Oswald, who was shot by Jack Ruby on national television on Sunday, November 24, 1963. This in itself pointed to conspiracy - someone wanted him quiet!   Lee Harvey Oswald has been linked to the CIA, the FBI, anti-Castro Cubans, and the New Orleans underworld. New Orleans attorney Jim Garrison discovered he was trained in Russian while in the U. S. military! If he truly defected to Russia, how could he immediately get back into the country without prosecution?!

Jack Ruby had pleaded for his safety with members of the Warren Commission. Jack Ruby had been sighted in Dealey Plaza before the shooting by Julia Ann Mercer, and during the shooting by Jean Hill and Mary Moorman. Dorothy Kilgallen, a well-known New York columnist, interviewed Jack Ruby in jail. She excitedly announced she was going to break the case "wide open." A few days following her announcement, she died of a massive barbiturate drug overdose in November 1965.

Jim Garrison reopened his investigation three years later against David Ferrie, after studying the Warren Commission Report. In addition to being an associate of Jack Ruby and Lee Harvey Oswald, David Ferrie knew Mafia New Orleans underworld leader Carlos Marcello. David Ferrie died suddenly of a brain hemorrhage on February 22, 1967 just before his arrest. Another key witness, Emilio del Valle, was murdered in Florida the same day.

Jim Garrison was impressed with the fact that the route of the motorcade had been changed from going straight down Main Street to making the loop down Houston and Elm Street, requiring the motorcade to slow down. What about the inadequate security precautions and all the issues about the autopsy?! In his book, *On The Trail of the Assassins*, he discounted the many theories of Mafia involvement in the shooting. Even if the Mafia supplied the "labor," surely they could not have organized the overall plot and the subsequent cover-up.

Jim Garrison had no one left to prosecute but Clay Shaw. Clay Shaw was a powerful New Orleans businessman and was linked to the CIA. He owned the international company Permindex, which reportedly had funded a group that attempted to assassinate French President Charles DeGaulle. With his key witnesses dead, Jim Garrison lost his case against Clay Shaw. The only trial that ever has taken place on this whole episode, he was able to convince the jury that a conspiracy was involved in the death of President Kennedy.

Many private researchers, such as Dallas journalist Jim Marrs, author of the 1989 book *Crossfire*, believe that the Warren Commission simply accepted the pre-conceived notion of the FBI that the assassination was the work of a lone gunman, and not a conspiracy, in spite of overwhelming evidence to the contrary. This is quite reasonable.

The letter of Lyndon Johnson appointing the Warren Commission, Executive Order #11130, dated November 30, 1963, clearly states in the very first sentence "The purposes of the Commission are to examine the evidence developed by the Federal Bureau of Investigation..." While the Warren Commission had the prerogative to do an independent study, J. Edgar Hoover essentially controlled what was brought to the Warren Commission.

For example, when published by the Warren Commission, the Abraham Zapruder film was reversed, to show the President falling forward, thus suggesting the head wound came from behind, from the Texas School Book Depository. J. Edgar Hoover, the Director of the FBI, later explained in 1965 that this was a "printing error."

The question remains, *who* is responsible for the death of President Kennedy? And *why* was President Kennedy killed? And **who** ultimately was behind it all? The summer of 1964, my friends Frank Santoro, George Reed and I hitchhiked through Europe. President Kennedy was universally loved all over Europe, and the subject always came up. One night in Austria an innkeeper let me stay if I gave him my Kennedy half-dollar, which I promptly did. He asked me an interesting question - *who had the most to gain by the death of President Kennedy?*

The erosion of public trust progressed with the quagmire in **Vietnam**, a war which never made any sense. President Kennedy had issued a directive to disengage from Vietnam just before his death on November 22, 1963. As permanently recorded in his National Security Action Memorandum (NSAM #263) of October 11, 1963, the President had planned to bring 1000 military men home by Christmas and to have the remaining military advisors out of Vietnam by the end of 1964! At the time of the President's death, there were strictly military advisors and no fighting troops present in Vietnam. The President had become wary and disenchanted about the prospects for any resolution in Vietnam, and his goal was **disengagement**!

Retired Colonel L. Fletcher Prouty points out in his book *JFK. The CIA, Vietnam and the Plot to Assassinate John F. Kennedy,* withdrawal from Vietnam would have been devastating to the power and finances of the military-industrial complex!

However, with the death of President Kennedy, Lyndon B. Johnson *escalated* the war in Vietnam. On November 26, 1963, **4 days** *after the death of President Kennedy, and the day following his burial,*   Johnson signed National Security Action Memorandum #273, which changes the direction of the Vietnam conflict, by stating the "central object of the United States in South Vietman (is) to assist the people and Government of that country to **win** their contest against the externally directed and supported Communist conspiracy."   This is quite different from President Kennedy's memorandum of October 1963 calling for complete American withdrawal by the end of 1964! It seems a prudent and independent leader would study a situation longer than 4 days before he would commit his country to war!

On March 17, 1964, Johnson signed a new directive for deepening involvement in the Vietnam War, and America soon became engulfed in the most meaningless war in its history, not to mention the only war we ever lost.   No matter - the military-industrial complex ended up with the money and power they sought. The Vietnam War cost $220 billion dollars! Did they care that 58,000 Americans died in the war? Did they care that nearly a million American soldiers are partially disabled because of injuries or Agent Orange?

Nobody wanted the war in Vietnam. The general feeling at the time was "Why are we involved in Vietnam which is 10,000 miles away and on the other side of the world, when we let Cuba go which is 100 miles off our coast?"

July 1, 1967 we moved to Chapel Hill, North Carolina where I began an internship. Our first son, Matthew, was born August 3, 1967, shortly after our move to Chapel Hill. Since I had to work every other night, and made only $4,000 a year, we lived a very simple life. We enjoyed our son Matthew, friends, and music. One of our favorite television shows was "The Fugitive," about Dr. Richard Kimble, played by David Janssen, who was continuously on the run after he had been falsely accused when his wife was murdered by a one-armed man. He often helped others while he was on the run. He was kind of a modern Lone Ranger. The show ran only during my years in medical school, from 1963 to 1967, but the final episode on August 29, 1967 was the most-watched television show in America up until that time.

Our year in Chapel Hill, North Carolina was marred by the tragic deaths of Martin Luther King and Bobby Kennedy. Were the assassinations of Martin Luther King and Bobby Kennedy also the work of "lone gunmen," or conspiracy?

Robert F. Kennedy, brother of the President, served as Chief Counsel to the Senate Rackets Committee from 1957 to 1959, and exposed the underworld connections of Teamsters Union leader Jimmy Hoffa. Over 300 indictments and convictions were brought against Jimmy Hoffa. As U. S Attorney General from 1961 to 1964, he was a formidable opponent of the Mafia underworld. Bobby Kennedy was fortunate when Joseph Valachi, fearing for his life, "sang" on the Mafia underworld on September 25, 1963 before the Senate committee.

Robert Kennedy decided to run for President in March of 1968, and gave a stirring speech against the Vietnam War. Bobby Kennedy was met with tremendous enthusiasm by the public. Two weeks later, Johnson announced he would not run again.

Martin Luther King, in addition to his cause for civil rights, also began to speak out for the cause of peace, and against the Vietnam War. He was shot dead in Memphis, Tennessee on April 4, 1968. America was again told it was the work of a "lone gunman," James Earl Ray. That evening, Senator Robert Kennedy delivered a speech in honor of the slain man: "Martin Luther King dedicated his life to love and to justice for his fellow human beings, and he died because of that effort...What we need in the United States is not hatred; what we need in the United States is not violence or lawlessness, but love and wisdom, and compassion towards one another, and a feeling of justice towards those who still suffer within our country, whether they be white or they be black."

Robert Kennedy was favored to win the 1968 Presidential election! After easily winning the California primary in Los Angeles, Bobby Kennedy was shot and killed that night, June 5, 1968. America was told it was the work of a "lone gunman," Sirhan Sirhan, although 13 bullets were identified in the Ambassador Hotel pantry, and Sirhan's gun only held 8 bullets.

Chaos reached a peak at the Democratic National Convention in the summer of 1968, when 178 demonstrators were arrested protesting the Vietnam War. The unpopular Vietnam war, coupled with the loss of our two favorite leaders, and the loss of order in our cities, proved unsettling to American society.

We moved back to Washington, D. C. after completing internship. Our second son Stephen was born June 29, 1968. I received orders from the U. S. Navy and we were shipped off to the island of Bahrain on the other side of Saudi Arabia, in the Arabian or Persian Gulf.

At the time physicians had to serve two years in the military, and we were grateful for the assignment in Bahrain, for at least I was assigned to somewhere other than Vietnam, and that Marilyn, Matthew and Stephen could come with me. Bahrain had no television, and it really cured us both of the television habit. Fortunately, we had music, and Marilyn was an avid reader. I was the movie officer, and we used to bring home movies to watch. Everyone's favorite movie, including officers, the enlisted, and the local Bahrainis was "The Good, The Bad, and The Ugly." One weekend we played it 3 times for different guests!

We also organized a rock band called the Exploding Soul Machine from the enlisted guys on ship. Dale Grimm, my hospital corpsman, was the lead singer - he was from West Virginia and sounded just like John Fogarty of Creedence Clearwater Revival. Steve Smith was the soul singer with a high voice, and the two of them were a great duo on Righteous Brothers songs. Ed Scolforo was lead guitar, Mike White was rhythm guitar, Pete Munsell was base guitar, and Craig Baylor played drums. These guys were great! I would arrange places for them to play, and Marilyn and I had great fun dancing and partying with our friends. One time we played in Africa, and the local people loved "Proud Mary," "Satisfaction," and "Sitting on the Dock of the Bay." "Hey Joe, "Green River," and "Unchained Melody" were also audience favorites, and "Born To Be Wild." One time in 1969 we played in Bombay at the Blowup, the Taj Mahal Discotheque, when a touring group didn't show up.

We returned home in 1970, and I began residency at Georgetown University in Washington, D. C. Our third son, Joseph, was born January 16, 1971 at

Georgetown University Hospital. I started Emergency Medicine in July 1971 at Arlington Community Hospital in Virginia. Marilyn was expecting our fourth child at that point, and I took a year off from residency because we needed the income. Dr. Douglas Koth offered me a position to work Monday through Friday 8:00 am to 6:00 p.m. for $30,000 a year, about six times the salary of a resident! Residents who "moonlight" in the Emergency Room normally have to work the nights and weekends, so this was a great schedule! Our first daughter, Jeanne, was born February 25, 1972.

I loved my year at Arlington Hospital and the variety of the patients you would see in the ER. A most unusual patient concerned a 30 year old white female who came into the ER very late at night in Arlington, and she was deeply troubled and wanted to talk. Since the ER was slow we went back in the office and I began to listen. She had dark hair and very soulful brown eyes. What she said completely shocked and overwhelmed me. She said that she could sense the spirit and feel what was in other people's souls. She could feel all the misery in their souls. And, she was terribly weighed down by all of this. I was at a loss for what to say. She then began to tell me that I had tremendous energy and that I was very restless. After the things she told me, I believed everything she said. I really didn't know how to help this patient except that listening to her for over an hour and letting her unburden her soul made her feel better. We talked about prayer for all those unhappy and miserable souls that she ran into. Three months later she came screaming into the ER brought by EMS. She recognized me and ran over to me, crying hysterically. She was completely insane and there was nothing I could do other than to commit her to a psychiatric hospital. I never saw her again. Nor have I ever met any other patient like her.

In the ER, you never know what is coming in the door, who your next patient will be, and what their condition would be. This was the life for me. While there were no emergency medicine residencies that were approved at the time, there was a general consensus that Emergency Medicine would be a three-year specialty training program. On July 1,1972 I went back and took a third year of post-graduate training at Georgetown University.

Emergency medicine has been a most wonderful career. I have just completed 27 years of emergency medicine, and I hope God gives me many more. Emergency medicine is the most challenging medical specialty there is.

We have to know how to handle every emergency in every field. We are also the only specialty that consistently takes patients regardless of their ability to pay. This is what has sustained me all these years, as we truly help people. A physician I met in Australia called us "modern missionaries."

Emergency medicine is tough, because we have to work days, nights, and weekends. Unfortunately I was often in a terrible mood after working all night and coming home exhausted. And when my wife wanted to do something on weekends I had to work, leaving her with all the children.

Frank Wills, an $80-a-week security guard in the plush **Watergate** apartment complex in Washington, D. C., arrived at work after midnight, June 17, 1972. He was making his rounds when he noticed lightly colored masking tape covered the lock of the stairway door, allowing it to stay open to the apartment complex; he removed the tape. Residents often open this door from the parking garage, so they wouldn't have to sign in or out at the security desk.

However, when Frank Wills found a fresh piece of masking tape holding open the door on his next rounds, he became suspicious. He also found three other doors taped and called the police at 1:47 a. m. The police found their way to the 6th floor, where they arrested James McCord, a former CIA employee; Frank Sturgis, who, according to Mark Lane and others, also was in Dallas with E. Howard Hunt on November 22, 1963, and is a suspect in the Kennedy assassination; Bernard Barker, who served as a CIA liaison with anti-Castro Cubans during the Bay of Pigs invasion; and two Cubans associated with the Bay of Pigs invasion, Rolando Martinez and Virgilio Gonzalez. They were caught with surgical gloves trying to "bug" the office of the Democratic National Headquarters.

E. Howard Hunt and Gordon Liddy were in the Watergate Hotel and were in contact with the five by radio. The Nixon White House tapes, finally released in 1974, disclosed this following conversation of Nixon on June 23, 1972: "this Hunt, that will uncover a lot of things...this fellow Hunt, he knows too damned much...if it gets out that this is all involved, the Cuba thing, it would be a fiasco. It would make the CIA look bad...make Hunt look bad, and it is likely to blow the whole Bay of Pigs thing..."

The Watergate scandal was a shocking eye-opener to the American people, as it was the first realization that the Federal government was capable of conspiracy at the highest level. It was then that America truly began to doubt the word of the Federal Government.

Our fifth child, Charlene, was born June 27, 1973 at Georgetown University Hospital in Washington, D. C. In July 1973 our family moved to Savannah, Georgia and I started the practice of emergency medicine at Memorial Medical Center. One of the first patients I had was a patient with multiple trauma, a pedestrian hit by a truck. He had several mortal injuries, presented in shock, and even though we had surgery residents to help with the patient's care, the patient rapidly succumbed and died in the emergency department. The family realizing it was a mortal injury were most thankful "for all that we had done."

Our move to Savannah required many trips up and down Interstate -95, and listening to the car radio, we all become quite aware of the music that year. 1973 was an interesting year in the music world. A British group, Pink Floyd, released an album called "Dark Side of the Moon." While the album was number #1 for only one week, it survived as the longest-running album on the charts in all of music history, remaining on the charts for 741 weeks, from 1973 to 1987. Other popular songs that year included Elton John's "Daniel", Steely Dan's "Reelin' in the Years", Jim Croce's "Time in a Bottle" and "I Got A Name," America's "Ventura Highway", the Carpenters "Yesterday Once More", Grand Funk Railroad's "We're an American Band", Gladys Knight and the Pips, "Midnight Train to Georgia", and Paul McCartney and Wings, "Live and Let Die" and "Band on the Run". Eric Clapton had just released "Layla" with Derek and the Dominoes.

Savannah, which lies on the Atlantic Ocean, has a very moist climate. The hallucinogenic mushroom *Psilocybe cubensis* is usually found in moist tropical climates, such as the coasts of Georgia, South Carolina, and the Gulf coast. There is an orphanage in Savannah called the Bethesda Home for Boys. They have a farm with a cow pasture. One afternoon about 4:00 some high school students brought in a friend of theirs who was hallucinating. He had eaten some psilocybe mushrooms that he had harvested from the orphanage.

The patient was aware of his condition and said that he could control his hallucinations. He then presumed to point in my direction and exclaimed, "Wow, I am making you melt to the ground." We put him in the quiet room and I gave him some Valium and in an hour or two he had calmed down and in fact was quite morose. He actually was resentful that we had ended his "trip." His parents were going through a divorce and the only joy he said he had was eating "magic mushrooms."

Marilyn and I were blessed with a beautiful family of eight children. Daniel was born January 22, 1975, Elizabeth Anne was born November 24, 1977 on Thanksgiving Day, and Madeleine Mary was born March 20, 1979, all in Savannah. We were also quite busy raising our big family. We moved from our first house to Bluff Drive at Isle of Hope in March of 1979 in anticipation of being able to build and expand the Isle of Hope home.

Marilyn was a natural in raising a big family. She was loving and generous and ever-patient. As it was a tremendous effort and a great deal of work, we were grateful to have Ernestine help her. Imagine the effort of raising so many children! Even though the woman's liberation movement and the need for additional income was taking the American woman from the home, all you had to do is come to our home and spend one day - you would quickly realize that the most productive and individual effort a woman can make is raising a family!

One can easily understand why the family is the basic building block of our society. It gives the individual love, comfort, meaning, values, direction, a sense of belonging, and a place in the world.

It was a lot of fun for me, because I would come home and play chase around the house and play board games like Clue, Monopoly, and Candyland with the gang. Clue was one of our favorite board games. Daniel had a favorite red chair, and we used to sit on the upstairs porch outside overlooking the river, playing Clue. Most of the time it was Miss Scarlett who committed the crime.

Jeanne and Charlene especially liked to dance, and play with our two little ones, Elizabeth Anne and Madeleine. Jeanne is our sweet angel. She is thoughtful and everyone's big sister. The whole family looks to Jeanne. Charlene has a beautiful smile. I had trouble correcting her, because her smile would make me melt. One time when the neighbors had their home broken into, Charlene found the stolen equipment in the bushes near her lemonade stand on Bluff Drive.

One time when Elizabeth Anne was two she woke me up in the middle of the night. She couldn't sleep because the wind was whistling underneath the front door. She knew something was amiss. The next day, on September 4, 1979, Hurricane David struck Savannah at 98 miles per hour, and we were without water, electricity, and phone for nine days! One of the pine trees fell in the back yard, and became known as the "hurricane tree." It became a favorite place for the children to play games and a place to hide eggs for the annual Easter egg hunt.

Our first son Matthew was quiet and a deep thinker. The nuns at school said he had an exceptionally spiritual nature, and one day would be a priest.

All of us used to play baseball in the back yard, and Matthew, Joseph and I would play football with the neighborhood kids. One of our favorite family games was a version of Hide and Go-Seek in the dark, called "Close Encounters." I put on the movie song "Close Encounters of the Third Kind", and when the music stopped, the person who was "it" would look for everybody with a flashlight.

From an early age Joseph had a protective nature about him, and would risk his own safety for his family -he was there in an emergency. One time Elizabeth Anne was two, and she walked out on the dock, and wanted to dive in the water like the other children. Joe was there to catch her. One time we were pulling our boat into the dock, and a line tangled in the motor, and choked it out, and we began drifting towards thc marsh. Joe instinctively grabbed a knife and dove in the water and cut the line and removed the rope, just in time. One Easter, I gave the family a bunny rabbit, which they named Thumper. We were all outside, and a water moccasin threatenly appeared. I told everyone to back away, but the girls were worried about the rabbit's safety and stayed. The snake, almost sensing the uproar, became more aggressive and approached even closer. Guess who ran into the house, grabbed a rifle, gave me the gun, and told everyone to back off. Needless to say, everybody scattered.

Sunday was our family day. We would all go to Sunday Mass at St. James Catholic Church, and receive Jesus in Holy Communion. Those were happy days, all nine of us in Church together.   When they were very young, one or two of them somehow started to giggle. We would then go to the beach in the summer and stop by for ice cream on the way home.

On Sunday nights we all used to watch "The Hardy Boys," with Shaun Cassidy playing Joe Hardy and Parker Stevenson playing Frank Hardy. Television was limited during the week, but the children used to love "Happy Days" with high school drop-out "Fonzie" Fonzarelli (Henry Winkler), who started a national symbol with this "thumbs-up" gesture. Other family favorites were "Little House on the Prairie" with Michael Landon, and "The Brady Bunch." One of our favorite TV shows began in 1983, "The A-Team." George Peppard played the leader Hannibal; Mr. T was B. A. Baracus, the tough mechanic with a fear of airplanes; Dirk Benedict was the smooth-talking Faceman, and Dwight Schultz played the comic and pilot Murdock. Wrongly accused by the U. S. military while serving in

Vietnam, these fugitives saved the world from all sorts of madmen. Not one drop of blood was ever shed, and the episodes were hysterically funny.

Everyone's favorite time was reading bedtime stories. While they resisted going to bed, and for us to get them ready for bed was clearly a chore, anticipation of bedtime stories made it all the more tolerable for all of us. Probably the universal favorites of all were *The Little Engine That Could, The Littlest Angel* and *The Night Before Christmas* .

Some of the children liked to read stories as soon as I came home. When they were very young, they liked the Mother Goose Fairy Tales, and reading from books such as Richard Scarry's *ABC Word Book*, and *Cars and Trucks and Things That Go*, and *What Do People Do All Day?* Charlene liked Stan and Jan Berenstein's Bear Family stories. Daniel liked Dr. Seuss'*Green Eggs and Ham* and *The Cat in The Hat* and Jean de Brunhoff's *Babar the Elephant.*

The girls especially loved to hear the classic romantic stories, such as *Rapunzel* by Brothers Grimm, *Cinderella* by Charles Perrault, and *Beauty and the Beast*, by Madame de Beaumont. Popular Bible stories included the *Creation, Adam and Eve, Noah's Ark, David and Goliath, Samson and Delilah, Daniel in the Lion's Den* , and *Jonah and the Whale.*

Family celebrations centered around Christmas, Easter, and birthdays. On birthdays, the birthday person chose where to have dinner. Major life events in the children's lives, such as Baptism as infants, Confession and First Communion in the second grade, and Confirmation in eighth grade were important family occasions. The family especially enjoyed Thanksgiving, because Elizabeth Anne's birthday fell on that day when she was born. And we always had the neighborhood Fourth of July fireworks celebration!

Every summer we took a family vacation, all nine of us in one station wagon. All of them loved places with rides. Actually the girls were more adventuresome than the boys: when all the girls were riding on Space Mountain at Disneyworld, the boys and I played some of the early video games such as Pac-Man and Elevator Action. One time when all of us took a ride on Small World, Daniel, who was five, waited outside and stood by the water fountain and turned it on for people to drink. A lady gave him a quarter. He decided he would get a job at Disney World when he grew up.

Prayer was part of our family life. Before dinner, we said grace.
Bless us, O Lord, and these thy gifts, which we are about to receive, from thy bounty, through Christ Our Lord, Amen.

When we finally got them all in bed, we ended the day with prayer, sometimes with a prayer to our Guardian Angel. Marilyn has a great belief in guardian angels.

>*Angel of God, my guardian dear,*
>>*to whom God's love commits me here.*
>*Ever this day be at my side,*
>>*to light the way and truly guide, Amen.*

We would always end the day with this prayer:

>*Now I lay me down to sleep;*
>>*I pray to the Lord my soul he will keep*
>*If I die before I awake,*
>>*I pray to the Lord my soul he will take.*

Then we asked God to bless each member of our family, the grandparents, Ernestine and everybody else.

Several of my colleagues began to change the name "Emergency Room" to "Emergency Department", or "ED" around 1980, when Emergency Medicine was named a "conjoined specialty", and the American Board of Emergency Medicine offered the first certifying examination. They wanted to show that we were a sophisticated department run by specialists in Emergency Medicine. The sense of being a proud new specialty was a healthy one. Emergency Medicine was formally recognized a primary specialty September 21, 1989 by the American Board of Medical Specialties, ironically the same day Hurricane Hugo struck Charleston! Now that our specialty has matured, we notice that surgeons never renamed the OR, the operating room! Perhaps now emergency physicians will be comfortable working in an "ER!"

The loss of respect for the Federal government spread to loss of respect for authority, and loss of respect for the next person. Somewhere in the 70s everyone began locking their doors at night and installing alarm systems. It used to be you could sleep with the windows up and get a nice breeze at night and you didn't need air conditioning as much. Your neighbors were your friends and part of your extended family. As crime escalated, and trust between people began to break down, locking the doors to your car and home became part of life. Everybody began installing those crazy alarm systems that in early days rarely worked.

Fortunately, we never installed one, even after the following incident:

One night about four in the morning, good old Mrs. Keebler, our night nurse, woke me up. I knew something was wrong because in those days they would let the doctors sleep, and would wake us up only for EMS and the critical patients and would not wake us up for all of the trivial cases that came in the ER. If someone had insomnia, Mrs. Keebler would give them a sleeping pill. If someone had a fever for less than 24 hours and was alert and with the program, Mrs. Keebler gave them Tylenol and gave them a choice of waiting until 6 am when she would wake up the doctor or they could go to see their own doctor in the morning. If someone had constipation, Mrs. Keebler would give them a laxative. We all trusted Mrs. Keebler, because she had common sense, and rarely if ever made a mistake.

This time Mrs. Keebler said that a robber had broken in this man's home and beaten him up. She was very upset at the way things had become in our society. Most of the time after being awakened at four in the morning I was semi-conscious, but her concern for the situation caught my attention, and I went to see the patient.

He was an average-sized man, all bruised up. The patient said that he was asleep on the second floor of his home when he heard a noise in the bushes outside . He got up and looked out his second story window and saw someone trying to break in his house! This patient happened to belong to a rifle club and was a sharpshooter.

He ran over to his gun case and grabbed a loaded rifle and a 9 millimeter Browning automatic. He tiptoed down the stairs and crawled over to the dining room window where the man was breaking in. At first he was angry at this assault on his house, property, and family, and when the man had finally jimmied open the window and was about to climb in, he realized that he could kill this man and he wouldn't go to jail. The patient stopped talking and looked up at me and then he said, "Doc, as angry as I was and wanting to shoot this man for what he was doing, in my heart I didn't want to have his blood on my conscience." He said that he laid the guns down and as the man was climbing into the window he decided to tackle him. The robber, at first surprised, became furious when his well-laid plans were frustrated and he began beating the homeowner, striking him senseless. Luckily, one of his sons woke up and came downstairs and on hearing this the robber jumped out of the window and ran. Fortunately, the patient had no fractures and, aside from multiple contusions and abrasions he was okay.

Figuring the patient had had a bad enough night I didn't charge him. But I kept wondering if I were in that same situation what would I have done. All of us began to ask ourselves what we would have done in that situation. All of us considered the patient lucky that the robber didn't grab one of the guns and kill him.

What would you have done?

Clark Hodgson was a young Chatham County police officer who was very idealistic. He was a gentleman, and the nurses thought he was very handsome and had great respect for him. Clark came up to the ER and gave a morning lecture to all the ER nurses. It was a Tuesday morning, and Clark told the nurses that he had been trained in psychology and that he would use psychology on the criminals and disruptive individuals when he was called to a scene. By listening to the person in distress, and showing concern Clark had learned to talk people down and make them calm and rational, and they would "come around." He had been in several dangerous situations and had had people turn guns over to him or prevented them from inflicting any self-harm. Clark also was very sincere and had a heart. All of us were very impressed with Clark Hodgson.

Saturday, that same week, was the worst day I ever had at Memorial Emergency. We had nine gunshot victims in a 12-hour shift. Only one patient died--a patient who had sustained three gunshot wounds at a standoff in Chatham County. The patient was Clark Hodgson. A patient had been released earlier in the week from a psychiatric hospital, and somehow was able to purchase a gun. Clark Hodgson was called onto the scene when this patient went berserk and began opening fire. Clark Hodgson had tried to reason with him. All we have left of a wonderful police officer is a street named after him.

The 1960s and 1970s brought a dramatic upswing in use of illicit drugs, as our younger generation, feeling disenfranchised from the federal government, and the loss of direction of our society, increasingly "tuned in, turned on, and dropped out."

Marijuana became very popular among college age students and young adults in the 1960s and peaked during the late 1970s when more than 60% of high school seniors reported having smoked marijuana at least once in their lifetime. Marijuana is the hemp plant, *cannabis sativa*. THC, or delta-9-tetrahydrocannabinol, is the principal active ingredient in the cannabis sativa plant. Marijuana generally refers to tobacco-like preparations of the leaves and flowers. Hashish is the resin extract from the tops of the flowering plants. Hash oil is a specially prepared extraction from the cannibis plant that can provide a THC concentration of 20% or higher. An average marijuana cigarette contains 15 to 30 milligrams of THC.

Marijuana has extensive physiologic effects on the human body. A major concern society must face is the effect of marijuana on the performance of an individual on the job, in the classroom, and on the highways. Its reputation as a cause of automobile accidents is well-deserved, as it slows one's reaction time. Marijuana interferes with short-term memory, affecting college and high school students in learning and testing, and in job workers learning new skills or trades. Marijuana has long-term effects on the respiratory system and the reproductive system, especially in the male.

Marijuana has excellent therapeutic properties. It is effective in reducing intraocular pressure in patients with glaucoma. It is effective in reducing nausea and vomiting in patients on chemotherapy. It is useful in the AIDS wasting syndrome. A 1996 referendum in California legalized marijuana for medicinal purposes, and three more states voted for legalization of marijuana for medicinal purposes on November 3, 1998, but the Federal government has thus far frustrated its use.

The use of **Cocaine** did not become prevalent until the 1980s in the United States. The late 1970s found cocaine, expensive and scarce, a status symbol, its use largely confined to the wealthy and socially prominent. With the introduction of inexpensive crack cocaine that could be smoked in cigarettes, cocaine abuse grew at an alarming rate. "Ice" and other amphetamines have effects similar to cocaine.

Cocaine, an alkaloid of the plant *Erythoxylon coca,* grows extensively in the Andes mountains. Coca leaves mixed with lime were chewed by Peruvian Indians as early as the sixth century and were an essential part of the Incan religion.

Although explorers introduced the leaves to Europe, it was not until 1860 that Niemann isolated the alkaloid cocaine. Sigmund Freud, the Viennese neurologist, began experimenting with cocaine in 1884 to relieve his own depression and became ecstatic about its curative abilities. It was not until Freud had used cocaine extensively for years that he wrote his great psychiatric works!

In 1884, Freud's close friend Karl Koller was the first to use cocaine as a local anesthetic in eye surgery and thus forever legitimized the use of cocaine in the medical profession. Today, cocaine is used in nasal surgery by plastic surgeons and Ear-Nose-Throat specialists, and by emergency physicians in emergency nasotracheal intubation.

In 1886, John Styth Pemberton of Atlanta marketed an elixir containing cocaine from the coca leaf and caffeine from the African kola nut and appropriately named it "Coca-cola." Coca-cola rapidly became one of the most popular elixirs in the country. Not until 1906 did the Coca-Cola Company agree to use decocainized coca leaves.

Cocaine was thought at one time to be a possible cure for tuberculosis. Indeed, in 1895, Robert Louis Stevenson, while undergoing cocaine therapy in a sanitarium, wrote the novel Dr. Jekyll and Mr. Hyde in only three days.

Cocaine came under the strict control of the Harrison Narcotic Act and is listed as a narcotic and dangerous drug. Its illicit use is subject to the same penalties as those applied to opium, morphine, and heroin.

Cocaine is also lethal. Cocaine as a cause of cardiac arrest presenting to an emergency department was described in 1979. In 1996 the National Institute on Drug Abuse reports that cocaine is the most common cause of death from drugs in the United States.

Hallucinogen abuse first appeared with the emergence of the drug culture in the 1960s, but has recently experienced a resurgence, especially in adolescents, on college campuses, at rock concerts, and at "rave" parties.

LSD, or D-lysergic acid diethylamide, was discovered by Dr. Albert Hofmann, a Swiss chemist, who was doing research on synthesis of ergot as found in Claviceps purpurea. On April 16, 1943, he discovered that the ergot derivative LSD-25 caused an "intense kaleidoscopic play of colors and fantasies." Further experiments by Dr. Hofmann and psychiatrists at the University of Zurich established that as little as 50 to 100 micrograms could produce a full-scale LSD "trip."

LSD has been intensively studied in the scientific community for possible legitimate use. LSD is a remarkable drug in that it makes cats afraid of mice, causes fish to swim backward, and produces fever in rabbits but hypothermia in pigeons. LSD was experimentally tried by the psychiatry community to bring to consciousness repressed thoughts and memories, but this practice has obviously fallen into disfavor. Reports of chromosomal damage from LSD in the late 1960s received sensational media attention, and the LSD "chromosome scare" dramatically curtailed the casual use of LSD.

Other hallucinogens include peyote, the common name for the North American cactus *Lophophora williamsii,* found in the deserts of the Southwestern United States and Mexico. The legal use of peyote and mescaline in the United States today is limited to Indian tribes in the Native American Church, which use the peyote as part of their religious ceremony. Peyote is a spineless cactus, which forms buttons with 7 to 10 ribs.   Peyote buttons are the round fleshy tubercles from the cactus, which maintain their hallucinogenic potency while in storage for later usage.

Mescaline, the active phenylethylamine alkaloid, was first isolated from peyote in 1896; the average hallucinogenic dose of synthetic mescaline is 5 mg/kg. Mescaline is the major active alkaloid of peyote. The cactus contains about 6% of mescaline when dried. One peyote button contains about 40 to 50 mg of mescaline, which explains the tradition of consuming 4 to 12 peyote buttons during each Indian ceremony. Mescaline sold on the street is usually LSD, PCP, or a designer drug.

The clinical effects of peyote and mescaline usually occur approximately one hour following ingestion, and begins with a gastrointestinal phase, predominantly nausea and vomiting.   This is followed by the psychoactive phase, which generally peaks 4 to 6 hours and resembles LSD intoxication. This temporal pattern of transition from the gastrointestinal phase to the psychoactive phase is markedly uniform and is characteristic of mescaline intoxication.

Symptoms usually resolve within 12 hours of ingestion. Deaths are rare, and are usually associated with accidents due to altered perception of the user.

Dimethyltryptamine (DMT) is known as Yurema in Brazil and is basic to the Brazilian Indian Kariri religion. DMT is prepared as snuff from the seeds, leaves, and pods of *Piptadenia peregrina, Prestonia amazenicum,* and *Mimosa hostilis.*   DMT intoxication closely resembles LSD, except that its effects last only 30 to 60 minutes.

Morning glory is the common name for plants of the *Convolvulaceae* family, many of which have been used for their hallucinogenic properties. A garden morning glory is a beautiful flower shaped like a funnel with heart-shaped leaves. The toxic part is the seed, which the American Indians ground into flour, then soaked in cold water, and strained with a cloth. The filtrate was then consumed during a religious ceremony. Mexican ololiuqui was the derivative of the morning glory *Rivea corymbosa.* *Ipomoea violaceae* is one of the common morning glory plants sold in garden catalogues in the United States; those with blue flowers are called Heavenly Blue, those with crimson flowers Scarlet O'Hara, and those with white flowers are known as Pearly Gates. The Hawaiian baby woodrose (*Argyreia nervosa*) and Hawaiian woodrose (*Merremia tuberosa*) also have hallucinogenic properties, but are considerably more potent.

Psilocybe mushrooms are found throughout the United States, and have hallucinogenic properties. Phencyclidine (PCB), or "angel dust", is a manufactured hallucinogen that was popular in the 1980s, but because of its long lasting and dangerous effects, has fallen into disfavor. Two psychotomimetic amphetamines commonly found at rave parties are "ecstasy" (MDMA) and "eve" (MDEA).

Heroin abuse, nearly erased from intravenous abuse because of the AIDS epidemic, is becoming more common with nasal "snorting" of the drug. Heroin is so addictive that it eventually leads to intravenous abuse, or "mainlining" the drug, leaving the abuser vulnerable to contacting the AIDS virus. Patients who abuse heroin are usually identified in the ER by needle marks or "tracks" where they "shot up" the drug. Heroin is a synthetic opiate with the chemical name of diacetylmorphine.

Morphine belongs to the Opium family of drugs, derived from the juice or sap of the opium poppy, *Papaver somniferum.* The red and white, pink and purple poppy flowers are grown extensively in the Orient, especially in China and India since ancient times. Opium sap from the heads of immature poppies, contains the natural alkaloids morphine, codeine, and numerous other naturally occurring opiates.

The term "opioid" refers to all drugs, natural (such as morphine) and synthetic (such as heroin) that have similar actions on the human body and which act on the opioid receptors of the brain.

Alcohol is still the leading toxin and remains the number one cause of emergency department visits. Ethanol is derived from fermentation of sugars in fruits, cereals, and vegetables. The blood ethanol concentration that defines legal intoxication in most states is 100 milligrams percent or 0.1%. However, in people who are not habitual drinkers, decreased reflexes, increased reaction time, and poor coordination may be seen at levels from 50 to 100 milligrams percent. Habitual drinkers have an increased tolerance.

Nicotine is an alkaloid obtained from the dry leaves and stems of the

Nicotiana plant species. These include *N. tabacum* (cultivated tobacco), *N. attenuata* (wild tobacco), and *N. glauca* (tree tobacco). Lobeline, the chief constituent of Indian tobacco, is obtained from the leaves and tops of *Lobella inflata.*

Cigarette smoking is the number one cause of preventable death in the United States.

Since educators cannot render effective discipline in schools, and parents give way to psychologists and social workers, there has been an alarming trend in the prescription of drugs such as Ritalin, Prozac, and Tofranil, for children "to modify behavior." *Children are being raised to go by their feelings.* When I was growing up and someone was disruptive in class it was said, "Well, he's just all boy." But now, for children today, they have a behavior disorder and are placed on medication. The child then thinks if he gets upset he needs a pill. And, since doctors and psychiatrists charge $50 to $100 a visit, in this time of consumerism, physicians feel obligated to give a prescription of something just to justify their fee. When the child becomes a teenager, there is no wonder that he or she turns to illicit drugs to *feel good*. The need to feel good helps to explain the rampant teenage drug abuse prevalent today in our society.

The prescription of mind-altering medications to adults has dramatically risen in the past 20 years. The anti-anxiety drug Valium was the number one prescription drug for seven years in the 1970s. Then the 1980s saw the anti-ulcer drugs Tagamet, Zantac, and Pepcid become leading drugs as stress levels reached new levels in our fast-paced society.

Society has become ever more confining and less tolerant of the individual and the ebb and flow of his or her emotions. We have night and day, high tide and low tide, and our own biorhythms. But God help you if you have a mood at work!

As more and more people feel overwhelmed with our fast-paced society, depression has become a leading mental illness, so that now, two of the top selling drugs in the United States today are the major antidepressants Prozac and Zoloft! Frankie, one of our ER nurses, commented, "It seems like nearly everybody is on something these days." Chemical dependency, whether pre-scribed drugs or illicit drugs, is commonplace in American society today.

Prozac (Fluoxetine) has the ability to inhibit the uptake of serotonin at nerve connections (synapses), and thus produces increased serotonin at nerve endings. This has proven safe and effective in alleviating depression. Prozac, and related drugs such as Zoloft and Paxil, have become the drugs of choice for depression.

While there is no doubt that there are definitely patients who can benefit from Prozac in selected instances, I personally feel these drugs are horribly over-prescribed by our profession.

Anxiety and mild depression are normal human responses to situations in one's life, but because they are unpleasant, they serve as catalysts to change one's environment. Once the unpleasant situation is solved, the anxiety and depression lift, and a sense of peace and relief set in. Some patients on Prozac just feel good all the time, no matter what situation they are in! It is as if they don't care any more, and since they feel good, there is no stimulus to change.

Furthermore, there are significant social ramifications to having millions of Americans dependent on medication, psychiatrists and psychologists. These patients become so dependent on their medication they are subject to manipulation and control by anyone with unethical intent.

A 29 year old white female was brought in one night about 2:00 in the morning during the week in seizures. EMS had picked her up. EMS had gone to her home and called us and we had ordered intravenous Valium (which in addition to helping patients calm down is an excellent medication for seizures). When EMS arrived, the patient was still seizing in spite of 10 milligrams of intravenous Valium. One of the paramedics told me that the patient's husband had a reputation for being a drug pusher and was thought to be a distributor of cocaine. The patient continued to seize and we had to give her another 10 milligrams of intravenous Valium to stop the seizure. Fifteen minutes later she began seizing again and we gave her another 5 milligrams of intravenous Valium to stop the seizure. We call patients with recurrent seizures over a 30 minute period as having status epilepticus, a true medical emergency. She stopped seizing for another 15 minutes and an anonymous phone caller told us that the patient had snorted some very pure cocaine. The patient began seizing again. I had never seen status epilepticus from cocaine before, and being in the 1970s, there had not been much in the medical literature concerning this subject. I gave her 5 more milligrams of Valium (for an unheard-of total of 30 milligrams of intravenous Valium), which briefly stopped her seizures. All I could think of at this point was to paralyze the patient with an intravenous anesthetic. I called an anesthesiologist who recommended we give the patient pancuronium bromide, a synthetic derivative of naturally occurring curare, the arrow-tip poison used by South American Indians. We intubated the patient, and placed her on a ventilator, and then gave her pancuronium bromide. This stopped the patient's seizures. We also gave her intravenous phenobarbital which would stop the abnormal electrical activity in the brain. By this time, the patient had a fever and a build-up of acid after having nearly an hour of seizure activity. The excessive muscle activity caused by the seizures causes a buildup in the blood of lactic acid, and we corrected this by giving her a base, intravenous sodium bicarbonate. We admitted the patient to the hospital. No one, including her husband, ever came to visit this patient.

Then, there is this 40 year old patient in Trauma 3 who had a laceration on his right hand. You realize in the ER there are all kinds of people in this world. Mr. James set up the suture tray. The wound appeared pretty superficial and he had good hand function. I introduced myself, gave him some Lidocaine to numb the wound, and started to suture. To make conversation, I asked him how this happened. The patient went on to tell me that he had bought a German submarine from World War II Germany and he was taking the German submarine from New York to Florida. He was having some engine trouble and so he pulled into the Savannah port. The patient was very proud of his prized collection, and he was trying to fix it himself and he had cut his hand. He said there were only seven of these submarines left in the world! I could tell the man's submarine meant a great deal to him and might have been all he had in the world as he had no crew or family to help him. The patient asked me if I lived in Savannah and knew of anywhere that he could stay that wouldn't be too expensive. The patient then laughed and said, "You know, Doc, I might be here for a while because it's not too easy getting spare parts for my submarine."

Stingrays are a common cause of emergency department visits along the coast. Three common stingrays are the round stingray, *Urolophus halleri,* found along the Pacific coast from California to Panama; the blunt-nosed stingray, *Dasyatis sayi,* found along the eastern Atlantic coast of North, Central, and South America; and the spotted eagle ray, *Aetobatus narinari,* found throughout tropical waters from the Atlantic to the Pacific.

There are several families of rays, such as the manta rays, the electric rays, and sting rays. Some stingrays display an interesting characteristic: They have a sense of territory and usually do not stray too far from their claimed "turf." The Dasyatis stingrays are difficult to detect because of their habit of lying buried in the mud or sand with only a portion of the body exposed.

Accidents usually occur when bathers step on a buried ray. The ray then whips its tail up and forward, driving the stinger into the foot or leg. Shuffling the feet in murky water causes stingrays to swim away from the immediate area. Commercial fisherman are sometimes stung in the hand or arms when emptying nets. Divers may be stung on the chest or abdomen.

A patient named Claude came hobbling through the ER front door screaming in pain. He had just been attacked by a stingray at the beach. He had a deep puncture wound near his ankle and was in severe pain. Our ER technician, Sammy Marsh, was born in Savannah and grew up on the waterways. He was a wonderful naturalist, and knew a lot of marine first aid. Sammy told me to place the injury in a bucket of hot water, as hot as the patient could stand it. At first the patient objected and wanted a pain shot, but I trusted Sammy and told the patient we should give it a try. Amazingly enough, it gave the patient great relief.

Hot water immersion has become a standard of care for stingray envenomation, and is also used as well for first aid therapy for injury from sea urchins, starfish, catfish, weaver fish, stone fish, and scorpion fish.

One morning about 10:00 someone came running through the ER front door, shouting that a young electrician who was working on the Memorial grounds near the entrance had been electrocuted by high voltage electric lines. So, I ran out of the ER and dashed down to where the patient was laying. He was in full cardiac arrest, laying on the ground right next to the entrance on Waters avenue. Pam, our head nurse, said that she would follow with a defibrillator. One of his fellow co-workers was giving him mouth-to-mouth resuscitation and CPR. Pam arrived and we shocked the patient. He immediately responded and developed a normal heart rhythm and a good pulse and blood pressure. By the time we had him transferred back to the ER, he was beginning to stir. I called a colleague in cardiology, and he placed the patient in the coronary care unit. The patient fully recovered and went home the next day. We were all very happy and felt the patient was truly blessed to have a co-worker who gave him CPR. It is the first 5 minutes that count!

One occasionally sees victims of snakebite in Savannah. In North America, two snake families have venomous members: the pit vipers (Crotalidae), which include the rattlesnakes, copperheads, and water moccasins; and the coral snakes (Elapidae). The crotalids primarily are toxic to the cardiovascular and blood systems of the human body, while the elapids are primarily toxic to the nervous system.

One afternoon a 35 year old patient had been bitten twice by an Eastern Diamondback rattlesnake. He had picked up the rattlesnake by reflex, when he saw the rattlesnake slithering over to where his little girl was standing. He had driven straight over to St. Joseph's Hospital and had arrived there 20 minutes after the bite. He was quite pale looking but otherwise his vital signs, including blood pressure and pulse, were stable. An intravenous line was begun, but within 45 minutes, the patient began to deteriorate.

An internist colleague immediately rushed to the hospital, and admitted the patient, and asked me to consult with him. We found the patient in shock. He was semi-conscious, and his muscles were quivering. The laboratory technician informed us one of his clotting studies was out to "infinity." We spent the next 8 hours in the intensive care unit, through the middle of the night, treating one of the most critical patients we have ever faced. A hematologist and a plastic surgeon helped care for the patient. In addition to fluid resuscitation and the administration of several blood products, the patient required 20 vials of snake-bite anti-venin. Fortunately, the patient did well, and went home a week later.

We moved back to Washington D. C. in 1983 when my father was ill. A great friend of mine gave me work at Greater Southeast Hospital in Washington, D.C., and I joined an excellent staff of well-trained emergency physicians. Greater Southeast Hospital was as busy as Memorial and we saw over 50,000 patients a year. We had double coverage there at Greater Southeast Hospital.

My first day at Greater Southeast Hospital we had a pedestrian hit by a truck, and because I was new the other emergency physician took the patient. The patient had multiple life-threatening injuries and presented in shock. And, even though the attending emergency physician had help from several specialists, the patient died. When the family, who was gathering outside, heard the news, they erupted in anger. One of the family members came in the ER doors and screamed, "I'm gonna sue." What a difference from my first day in Savannah in 1973!

We did enjoy going home to Washington. We moved to a great neighborhood with loads of youngsters for our children to play with, just off George Washington Parkway towards Mount Vernon in Alexandria. Matthew, Joseph, Dan, and I liked to go to the Washington Redskin games. Jeanne and Charlene especially had many friends their age. Elizabeth Anne and I used to bike down the path by the Potomac River over to visit our cousin Pat Whiteford and her family. We alternated Sundays, either visiting my father, or taking a tour of Washington's many historic treasures.

Madeleine is a beautiful joy, as well as a surprise. She brings happiness to those around her. Exceptionally bright, she has a wonderful sense of humor. Even at a young age she could create the most outlandish stories, such as on April Fool's Day, and have you believe them! When Madeleine was 5 years old she found and adopted our cat Mopsy.

One of the major changes we had to make in our raising of the children was to diminish the influence of television. The media has become a major influence in our society. Every family today watches hours upon hours of television. Whereas television once portrayed men of great character, and ideal families with high moral standards in the 1960s and early 1970s, television has become an evil influence in our society. The television show *Dallas* was probably the first to portray sleazy and immoral characters as the heroes. As competition for advertising grew, sex, violence, and aberrant relationships were added to increase ratings.

Gossip has become a major industry in the media. In spite of their human failings, President Kennedy was an exceptional President and Princess Diana was an outstanding humanitarian. But today the media portrays everything negative about anyone, such as the verbal assassination of President Kennedy, whether there is any truth or not. Of course, it is better if they are dead, because they cannot refute it. There was a time that individuals were judged on their merits, and everything negative was left unsaid.

One of the better decisions we made for our family was to move the television set out of the living room, stop cable, and have only one television set. While we all went through withdrawal for a while, in one or two weeks we all began to visit, communicate, converse, listen to music, play with the family pets, and enjoy family life!

Dad loved his grandchildren. On Father's Day, 1984, I will always remember how his eyes lit up and his face broke out in a big smile when he saw all the children hop out of the station wagon and run up to him. It was the last time he went out to dinner.

September was a rough month. Dad had to go into the hospital on September 4th. Somehow he held on until my birthday on September 7. When I got off work and walked in the room, he wished me Happy Birthday, and told me to take care of Mom. Those were the last words he ever spoke. He then lapsed into a coma, never to awaken. My father passed away on September 8, 1984.

We moved back to Savannah in 1986, and I began practicing emergency medicine in South Carolina. In 1988 I was invited to participate in a seminar on Emergency Medicine in Brisbane, Australia, the site of the World Fair. I took our youngest son Daniel with me, who was thirteen. Daniel and I had a wonderful time together, and had a chance to become really close.

Crossing the international date-line is an experience. On the way over we skipped a day, and on the way home we lived the same day twice! After a 26-hour flight, we crashed in our hotel and slept 16 hours. We woke up and were wide awake over there at 3 in the morning. Daniel was up first, and was washing up, and excitedly called me over to the sink - "Watch, Dad." I could tell something was unusual, but couldn't put my finger on it. Daniel explained that the water was going down the drain clockwise, whereas in the United States, it goes down the drain counter-clockwise. He explained it has something to do with the differences in the hemispheres, and the influence of the magnetic fields of the North and South poles.

The next day we saw the koala bears and the kangaroos, and that afternoon we went to the Brisbane World Fair. While I was touring all the countries with exhibits, Daniel was having a great time playing all the latest video games from Japan that had not yet reached the States, such as Super -Contra. It was after Papua New Guinea that a great truth came upon me.

I was sitting outside thinking about the Papua New Guinea exhibit, watching the crowd go by. I realized every country and every group has specific customs and special dress to make them feel special and unique. This is not much different than Americans who live in special residential areas with gate guards, drive BMWs, and wear the latest fashion clothes.

The sweepers came by cleaning up, much like in Bombay, where the sweepers come every morning to sweep away the people who died of starvation on the street during the night. If I died right then, I had no identification. They might as well sweep me away also. I then felt totally meaningless, one of five billion people on this planet.

But then I realized in a flash that there was only one me, one of five billion, and I must be here for a purpose. All I have to do is be myself, and use the talents God gave me!

We also had a chance to visit New Zealand, which is a most beautiful country. We flew into Wellington on the North Island, and then crossed the scenic Cook Straight to the South Island, and then took the train along the coast to Christchurch, where we spent most of our time in New Zealand. There we visited the U. S. exhibit on Antarctica. It was those quiet evenings in the hotels after dinner that we had a chance to visit and talk and listen to each other. Daniel is a very gentle soul.

One day a 19 year old white female came in after having taken a multiple drug overdose. We pumped her stomach and gave her activated charcoal through the gastric tube we had placed through her nose. Activated charcoal adsorbs the toxin and prevents the drug from being absorbed into the blood stream. Because she had taken mild sedatives, we placed her in our observation room in the Emergency Department until she woke up. A few hours later she woke up and became responsive.

I went over to talk to her. I was very curious as to why she had done this. After all, she was the same age as two of my daughters. And, my heart went out to her. She told me she had nothing to live for. She said she didn't talk to her mother, and she didn't know where her father was. She said that she had done everything there was to do in this world. She began having sex when she was 13 years old. She had sex with many different guys both for love and for kicks. She said that she even tried it with a girl to see what it was like. She also had tried every single kind of drug that had been made, both legal and illegal, by every kind of route there was. She had smoked drugs, inhaled drugs, and shot drugs. She had tried sex and drugs in kinky ways. She had done it all and there was nothing left to do.

I asked her if she ever thought about helping somebody else. She could try that for a change. Somebody else might appreciate if she cared for them. She began crying and said that nobody ever really cared about her. This is 1993. It was then I realized that we now have a whole generation of young Americans, many of whom have no belief system. They are only here for self-gratification. A whole generation of lost and rootless souls exist.

The younger members of the family inform me that alternative rock groups, representing "Generation X" of the 1990s, such as Pearl Jam ("Ten") are in vogue.   Popular singles include the Soul Asylum's "Runaway Train", the Gin Blossoms "Hey Jealousy", and Guns 'n' Roses "November Rain." Fortunately, country music is still romantic, and Whitney Houston has a romantic song, "I Will Always Love You." Madeleine likes classical music. The college-age group seems to like a group called Widespread Panic. Is this name prophetic? They had one single called "Hope in a Hopeless World."

Fortunately, there was still something left for the parents of Generation X. An unknown playwright named Gaston Leroux was born in Paris in 1868.   He did achieve some success in France with his detective novels, such as *The Mystery of the Yellow Room*, starring the detective Joseph Rouletabille. How-ever, his plays never achieved any recognition during his lifetime. It was not until nearly 1990 that his genius was discovered with *The Phantom of the Opera.* Not only was the play an international success, the recording became one of the longest running albums in history on the music charts.

On December 1, 1997, following an informal prayer meeting of 35 Chris-tian high school students in the school lobby at Heath High School in West Paducah, Kentucky, a 14 year-old student opened fire on them, killing 3 students, and wounding 5 more.

A 28-year old mother of five came home at 7 in the morning after staying out all night abusing crack cocaine, and, after a heated argument with her husband, took an overdose of 60 capsules of her mother's blood pressure medi-cation. The medication was a calcium-channel blocker, the most common blood pressure medication on the market today, products such as Procardia, Calan, Cardizem, Norvasc, and over 10 other similar products. She rapidly fell into coma, and was transported to Charleston Memorial Hospital with early shock.

Upon arriving at the ER, she lost her blood pressure and pulse as she was transferred to our stretcher. Thanks to the heroic efforts of our nurses Doris, Anne, Susan, and other staff-members, she was quickly evaluated and placed on a cardiac monitor, and one ampoule (one gram) of intravenous calcium chloride was rapidly administered. A carotid pulse returned. We eventually gave her 4 grams of calcium chloride in the first hour.   She was then admitted to the Intensive Care Unit, where intravenous calcium chloride was continued until she stabilized. She went home the next day.

And so, here we are, America, March 24, 1998.

Today in America our children are not allowed to pray or learn the Ten Commandments in public school.

Today our children are being raised by one parent or two parents, but, either way, they are probably at work.

Today our children watch sex and violence and learn about drugs and homosexuality on television.

Today our children listen to satanic music on the radio, and listen to chants after Marilyn Manson rock concerts, "We hate to love, we love to hate."

Today our children see the President, our leader, immersed in a live soap opera in Washington, D. C, and watch him fly to Africa to escape the pressure. The President is from Arkansas.

Today, in Jonesboro, Arkansas, 4 children ages 11 to 12, Brittany Varner, Stephanie Johnson, Paige Ann Herring, and Natalie Brooks, and a teacher, Shannon Wright, were killed by gunfire by two children, Mitchell Johnson, age 13, and Andrew Golden, age 11. Ten were injured.

On April 20, 1999, at Columbine High School in Littleton, Colorado, two high school students, who reportedly played the video game "Doom" and considered themselves neo-Nazis, entered the school with semi-automatic weapons. Their rampage slaughtered a teacher and 12 students, and wounded at least 23, some of whom remain paraplegic or in serious condition at the time of this writing. Following the massacre, the two committed suicide.

They asked one student, Cassie Bernall, if she believed in God, and when she answered yes, they shot her in the face and killed her.

The thirteen slain at Columbine were Cassie Bernall, Steven Curnow, Corey DePooter, Kelly Fleming, Matthew Kechter, Daniel Mauser, Daniel Rohrbough, the teacher William "Dave" Sanders, Rachel Scott, Isaiah Shoels, John Tomlin, LaurenTownsend, and Kyle Velasquez.

A truly unique experience in my medical career was to see an entirely new disease unfold and develop into a world-wide pandemic - AIDS, the Acquired Immunodeficiency Syndrome. In 1981 the Communicable Disease Center identified unexplained occurrences of *Pneumocystis carinii* pneumonia and Kaposi's sarcoma in homosexual men. l982 saw the first pediatric case of AIDS. In 1983, the Human Immunodeficiency Virus (HIV) was first isolated from a patient with lymphadenopathy (swollen lymph glands). HIV testing was begun in 1985.

The Human Immunodeficiency Virus attacks a key component of the immune system, the CD4 T lymphocyte white blood cell, which helps the body to fight infection. The virus invades the CD4 T lymphocyte, and takes over the cellular machinery of the cell to reproduce itself, and thus destroys the cell. When new virus particles are reproduced and the cell dies, the virus particles are released to invade more CD4 T lymphocytes, and the cycle continues, until the patient can no longer fight infection and dies. There has been some breakthrough in the management of AIDS, with the development of the new and powerful antiretroviral agents. While the new drugs can prolong the patient's life and sense of well- being, there is no cure yet in sight, because of the ability of the virus to rapidly mutate.

In 1997 there were 30 million patients worldwide living with AIDS. There were also 5.8 million new cases of AIDS, and 2.7 million patients died of AIDS in 1997!   AIDS is now the leading cause of death in the United States among ages 25-44 years.

The primary means of transmission of the HIV virus is sexual transmission. Blood and blood products are another major source. In the United States, which primarily has the **B** strain (or clade), 50% of patients are homosexual men, and 25% are intravenous drug abusers. Patients also contracted AIDS by receiving contaminated blood transfusions, by an occupational needle-stick from HIV-infected patient in hospitals, and by birth as infants to HIV-positive mothers.

In Asia, such as the country of Thailand, which primarily has the **E** clade, transmission is primarily heterosexual, as in Africa, which primarily has the **A** strain. Heterosexual transmission is on the rise in the United States, particularly in prostitutes, partners of intravenous drug abusers, and promiscuous young adults.

He checked into the ER late at night with a fever of 103 degrees and a cough. He was thin, and short of breath. Some of the staff made fun of him because of his bizarre appearance. He was wearing a dress, had high-heels on, and had long fingernails painted purple.

I felt uncomfortable going in to see him, but actually he was quite thoughtful and pleasant. He was 27 years old, and had been losing weight for the last six months, and had been coughing for about three weeks. The fever and shortness of breath occurred in the past twenty-four hours.

I suspected AIDS, but hesitated to ask him about his personal life. Almost reading my mind, he asked, "You have some questions, doctor?"

His name was William. His mother ran away when he was an infant, and his father had many women move in and out during his childhood. The first woman that moved in used to dig her fingernails into his arm and shake him mercilessly when she was angry. One time she burned him with a hot iron on his thigh. William pulled up his dress and exposed himself to show me the burn.

The next woman used to lock him in a dark closet - she didn't stay long, because his Dad came home early one day and there was another man there. Another woman had her girl friends over, and gave William a pill, and they all laughed at him when he began to act funny.

William endured all this because he loved his father. His father worked construction, and even though he loved sports, he never pushed or teased William because of his lack of physical prowess. Inept as his father was at being a parent, he loved William and was nice to him. Looking at the female figures in his life, it was no wonder that William was gay.

Aside from his fever, his physical examination was unremarkable. However, his chest X-ray did reveal a pneumonia, probably *Pneumocystis carinii*. I began an intravenous antibiotic called Septra, and admitted him to the Hospital. He did poorly, and, as this was before the new AIDS drugs, William died within six months. Knowing William changed my attitude to these patients - from then on, I took an interest in AIDS and did all I could to help AIDS patients.

Treating these young patients with tragic lives created within me a sadness, and a concern for the future of our children and grandchildren, and for the future of American society. The inquisitive nature of our seven children led me to search for answers concerning the meaning of life.

And then there was Nick.

CHAPTER 3
An Emergency Physician's Viewpoint on Near-Death Experience

Death, be not proud, though some have called thee
Mighty and dreadful, for thou are not so;
For those whom thou think'st thou dost overthrow
Die not, poor Death; nor yet canst thou kill me.
From rest and sleep, which but thy picture be,
Much pleasure; then from thee much more must flow;
And soonest our best men with thee do go -
Rest of their bones and souls' delivery!
Thou'rt slave to fate, chance , kings, and desperate men,
And dost with poison, war, and sickness dwell;
And poppy or charms can make us sleep as well
And better than thy stroke. Why swell'st thou then?
One short sleep past, we wake eternally,
And death shall be no more: Death, thou shalt die.
Death, Be Not Proud
John Donne, 1573-1631

In the early days of medicine up until the 1950s and early 1960s, patients died a natural death either at home or in the hospital. All doctors could ever do was quite literally hold the patient's hand, comfort the patient and the family, and provide relief of pain in the final days and hours of the patient's life. Today, it is a blessing if you are fortunate enough to die in such a peaceful fashion.

An American physician Dr. Claude Beck successfully performed electrical defibrillation of the heart on a 14 year old patient during open chest surgery in 1947. Dr. Paul Zoll performed the first successful closed-chest cardiac defibrillation in 1955. Dr. Lown of Boston published further work on electrical defibrillation of the heart with the use of direct current in 1962. As I went through medical school and residency at Georgetown University Hospital, we gradually began to replace alternating current (AC) defibrillators with the safer direct current (DC) defibrillators to resuscitate a patient.   Direct current defibrillators are still in use today.

Open heart surgery also had a profound effect on the management of critical patients. Dr. Charles Hufnagel performed the first successful open heart operation in 1951, when he replaced a leaky aortic valve with a plastic ball valve. He was chairman of our Department of Surgery at Georgetown University Hospital in Washington, D.C. There were times when a "Dr. Heart" or "Code Blue" was called, and Dr. Hufnagel and his cardiovascular team would respond and open the patient's chest in the patient's room and perform open and direct massage of the heart, and then take the patient to the OR for open-heart surgery.

Patients who once died were now living because of defibrillation or open-heart surgery. Now, after a period of apparent death, which could last 15 to 30 minutes of having no vital signs, no blood pressure, pulse, or heartbeat, we were beginning to see some patients achieve full recovery and mental function and leave the hospital and go home. Also, some patients had some fascinating and unusual memories about their near-death experiences, patients such as Nick.

Nick was an orderly at one of the hospitals where I practiced emergency medicine. He was one of the nicest guys I had ever met, but he had a miserable personal life. He was about 30 years old and divorced, had three children, and just didn't seem to have very good judgment. Worst of all Nick had a terrible problem with cocaine. One Sunday evening he presented to the emergency room as a patient with a sore throat. Nick then preceded to have a cardiac arrest. Considering his age and his initial complaint, this was completely unexpected by the Emergency Room staff. A valiant effort ensued, and they were finally able to resuscitate Nick. They flew him to Memorial Medical Center in Savannah by helicopter.

I always liked Nick and went to the coronary care unit the following day to see him. He was awake and recognized me. He was very glad to see me and reached out his hand. I was deeply moved to see him alive and awake because I heard it was a very prolonged resuscitation, and they were not sure if Nick was going to make it.

Nick then told me that he had seen Jesus Christ. He also must have read the skepticism in my mind because he repeated, "Les, I really did see Jesus and He is real. He is filled with love and He is going to have mercy on me. But I need to come back for a little while and settle a few things, and He has given me that chance and I am so grateful."

Nick told me that he had come out of his body and could see everything in the emergency room that happened. He said, "Things are different." He could see people and hear conversations in the department as well as his own patient room.

Nick eventually became well enough to leave the hospital. When he came back to work, he was a changed man, a man of peace. He made a gesture of love towards his wife and family and settled his affairs, and then died shortly thereafter.

In 1975 Dr. Raymond A. Moody wrote the book *Life After Life* (Mockingbird Books, Marietta, Georgia, 1975), in which he described the phenomenon of near-death experiences. The book became a world-wide best seller and is still available in our nation's book stores. Several similar books have followed, but Dr. Moody is recognized as the pioneer in this field. Dr. Moody describes 15 different phases that evolve during the experience of dying. Not all of these occur in every patient that lives to tell us about their experience.

One of the characteristics of the near death experience is *ineffability*, or the inability to explain the experience. Patients always start off by explaining it is impossible to explain what happened, because "it's like in a different world."

Some describe *hearing the news* that they have been pronounced dead, followed by *feelings of peace and quiet*. For example, an ER nurse related to me what had happened to her when she was about 11 years old. She was playing with friends in a swimming pool and one of them held her under the water. She became frantic because she could not get to the top and became more frantic as she was losing consciousness. Then she remembers feelings of peace and quiet come through her and then she saw, like on a movie screen, her whole life appear before her. And, then she began to see a white light. It was then that she woke up laying on the side of a pool being given mouth-to-mouth resuscitation. Dr. Moody describes some of the patients he interviewed *hearing a noise.* A common experience is being transported through *a dark tunnel.*

Many patients describe coming *out of the body.* This is the phenomenon that is the most difficult for physicians to dismiss, because patients often describe events during resuscitation and other facts that are impossible to refute. Dr. Michael Sabom, in his book *Recollections of Death: A Medical Investigation* (1982), studied 32 patients who had near-death experiences (NDE), many of whom were medically unsophisticated. He performed his study before there was much publicity concerning NDE. He asked them to describe what went on during their own resuscitation. Not one of them made a mistake. This presented very strong evidence to Dr. Sabom that these patients were actually outside of their body and looking down and watching what was going on.

Either while in the tunnel or out of the body, patients describe *meeting others*, who frequently serve as guides for the rest of the journey. Often it is their guardian angel, or someone they had loved very much and who had passed away.

The most beautiful experience is seeing *The Light.* Patients have an overwhelming feeling of love and awe, and say they are in the presence of God or Jesus when they see the light. Once they see the light they want to stay there forever, as the feeling of peace and love is all embracing and comforting.

Patients describe a *review* of their whole life plays before them. They often feel the hurt they have caused others during this life review, but also the joy they have given others in their life.

For patients that return they meet a *border or limit.* They are often asked if they want to stay or to go back, but in other cases they do not have a choice and feel themselves being drawn back. They often realize that they have a purpose or mission they need to accomplish. Some actually describe the experience of *coming back.*

Upon their return, patients may or may not *tell others*, but the experience generally has a profound *effect on their lives*. They have a *new view of death,* as they realize it is just a transition or a passage to a new existence. There may or may not be *corroboration* of the events.

An afterlife has been described in many diverse cultures and civilizations. It is important to note that each culture discovered this phenomenon on their own, as world-wide communication did not exist in ancient history. The oldest civilization with recorded manuscripts is the Hebrew culture: the ancient *Torah* comprises the first five books of the Old Testament of our modern Bible. Although these books were composed in different time periods and in geographically distant regions of the world, the *Egyptian Book of the Dead ,* the *Tibetan Book of the Dead ,* and the *Aztec Song of the Dead* all show belief in an after-life in these ancient cultures. The Grecian writer Plato believed the soul is imprisoned in the body and separates from the body at the time of death to live in eternity. In fact, Plato describes the equivalent of a near-death experience in his famous work, *The Republic!* Since the Biblical ethic is the foundation of our Western civilization, it is appropriate to review the Bible as a source of information on the afterlife. Scripture quotations are from 4 major Christian Bibles, Catholic and Protestant.

One of the earliest references to the after-life in the Old Testament occurs in the book of Isaiah:

"But your dead shall live, their corpses shall rise;
awake and sing, you who lie in the dust.
For your dew is a dew of light,
and the land of shades gives birth."
Isaiah 26:19 [New American]

The book of Daniel also refers to the after-life:

"Many of those who sleep
in the dust of the earth shall awake,
Some shall live forever,
others shall be an everlasting horror and disgrace."
Daniel 12:2 [New American]

The last book of the Greek Septuagint Old Testament, the Second Book of Maccabees, refers to the resurrection of life. Chapter Seven describes the cruel murder of seven sons and their mother by King Antiochus Epiphanes, after he plundered Jerusalem and the Temple in the second century B. C.

When the second son was about to die after being tortured, he said:

Thou indeed, O most wicked man,
destroyest us out of this present life ;
but the King of the world will raise us up,
who die for his laws, in the resurrection of eternal life.
2 Maccabees 7:9 [Douay-Rheims]

As the fourth son was near death, he spoke:

It is better, being put to death by men,
to look for hope from God,
to be raised up again by him;
for, as to thee thou shalt have no resurrection unto life.
2 Maccabees 7:14 [Douay-Rheims]

When the seventh son was about to suffer the same fate, his mother bravely encouraged him:

> *I know not how you came into being in my womb.*
> *It was not I who gave you life and breath ,*
> > *nor I who set in order the*
> > > *elements within each of you.*
> *Therefore the Creator of the world,*
> > *who shaped the beginning of man*
> > > *and devised the origin of all things,*
> *will in his mercy*
> > *give life and breath back to you again,*
> *since you now forget yourselves*
> > *for the sake of his laws.*
> *2 Maccabees 7:22-23*
> *[Revised Standard Version, or RSV]*

The Lord God is frequently referred to in the Bible as the **Light**. As early as the Book of Exodus, God became a pillar of fire to guide his people from the land of Egypt:

> *And the Lord went before them*
> > *by day in a pillar of cloud to lead them along the way,*
> > *and by night in a pillar of fire to give them LIGHT,*
> > > *that they might travel by day and by night;*
> > > > *Exodus 13:21 [RSV]*

The Book of Psalms contains many references to God as the Light, for example:

> *Lord, Lift thou up the LIGHT of thy countenance upon us.*
> > *Psalms 4:6*
> > > *[Authorised or King James Version, or AKJV]*

> *For thou will LIGHT my candle*
> > *The Lord my God will enlighten my darkness.*
> > > *Psalms 18:29 [AKJV]*

> *The Lord is my LIGHT and my salvation;*
> *whom shall I fear?*
> *Psalms 27:1 [King James]*

> *For with thee is the fountain of life;*
> *in thy LIGHT shall we see light.*
> *Psalms 36:9 [King James]*

The prophet Isaiah continues this theme:

> *"No longer shall the sun be your LIGHT by day,*
> *Nor the brightness of the moon*
> *shine upon you at night;*
> *The LORD shall be your LIGHT forever."*
> *Isaiah 60:19-20 [New American]*
> *(emphasis added)*

Jesus describes himself as the Light of the World.

> *I am the LIGHT of the World.*
> *John 9:5 [King James]*

One of the most famous episodes in the Bible describing the light is from the New Testament, when Saul was on the road to Damascus:

> *"At midday, along the way. O King,*
> *I saw a LIGHT from the sky,*
> *brighter than the sun,*
> *shining around me and my traveling companions.*
> *We all fell to the ground, and I heard a voice*
> *saying to me in Hebrew,*
> *'Saul, Saul, why are you persecuting me?...'*
> *And I said, 'Who are you, sir?'*
> *And the Lord replied,*
> *' I am Jesus whom you are persecuting'".*
> *Acts of the Apostles 26:13-15 [New American]*

The epistle of John in the New Testament also describes God as the Light:

> *"This is the message*
> *we have heard from Him and proclaim to you, that*
> *God is LIGHT and in him is no darkness at all.*
> *I John 1:5 [RSV]*

As early as the Book of Genesis, we read that God the creator of heaven and earth, lives in heaven:

> *Then the Lord rained upon Sodom and Gomorrah*
> *brimstone and fire from the Lord out of heaven ;*
> *and he destroyed these cities, and all the country*
> *about, all the inhabitants of the cities,*
> *and all things that spring from the earth.*
> *Genesis 19:24-25 [Douay-Rheims]*

Heaven is where God, the source of light, lives and watches over mankind, as noted in the following passage:

> *The Lord looks down from heaven,*
> *he sees all the sons of men;*
> *from where he sits enthroned*
> *he looks forth on all the inhabitants of the earth.*
> *he who fashions all the hearts of them all,*
> *and observes all their deeds.*
> *Psalms 33:13-15 [RSV]*

Jesus describes the kingdom of heaven in a parable from the Gospel of St. Matthew:

> *Another parable he put before them, saying,*
> *"The kingdom of heaven may be compared to a*
> *man who sowed good seed in his field; but while*
> *men were sleeping, his enemy came and sowed*
> *weeds among the wheat, and went away.*

So when the plants came up and bore grain, then the weeds appeared also. And the servants of the householder came and said to him, "Sir, did you not sow good seed in your field? How then has it weeds?'

He said to them, 'An enemy has done this.'

The servants said to him, 'Then do you want us to go and gather them?'

But he said, 'No; lest in gathering the weeds you root up the wheat along with them. Let both grow together until the harvest; and at harvest time I will tell the reapers, Gather the weeds first and bind them in bundles to be burned, but gather the wheat into my barn..."

Then he left the crowds and went Into the house. And his disciples came to him, saying, "Explain to us the parable of the weeds of the field."

He answered, "He who sows the good seed is the Son of man; the field is the world, and the good seed means the sons of the kingdom; the weeds are the sons of the evil one, and the enemy who sowed them is the devil; the harvest is the close of the age, and the reapers are angels. Just as the weeds are gathered and burned with fire, so will it be at the close of the age. The Son of man will send his angels, and they will gather out of his kingdom all causes of sin and all evildoers, and throw them into the furnace of fire; there men will weep and gnash their teeth.

Then the righteous will shine like the sun in the kingdom of their Father. He who has ears, let him hear.

Matthew 13:24-30, 36-43 [RSV]

Two of my favorite passages in the Bible come from St. Paul in the New Testament, which corroborate near-death experiences:

There are celestial bodies
    and there are terrestrial bodies;
        but the glory of the celestial is one,
        and the glory of the terrestrial is another.
There is one glory of the sun, and another glory of the
    moon, and another glory of the stars;
        for star differs from star in glory.
So is it with the resurrection of the dead.
    What is sown is perishable,
        what is raised is imperishable.
    It is sown in dishonor,
        it is raised in glory.
    It is sown in weakness,
        it is raised in power.
    It is sown a physical body,
        it is raised a spiritual body.
    If there is a physical body,
        there is also a spiritual body.
    Thus it is written,
"The first man Adam became a living being";
    the last Adam became a life-giving spirit.
But it is not the spiritual which is first
    but the physical, and then the spiritual.
The first man was from the earth, a man of dust;
    the second man is from heaven.
As was the man of dust, so are those who are of the dust;
and as is the man of heaven, so are those who are of heaven.
Just as we have borne the image of the man of dust,
    we shall also bear the image of the man of heaven.
    I St. Paul to the Corinthians 15:40-49 [RSV]

"I know a man in Christ above fourteen years ago
    (whether in the body, I know not, or whether
        out of the body, I know not, God knoweth);
such a one caught up to the third heaven."
    2 Corinthians 12:2 [Douay-Rheims]

Two phenomenon that gives one an awareness of our spirit while we are alive are (1) the feeling of *deja vu,* or the sensation of having been there before, and (2) mystical experiences. William James, in *The Varieties of Religious Experience ,* published at Harvard University in 1902, describes four characteristics essential to a mystical experience: ineffability (indescribable), noetic quality (insight), transiency (lasting only a few minutes), and passivity. By passivity William James meant the experience is uninvited and suddenly happens to the person involved. A person suddenly becomes overwhelmed with a great truth and insight into his experience of life.

Dr. Melvin Morse, a pediatrician in Seattle, Washington, was the first to study near-death experiences in children. He first published his work in the medical journal *The American Journal of Diseases of Children* in 1983, and then published two books *Closer to the Light* (1990) and *Transformed by the Light* (1992).

One of the most famous cases he describes is his 9 year old patient, Katie, a freshwater drowning victim. After she recovered from a horrible ordeal in the pediatric intensive care unit, Dr. Morse interviewed her later on in his office when she was feeling well. Dr. Morse was amazed when she accurately noted details during her period of lifelessness, and recognized Dr. Morse as the "doctor with the beard." Dr. Morse was most impressed when Katie described having nasal intubation, or a tube being placed down her nose so a breathing machine could be attached and breathe for her. Oral intubation is the most common way of intubation on television.

As reported by Dr. Morse, Katie's first memory was of darkness and the feeling that she was so heavy she couldn't move. Then, a tunnel opened and through that tunnel came "Elizabeth." Katie went up the tunnel with Elizabeth, who was "tall and nice and had bright golden hair." She saw her late grandfather and made two new friends named Andy and Mark, two young boys, "souls waiting to be born."

Then she met the Heavenly Father and Jesus. The Heavenly Father asked if she wanted to go home. Katie cried. She said she wanted to stay with Him. Then Jesus asked her if she wanted to see her mother again. "Yes," she replied. Then she awoke.

Dr. Bruce Greyson, a psychiatrist from the University of Michigan, has published several papers on near-death experiences. Dr. Greyson has devised a near-death experience scale, to evaluate the varieties of near-death experiences.

Some experiences feature more of the cognitive component such as a panoramic life review. Others relate the affective experience, the joy, the peace, and the Light. Others primarily remember the paranormal phenomenon of being out of the body, while others have the transcendental experience of travel to another place.

Not all near-death experiences are pleasant. Dr. Bruce Greyson published in the medical journal *Psychiatry* his article on distressing near-death experiences in 1992. In this article he described three types of distressing near-death experiences. The first type had elements of initial terror or panic, but these feelings soon gave way to the peace and joy that is generally described. This type is also true of all the patients with distressing near-death experiences studied by Dr. Michael Sabom.

The second type of distressing near-death experience involves an experience of nothingness or of an existence in an eternal featureless void. Dr. Greyson wrote of one of his patients who described hurtling upward into darkness and rocketing through space. To her left appeared some circles which were black and white, and made a "clicking sound as they snapped black to white, white to black... They were jeering and tormenting, and their was laughter on their parts, malicious."

This second type of experience is often related to anesthesia or during a reaction to drugs, and may be questionable as to whether this is truly a near-death experience. However, the following passage from the New Testament leaves one wondering:

> **"They are like wild waves of the sea,**
> **foaming up their shameless deeds,**
> **wandering stars for whom the gloom**
> **of darkness has been reserved forever."**
> **Letter of Jude, 13 [New American]**

The third type of distressing near-death experience are classical visions of hell. These experiences appear not to convert to a peaceful experience after time. Dr. Greyson describes a wood worker with no religious background who tried to hang himself from a utility shed. He was outside his body and could see his body hanging. "Demons were all around me... They chattered like blackbirds. It was as if they knew they had me, and had all eternity to drag me down into hell, to torment me."

The Bible has several passages referring to hell as a place of damnation for those who have led an evil life. From the Pentateuch of Hebrew scripture Moses repeated the following words of the Lord:

> *"A fire is kindled in my wrath,*
> *and shall burn even to the lowest hell:*
> *and shall devour the earth with her increase,*
> *and shall burn the foundations of the mountains."*
> *Deuteronomy 32:22 [Douay-Rheims]*

From the Old Testament Book of Psalms, come two passages:

> *The Lord is known by the judgement he executeth:*
> *the wicked is snared in the work of his own hands.*
> *The wicked shall be turned into hell...*
> *Psalms 9:17-18 [King James]*

> *Let death take them by surprise;*
> *let them go down alive to Sheol,*
> *for evil is in their homes and in their hearts.*
> *Psalms 55:16 [New American]*

Further references concerning punishment for evil ways comes from the Old Testament Books of Proverbs and the Book of Isaiah:

> *Correction is grievous unto him that forsaketh the way:*
> *and him that hateth reproof shall die.*
> *Proverbs 15:10 [King James]*

> *Therefore hath hell enlarged her soul,*
> *and opened her mouth without any bounds,*
> *and their strong ones and their people, and*
> *their high and glorious ones shall go down into it.*
> *Isaiah 5:14 [Douay-Rheims]*

The New Testament also refers to what happens to those who go astray:

> *"And if your hand causes you to sin, cut it off.*
> *It is better for you to enter life maimed*
> *than with two hands*
> *to go to hell, to the unquenchable fire."*
> *Gospel of Mark 9:43 [RSV]*

> *The rich man also died and was buried,*
> *and from the netherworld, where he was in torment,*
> *he raised his eyes and saw Abraham far off*
> *and Lazarus at his side.*
> *And he cried out, 'Father Abraham, have pity on me.*
> *Send Lazarus to dip the tip of his finger in water*
> *and cool my tongue,*
> *for I am suffering torment in these flames.'*
> *Abraham replied, 'My child, remember that*
> *you received what was good during your lifetime*
> *while Lazarus likewise received what was bad;*
> *but now he is comforted here,*
> *whereas you are tormented.*
> *Moreover, between us and you a great chasm*
> *is established to prevent anyone from crossing*
> *who might wish to go*
> *from our side to yours or from your side to ours.'"*
> *Gospel of Luke 16:22-26 [New American]*

The last Book of the New Testament, the Book of Revelation or Apocalypse of John, sums it up!

> *And he that sat on the throne said,*
> *"Behold, I make all things new!"*
> *And he said,*
> *"Write, for these words are most faithful and true."*
> *And he said to me, "It is done!*
> *I am the Alpha and the Omega,*
> *the beginning and the end.*

To him that thirsteth I will give
of the fountain of the water of life freely.
He that shall overcome shall possess these things,
and I will be his God, and he shall be my son.
But the fearful and unbelieving,
and the abominable, and murderers,
and whoremongers and sorcerers,
and idolators and all liars,
they shall have their portion in the
pool burning with fire and brimstone,
which is the second death.
Revelation (Apocalypse of John) 21:5-8 [Douay-Rheims]

Dr. Wilder Penfield, the father of modern neurosurgery, "mapped" the brain by electrically stimulating various areas of patients' brains using a local anesthetic while they were awake. He was able to do this because the brain has no ability to feel pain itself, but can only perceive pain from other areas of the body. For example, he would stimulate the motor portion of the brain and the patient would move his arm. What was amazing to Dr. Penfield was that the patient could distinguish moving his arm from an electrical stimulation from when the patient willed moving his arm! Dr. Penfield developed a belief that the conscious mind was separate from the brain. Dr. Penfield may have discovered the seat of the mind: when he stimulated the sylvian fissure in the area in the right temporal lobe located just above the right ear, patients frequently would have an out of body experience.

After all his neurophysiological research, Dr. Penfield made this amazing statement: "It is clear, then, to survive after death the mind must establish a connection with a source of energy other than that of the brain. If during life, direct communication is sometimes established with the minds of other men or the mind of God, then it is clear that energy from without can reach a man's mind. In that case, it is not unreasonable for him to hope that after death the mind may waken to another source of energy." Wilder Penfield speaks of the mind as an energy source.

Dr. Melvin Morse speaks of the soul as the energy source.

I believe that the soul is the source of energy to the human body. Now that we have computers, it is easier to understand this concept. A computer is lifeless until someone plugs it in to an electrical source and turns it on. So it is with the soul for the human body. During life, we have a source of energy that animates us. With death, our soul leaves the human body and hopefully joins the Light of God.

The scientific and medical communities have made tremendous efforts to disprove the phenomenon of near-death experiences. The scientific community consistently rejects anything that cannot be proven in our physical realm. Multiple theories have been put forth to explain away near-death experiences.

First, near-death experiences are thought to be pharmacologic hallucinations, such as with LSD or the anesthetic ketamine. Lysergic acid diethylamide, or LSD-25, as discussed, has been extensively studied in the scientific community for possible legitimate use.

Ketamine is a derivative of the hallucinogenic veterinary drug phencyclidine (PCP), and was once used as a human anesthetic. Ketamine is known as a "dissociative anesthetic" because patients would describe being "detached" from their body, similar to an out-of-body experience. Because patients on ketamine developed hallucinosis upon awakening from anesthesia, its use is now limited primarily to providing conscious sedation, such as the suturing of facial lacerations in pediatric patients in emergency departments.

Near-death experiences cannot be pharmacologic hallucinations because patients with drug-induced hallucinations are usually aware that they have ingested a drug or are under the influence of medication(Haddad, Shannon, and Winchester: *Clinical Management of Poisoning and Drug Overdose,* Third edition, W. B. Saunders, Philadelphia, 1998). Furthermore, patients on both licit and illicit drugs hardly ever are filled with a sense of inner peace, joy, and love.

Or, second, they have a neurophysiologic basis, such as from the brain being deprived of oxygen, or releasing brain chemicals in time of distress, such as endorphins; or, being the result of temporal lobe seizures. Third, perhaps these are purely psychologic in nature as seen in people who undergo sensory deprivation. Or, fourth, this has a psychiatric basis being episodes of depersonalization or hallucinations. These explanations seem quite unrealistic if not impossible. As pointed out by Drs. Owens, Cook, and Stevenson in the medical journal *Lancet* (Lancet 336:1175-1177, 1990), patients in cardiac arrest have no brain circulation, and thus, one would expect them to have little ability to think, or have psychologic, biophysiologic or psychiatric capability. But, in fact, they have dramatically <u>increased</u> powers of cognitive function, as they can recall great detail concerning the episode of cardiac arrest, as evidenced by Dr. Michael Sabom's study.

No one has yet been able to disprove patients' accurate descriptions of when they are out of the body. Nor has anyone been able to explain away "The Light."

While the scientific community cannot accept anything beyond the physical dimension, this obviously has its limitations. All the great scientific discoveries were made by men who went beyond the accepted physical boundaries of the time, such as Galileo, who said the earth rotated around the sun. All science ever does is discover what truly exists in our universe, and each discovery extends the accepted physical realm of the time.

However, we are so limited by our five senses! For example, our dog, Phoebe, lives in the physical dimension and has five senses. Phoebe lives in the back yard and enjoys life. Phoebe has her own little world of chasing squirrels, barking at cars, wailing when an ambulance comes by, and getting excited when food is put out, and especially gets excited when someone comes out to play. Phoebe thinks her world is the whole world, but her little computer brain, as much as I love her, just doesn't see the big picture.

I believe that that is the way it is with us--while we think we know everything, we can only comprehend the little picture around us. Just stand outside on a clear night and look at the vastness of the night sky! Our world is a small world in contrast to the entire universe. Looking at the universe, surely there must be a higher intelligence.

I originally read Dr. Raymond Moody's book on near-death experiences with enthusiam when it was first published in 1975. However, while I was always interested in near-death experiences, it was nothing more to me than a conversation piece. I never questioned patients who were near-death or who had been resuscitated about their experiences. I did have one or two patients volunteer that they had some sort of experience happen to them, but these never made much of an impression. Until Nick came along.

Maybe it's because I knew him. Maybe it's because of the facts he told me when he was out of his body. Maybe it is because I saw the change in him when he returned to work. For whatever reason Nick's experience has had a profound effect on my life. I decided to give a lecture on near-death experience.

I began to question patients who came close to death about their experience. I am amazed at what I am learning, and would like to share with you three more near-death experiences.

A 35 year old patient named Betty Jane who was 6 months pregnant nearly died following a spontaneous hemorrhage of the uterus on Mother's Day, after she bent over at home. She had a history in her family of sudden death from spontaneous rupture of arterial vessels. She was transported to a Chicago Hospital, and rapidly collapsed in shock and coma. At one point, she was completely lifeless, and later was told she was dead. She remembers coming out of her body and all of a sudden she was transported to the courtroom of Pontius Pilate. Pontius Pilate was asking Jesus questions and he refused to answer. The noise was terrible from the courtyard outside, as the crowd was yelling and screaming, "Crucify him, Crucify him." Jesus was being beaten with whips and suffering the scourging at the pillar. He had wounds all about Him. They then placed a crown of thorns on his head. At this she became very upset and instinctively moved to protect Him and help Him but He stopped her and said, "Be still, and know that I am God. I must endure this for the sins of man." She then realized she was also being judged just as Jesus, and her whole life went before her. Then she was told she had committed more sins of omission than commission. She then was in a long dark tunnel and saw a light at the end of the tunnel. She then felt herself surrounded with "an all-encompassing, completely penetrating love. Nothing like anything you have ever felt before from your mother, your spouse, or your child. You never want to return and no longer fear death." She wanted to go to the light, but her mother-in-law, who had recently died, told her to "Go back, Go back, take care of George (her husband) and Pam (her daughter). Go back, Betty Jane."

She then woke up, and it was a horrible experience. Her arms were so weak, and they had intravenous lines, and she was receiving blood. She had a tube in her nose, and a drain in her abdomen. She was so weak, she couldn't even move her finger. She was all alone. She then saw Jesus at the foot of the bed holding a lamb.

She was in so much pain, and had no strength. She begged his help. He said, "Ask the father, in the way I taught you." She started to say the Our Father, but when she got to the part "Thy will be done", she didn't want to say it. How could all of this happen to me? She was so upset. She had tried to lead a good life, and now she had lost her baby. She looked up at Jesus, and he was waiting. After stopping several times, she said 'Thy will be done', and burst into tears. She then felt like she was the lamb and Jesus was holding her, and she felt His compassion, and again felt that wonderful, all-encompassing love. And then Jesus was gone.

Even though this happened years before, she remembers every detail as if it had happened yesterday, and there is no question in her mind that this was the deepest and most realistic experience she has ever had.

One week before I was to give my 1995 lecture, an attractive middle-aged lady came to see me and toll mo hor story. Sho had lost much blood during a surgical procedure and went into critical shock in the intensive care unit of one of our hospitals. Her family describes her as being lifeless, and the doctors did not hold out much hope for the family. She remembers entering a gray mist and a very handsome man appeared, but with a seething look in his eyes and a smirk on his face. She immediately knew it was satan, the evil one. He said with a sneer, "You're no good; you come with me." While she may have initially felt overwhelmed with guilt for her sins, she then rebuked him and said, "No! Jesus will have mercy on me." He became very angry but left. And then the mist dissipated and rays of light and peace and joy came all around her, and she knew she was in the presence of God and became very happy. God asked her if she wanted to stay. She then remembered her 14 year old daughter and felt she needed to be home and raise her daughter. It was then that she woke up and made a full recovery.

A 53 year old man from Mullins, South Carolina named Don felt weak in Church on November 4, 1984. It was the last thing he remembered, until he found himself looking down on a car that was stopped in the middle of a country field. A man ran up from the highway and tried to break in the car, and after much effort the man pulled a lifeless body out of the car, and cut off the person's tie. Don then realized it was himself that was being pulled out of the car! He then felt himself pulled through a dark and cold tunnel with a light in the distance. He felt himself enter the light and felt the presence of God, and a sense of peace.

He kept going, however, through the light, and found himself at a fork in the road. The road to the left was wide and full of people. The road to the right was narrow and went nearly straight up. He found himself going down the wide road, and began to hear screaming and moaning, and he found himself at the gate of hell. Words cannot express how terrible it was. He seemed to recognize the horrible voices as people he once knew. He became afraid, and began to pray, and asked God to please have mercy on his soul.

Don suddenly heard a voice, "Look up!" He saw two white doves, and the voice said "Follow the doves." The doves went back up the wide road, and then he saw a chariot with two white horses and driven by an angel. The angel took him in the chariot and said, "I've come to take you home." He then went through the pearly gates of Heaven, and again felt the presence of God, and felt an overwhelming sense of love and peace, when God welcomed him to heaven, "Welcome home, my son."

Don then went to the home of his mother, who had died 14 years before in 1970. After joyously being reunited with his mother, Christ came and said that he wanted Don to go back, that he had something for him to do. When his mother objected, Christ said he would only have to go for a little while, but promised he would be back "soon." Christ then walked him back to the pearly gates of Heaven. Don became very emotional at this point: "I will never forget the love I felt when Jesus put his hand on my shoulder, and said 'I will never leave you or forsake you.'"

Don then woke up in a Florence Hospital, three weeks after his cardiac arrest! He was told EMS had finally arrived at the country field, and they called for a hearse, because they thought he was dead. When they couldn't get one, they took him to the hospital in Mullins. Because he was well-known, the physician decided to attempt resuscitation, but gave up. The nurses went out and told the family he was dead. However, the doctor for some reason found the door jammed and could not leave the ER suite! He began anew an attempt at resuscitation, and the patient responded. He remained unconscious at Mullins Hospital for one week before he was transferred to Florence, where he remained unconscious for two weeks. His family was taking a course on how to care for a man in a vegetative state. Don today is completely functional, and directs a large business in Mullins, South Carolina.

I found Don a gentle man at great peace. I asked him if he had any words of advice. He told me to **"Trust in the Lord."**

After 25 years of emergency medicine, listening to these patients, and reading the Bible, I believe in an after-life.   Our soul is the source of energy to our body during human life. With death, our soul leaves our body, hopefully to join the Light of God. If one is primarily a peaceful soul on earth, a generous soul, a spiritual soul on earth, and we ask for God's love, forgiveness, and mercy, we will hopefully join God in Heaven.

Dante Alighieri wrote *The Divine Comedy* in Italy from 1608 to 1620. After journeying through *Inferno* (Hell) and *Purgatorio* (Purgatory), Dante and Beatrice finally reach *Paradiso* (Heaven). In Canto XXXIII Dante speaks of God as the Eternal Light:

> *O Light Supreme who doth Thyself withdraw*
> *so far above man's mortal understanding,*
> *lend me again some glimpse of what I saw;*
>
> *make Thou my tongue so eloquent it may*
> *of all Thy glory speak a single clue*
> *to those who follow me in the world's day;*
>
> *for by returning to my memory*
> *somewhat, and somewhat sounding in these verses,*
> *Thou shalt show man more of Thy victory.*
>
> *So dazzling was the splendor of that Ray,*
> *that I must certainly have lost my senses*
> *had I, but for an instant, turned away.*
>
> *And so it was, as I recall, I could,*
> *the better bear to look, until at last,*
> *my Vision made one with the Eternal Good.*
>
> *Oh grace abounding that had made me fit*
> *to fix my eyes on the eternal light*
> *until my vision was consumed in It!*

I saw within Its depth how It conceives
        all things in a single volume bound by Love,
of which the universe is the scattered leaves.
Canto XXXIII, 67-87
Dante, Paradiso, 1608

My prayer for you, the reader, is that one day you will see the Light of God!

CHAPTER 4
THE BIBLE

Hearing the near-death experiences of patients and seeing the tragic lives of many young patients in the ER, I yearned to learn more about the spiritual life, and began reading the Bible.

The Bible is a book about God our Creator and his unfailing love for his creation mankind.

In the Book of **Genesis**, the first Book of the Old Testament, and the first of five Books which make up the Pentateuch, God creates the universe. He created mankind in his image and likeness with our first parents, Adam and Eve.

> *And God said: Let us make man to our image and likeness:*
> *And let him have dominion over the fishes of the sea,*
> > *and the fowls of the air,*
> > *and the beasts, and the whole earth,*
> > *and every creeping creature that moveth upon the earth.*
> *And God created man to his own image;*
> > *to the image of God he created him.*
> *Male and female he created them, saying*
> > *Increase and multiply,*
> > *and fill the earth, and subdue it,*
> > *and rule over the fishes of the sea,*
> > *and the fowls of the air,*
> > *and all living creatures that move upon the earth.*
> > *Genesis 1:26-28 [Douay-Rheims]*

He gave many gifts, above all, free will. God reveals his great love for us, and all he asks, is that we reciprocate by being faithful and obedient. He places Adam and Eve in the Garden of Eden, and all he asks is that they not eat of the Tree of Knowledge of Good and Evil.

But the serpent tempts Eve by a lie, and Adam and Eve eat of the fruit of the Tree of Knowledge. They become ashamed because they are naked, and cover their bodies with fig leaves. When God discovers what happened, they confess their deed. Adam lamely puts it on Eve, and Eve says she was deceived by the serpent. God curses the serpent for the fall of mankind, and makes a promise of a Redeemer:

> *I will put enmity between thee and the woman,*
>> *and thy seed and her seed;*
> *she shall crush thy head,*
>> *and thou shall lie in wait for her heel.*
>>> *Genesis 3:15 [Douay-Rheims]*

Adam and Eve are punished, and they are driven from the Garden of Eden, ever to labor and toil on the face of this earth.

Mankind continually makes the wrong choices! God has sorrow of heart over the wickedness of man, and regrets his creation. He vows to destroy mankind, but one man, **Noah**, finds favor with the Lord God, and is obedient to him. So God makes a covenant with him, and places him and his family and two of every kind of animal in the Ark and saves them from the Great Flood.

This pattern of God's love, man's disobedience, God's punishment, but saving mankind because of the goodness of a few is repeated throughout the Old Testament.

For example, God destroys Sodom and Gomorrah for their wickedness, but God is pleased with Abram. God makes a covenant with **Abraham**:

> *Then Abram fell on his face; and God said to him,*
> *"Behold, my covenant is with you,*
>> *and you shall be the father of a multitude of nations.*
> *No longer shall your name be Abram,*
>> *but your name shall be Abraham;*
> *for I have made you the father of a multitude of nations.*
>> *Genesis 17:3-5 [RSV]*

God makes a covenant with the people of Israel, now in Egypt, in the Book of **Exodus**, appearing to Moses in the burning bush:

> *Now Moses fed the sheep of Jethro his father-in-law, the priest*
> *of Midian; and he drove the flock to the inner parts of the desert,*
>> *and come to the mountain of God, Horeb.*

And the Lord appeared to him in a flame of fire
out of the midst of a bush;
and he saw that the bush was on fire and was not burnt.
And Moses said: I will go and see this great sight,
why the bush is not burnt.
And when the Lord saw that he went forward to see, he called
to him out of the midst of the bush, and said: Moses, Moses.
And he answered: Here I am.
And he said: Come not nigh hither, put off the shoes from thy
feet, for the place where thou stand is holy ground.
And he said: I am the God of thy father,
the God of Abraham, the God of Isaac,
and the God of Jacob. [3:6]
Moses hid his face, for he dare not look at God.
And the Lord said to him: I have seen the affliction of my
people in Egypt, and have heard their cry because of their
taskmasters, and knowing their sorrow,
I am come down to deliver them out of the hands of the
Egyptians, and to bring them out of that land into a good and
spacious land, into a land that floweth with milk and honey,
to the places fo the Canaanite, and Hethite, and
Amorrhite, and Pherezite, and Hevite, and Jebusite.
For the cry of the children of Israel is come unto me:
and I have seen their affliction,
wherewith they are oppressed by the Egyptians.
But come, and I will send thee to Pharaoh,
that thou mayst bring forth my people,
the children of Israel out of Egypt.
Exodus 3:1-10 [Douay-Rheims]

The Book of Exodus continues with the Lord delivering **Moses** and the Israelites from Egypt, following the Passover. He calls for the Passover Ritual to be a day of memorial. The Passover tradition of the unleavened bread and the wine cup of blessing at the end of the Jewish Passover meal is celebrated to this day. On Mount Sinai, God gives to Moses his Ten Commandments, the code of living for our human race:

The Ten Commandments
Exodus (Shemot) 20:1-17

I am the Lord thy God, who have brought thee out of the land of Mizrahim, out of the house of bondage. Thou shalt not have any other gods besides me.

Thou shalt not make for thyself any graven image (carved idol) or any likeness of any thing that is in heaven above, or that is in the earth beneath, or that is in the water under the earth; thou shalt not bow down to them or serve them; for I the Lord thy God am a jealous God, punishing the iniquities of the fathers upon the children to the third and fourth generations of those that hate me; but showing mercy to thousands of generations of those that love me, and keep my commandments.

Thou shalt not take the name of the Lord thy God in vain; for the Lord will not hold him guiltless that takes his name in vain.

Remember to keep holy the sabbath day; six days shalt thou labor, and do all thy work; but the seventh day is a sabbath to the Lord thy God; in it thou shalt not do any work, thou, nor thy son, nor thy daughter, nor thy manservant, nor thy maidservant, nor thy cattle, nor thy stranger that is within thy gates; for in six days the Lord made heaven and earth, the sea, and all that is in them, and rested on the seventh day; therefore the Lord blessed the sabbath day, and hallowed it.

Honour thy father and mother: that thy days be long in the land which the Lord gives thee.

Thou shalt not kill.

Thou shalt not commit adultery.

Thou shalt not steal.

Thou shalt not bear false witness against thy neighbor.

Thou shalt not covet thy neighbor's house.

Thou shalt not covet thy neighbor's wife, nor his manservant, nor his maidservant, nor his ox, nor his ass, nor anything that is thy neighbors.

Exodus 20:1-17

Thou shalt not covet thy neighbor's wife.

Thou shalt not covet thy neighbor's (goods) house or fields, nor his male or female slaves, nor his ox or ass, or anything that belongs to him.

Deuteronomy 5:21

The Book of **Leviticus** records the ancient laws of purity, holiness, and other traditions. The Book of **Numbers** outlines the order for the distribution of the Promised Land. The people do not obey, and wander in the desert for 40 years. Moses gives his final teachings in the final book of the Pentateuch, the Book of **Deuteronomy**, before he dies. He repeats the Ten Commandments, with the order of the words changed for the final commandment.

The Historical Books begin with **Joshua** and the next generation of the Twelve Sons of Jacob that cross the Jordan River into the Promised Land. Again mankind falls, and become idolators, and the people of Israel have a troubled history, through the period of the **Judges**, a time without strong leadership.

But God finds favor with David, who is obedient and serves God. The Books of **Samuel** tell the story of David. David conquers Goliath. God makes a covenant with David, speaking through the prophet Nathan:

> *Thus says the Lord of Hosts,*
> *I took you from the pasture, from following the sheep,*
> *that you should be my prince over the people Israel;*
> *and I have been with you wherever you went,*
> *and have cut off all your enemies from before you;*
> *and I will make for you a great name,*
> *like the name of the great ones on the earth.*
> *And I will appoint a place for my people Israel;*
> *and will plant them, that they may dwell*
> *in their own place, and be disturbed no more;*
> *and violent men shall afflict them no more, as formerly,*
> *from the time that I appointed judges over my people*
> *Israel; and I will give you rest from all your enemies.*
> *Moreover the Lord declares to you I will make you a house.*
> *When your days are fulfilled and you lie down with your*
> *fathers, I will raise up your offspring after you,*
> *who shall come forth from your body,*
> *and I will establish his kingdom.*
> *He shall build a house for my name,*
> *and I will establish the throne of his kingdom forever.*
> *2 Samuel 7:8-13 [RSV]*

This parallel passage in 1 Chronicles, which supplements the historical books of Samuel and Kings, takes a dramatic turn.

> *Now therefore thus shall you say to my servant David,*
> *'Thus says the Lord of hosts,*
> *I took you from the pasture, from following the sheep,*
> *that you should be prince over my people Israel;*
> *and I have been with you wherever you went,*
> *and have cut off all your enemies from before you;*
> *and I will make for you a name,*
> *like the name of the great ones of the earth.*
> *And I will appoint a place for my people Israel, and will plant*
> *them, that they may dwell in their own place, and be disturbed no*
> *more; and violent men shall waste them no more, as formerly,*
> *from the time that I appointed judges over my people Israel;*
> *and I will subdue all your enemies.*
> *Moreover I declare to you that the Lord will build you a house.*
> *When your days are fulfilled to go to be with your fathers,*
> *I will raise up your offspring after you, one of your own sons,*
> *and I will establish his kingdom.*
> *He shall build a house for me,*
> *and I will establish his throne for ever.*
> *I will be his father, and he shall be my son;*
> *I will not take my steadfast love from him,*
> *as I took it from him who was before you,*
> *but I will confirm him in my house*
> *and in my kingdom for ever*
> *and his throne shall be established for ever.'"*
> *In accordance with all these words, and in accordance*
> *with all this vision, Nathan spoke to David.*
> *1 Chronicles 17:7-17 [RSV]*

In this parallel passage in 1 Chronicles, the passage in 2 Samuel, which spoke of David, now speaks about the Messiah, the son of God!

David as King united the tribes of Jacob, and Israel became a great nation under his rule. The Ark of the Covenant was moved to Jerusalem, which became the center of the united kingdom.

But even David succumbs to sin when he sees Bathsheba, the wife of Uriah. David puts her husband Uriah in the front lines of a war, where he is killed. The child he has by Bathsheba dies, and troubles befall David. David is forgiven, but must endure punishment for his deed. Israel still prospers under the reign of King David.

The son of David is Solomon, noted for his great wisdom. But Solomon married women of foreign lands, and idolatry again spread throughout Israel, and Israel suffers. The Kingdom is divided under King Rehoboam, Solomon's son, in 931 BC. The northern Kingdom is conquered by the Assyrians in 722 BC.

Jerusalem is destroyed in 587 BC by the Babylonians during an attempted revolt. The leading citizens of Israel were forced into exile to Babylon.

Our most important literary sources for the formation of the Jewish religious community after the Babylonian exile are the Old Testament Books of Ezra and Nehemiah. This is known as the period of the Restoration.

The Wisdom Books include such books as Job, Psalms, Proverbs, and others. David wrote many of the **Psalms**, one of which makes a striking prophecy of the crucifixion of the Messiah, at a time when crucifixion did not exist:

> *They have pierced my hands and my feet;*
> *they have numbered all my bones.*
> *Psalms 22:17*

God does not forget wayward mankind, and he calls the **Prophets** such as Isaiah, Jeremiah, Ezekiel, and Daniel to lead his troubled people to salvation. It is important to understand that the new Kingdom of God is not of this earth, but the Kingdom of God is heaven! It is in Isaiah that God promises to his people and to all people the coming of the Messiah, known as Immanuel.

> *Therefore the Lord himself shall give you a sign:*
> *Behold a virgin shall conceive, and bear a son,*
> *and his name shall be called Emmanuel.*
> *Isaiah 7:14 [Douay-Rheims]*

The passage of the Suffering Servant in **Isaiah** actually prefigures the death of the Messiah for the atonement and salvation of mankind:

Who has believed what we have heard? And to whom has the arm of the Lord been revealed? For he grew up before him like a young plant, and like a root out of dry ground; he had no form or comeliness that we should look at him, and no beauty that we should desire him.

He was despised and rejected by men; a man of sorrows, and acquainted with grief; and as one from whom men hide their faces he was despised, and we esteemed him not.

Surely he has borne our griefs and carried our sorrows; yet we esteemed him stricken, smitten by God, and afflicted. But he was wounded for our transgressions, he was bruised for our iniquities; upon him was the chastisement that made us whole, and with his stripes we are healed. All we like sheep have gone astray; we have turned every one to his own way; and the Lord has laid on him the iniquity of us all.

He was oppressed, and he was afflicted, yet he opened not his mouth; like a lamb that is led to the slaughter, and like a sheep that before its shearers is dumb, so he opened not his mouth. By oppression and judgment he was taken away; and as for his generation, who considered that he was cut off out of the land of the living, stricken for the transgression of my people? And they made his grave with the wicked and with a rich man in his death, although he had done no violence, and there was no deceit in his mouth.

Yet it was the will of the Lord to bruise him; he has put him to grief; when he makes himself an offering for sin, he shall see his offspring, he shall prolong his days; the will of the Lord shall prosper in his hand; he shall see the fruit of the travail of his soul and be satisfied; by his knowledge shall the righteous one, my servant, make many to be accounted righteous; and he shall bear their iniquities. Therefore I will divide him a portion with the great, and he shall divide the spoil with the strong; because he poured out his soul to death, and was numbered with the transgressors; yet he bore the sin of many, and made intercession for the transgressors.

Isaiah 53:1-12 [RSV]

The prophet **Jeremiah** speaks of the New Covenant:

> *Behold the days shall come, saith the Lord,*
> *and I will make a new covenant*
> *with the house of Israel and with the house of Judah,*
> *not according to the covenant which I made with their fathers,*
> *the day I took them by the hand to bring them out*
> *of the land of Egypt; the covenant which they made void,*
> *and I had dominion over them, saith the Lord.*
> *But this shall be the covenant which I will make with the house*
> *of Israel after those days, saith the Lord.*
> *I will place my law within them, and I will write it in their heart;*
> *and I will be their God and they shall be my people.*
> *And they shall teach no more every man his neighbor,*
> *and every man his brother, saying: Know the Lord,*
> *for all shall know me from the least of them even to the greatest,*
> *saith the Lord, for I will forgive their iniquity*
> *and I will remember their sin no more.*
> *Jeremiah 31:31-34 [Douay-Rheims]*

The prophet **Ezekiel** has been called the father of Judaism. This passage is often quoted in the sacrament of Baptism:

> *Then will I sprinkle clean water upon you, and ye shall be*
> *clean: from all your filthiness, and from all your idols,*
> *will I cleanse you.*
> *A new heart also will I give you, and a new spirit will I put*
> *within you, and I will take away the stony heart out of*
> *your flesh, and I will give you a heart of flesh.*
> *And I will put my spirit within you and cause you to walk*
> *in my statutes, and ye shall keep my judgements,*
> *and do them.*
> *And ye shall dwell in the land that I gave to your fathers;*
> *and ye shall be my people, and I will be your God.*
> *Ezekiel 36:25-28 [King James]*

The apocalyptic Book of **Daniel** is often quoted today in this time of the Millenium; this passage alludes to Messianic Salvation:

> *I beheld therefore in the vision of the night, and lo,*
> *One like the Son of Man came with the clouds of heaven;*
> *and he came even to the Ancient of days:*
> *and they presented him before him.*
> *And he gave him power, and glory, and a kingdom:*
> *and all peoples, tribes, and tongues shall serve him.*
> *His power is an everlasting power*
> *that shall not be taken away,*
> *and his kingdom that shall not be destroyed.*
> *Daniel 7:13-14 [Douay-Rheims]*

Chapter Six relates the famous story of Daniel in the Lion's Den. The beautiful story of the virtuous Susanna in the Apocryphal or Deuterocanonical part of the Book reveals Daniel's wisdom in fighting evil. Here is a prophetic passage about the future, his vision of the four beasts, and the terrible fourth beast with ten horns:

> *He shall speak against the Most High*
> *and oppress the holy ones of the Most High,*
> *thinking to change the feast days and the law.*
> *They shall be handed over to him*
> *for a year, two years, and a half-year.*
> *But when the court is convened,*
> *and his power is taken away*
> *by final and absolute destruction,*
> *Then the kingship and dominion and majesty*
> *of all the kingdoms under the heavens*
> *shall be given to the holy people*
> *of the Most High,*
> *Whose kingdom shall be everlasting:*
> *all dominions shall serve and obey him."*
> *Daniel 7:25-27 [New American]*

The **Book of the Twelve a**re the twelve prophets whose writings are brief and are combined into one Book in Hebrew Scipture, but are now twelve books.

Amos, Hosea, and **Micah** were active in the eighth century B. C., at the time of Isaiah. The prophecy of **Zephaniah**, **Nahum**, and **Habakkuk** occurred in the seventh century B. C., about the time of Jeremiah. The remaining six prophets lived after the Babylonian exile. **Haggai** and **Zechariah** were active in the rebuilding of the Jerusalem Temple in 520 B. C. **Jonah, Joel**, **Obadiah**, and **Malachi** lived in the sixth through fourth centuries.

A common prophecy that runs through many of the Twelve is the **"Day of the Lord", the universal day of judgment.** The Day of the Lord is discussed in the Books of Amos,Joel, Obadiah, Zephaniah, Zechariah, and Malachi.

The story of Jonah and the whale is of course the most famous of the Twelve, published in innumerable story books for children.

It is the Book of **Hosea** that touches one's heart. Hosea was a fiery man, who changed from angry rage to the deepest tenderness in a flash. Troubled with an unhappy marriage to the adulteress Gomer, he lived a miserable life. But his tragic life led to the beautiful analogy of his Book, in which his marriage becomes the example for the marriage of God and his great love for his faithless spouse Israel. In spite of God's anger at the unfaithfulness of his people, he takes them back when they repent.

> *Again the LORD said to me:*
> *Give your love to a woman*
> *beloved of a paramour, an adultress;*
> *Even as the LORD loves the people of Israel,*
> *though they turn to other gods*
> *and are fond of raisin cakes.*
> *So I bought her for fifteen pieces of silver and a*
> *homer and a lethech of barley.*
> *Then I said to her:*
> *"Many days you shall wait for me;*
> *you shall not play the harlot*
> *Or belong to any man;*
> *I in turn will wait for you."*
> *For the people of Israel shall remain many days without king or prince,*
> *Without sacrifice or sacred pillar, without ephod or household idols.*
> *Then the people of Israel shall turn back*
> *and seek the LORD, their God,and David, their king;*
> *They shall come trembling to the LORD*
> *and to his bounty, in the last days.*
> *Hosea 3:1-5 [New American]*

It is in the **New Testament** that Salvation History comes to fruition, with the coming of the Messiah, the descendant of David, Jesus Christ, born on Christmas Day.

And it came to pass in those days, that there went out a decree from Caesar Augustus that all the world should be taxed. And this taxing was first made when Cyrenius was governor of Syria.

And all went to be taxed, every one into his own city. And Joseph also went up from Galilee, out of the city of Nazareth, into Judea, unto the city of David, which is called Bethlehem, because he was of the house and lineage of David, to be taxed with Mary, his espoused wife, being great with child.

And so it was, that while they were there, the days were accomplished that she should be delivered.

And she brought forth her first-born son and wrapped him in swaddling clothes, and laid him in a manger, because there was no room for them in the inn.

And there were in the same country shepherds abiding in the field, keeping watch over their flock by night.

And, lo, an angel of the Lord came upon them, and the glory of the Lord shone round about them, and they were sore afraid.

And the angel said unto them,

"Fear not: for, behold, I bring you good tidings of a great joy, which shall be to all people; for to you is born this day in the city of David a Saviour, which is Christ the Lord.

And this shall be a sign unto you: you shall find the babe wrapped in swaddling clothes, lying in a manger."

And suddenly there was with the angel a multitude of the heavenly host praising God and saying,

"Glory to God in the highest, and on earth peace, good will toward men!"

St. Luke 2:1-1 [King James version]

The Gospel of St. Mark presents the ministry of Jesus.   The Gospel opens with the pronouncement that this is the Gospel of Jesus Christ, the Son of God. John the Baptist heralds the coming of Jesus, and the first action of Jesus is to be baptized by John:

> *"After me comes he who is mightier than I, the thongs of*
> *whose sandals I am not worthy to stoop down and untie.*
> *I have baptized you with water;*
> *but he will baptize you with the Holy Spirit."*
> *In those days Jesus came down from Nazareth of Galilee*
> *and was baptized by John in the Jordan.*
> *Gospel of St. Mark 1:7-9[RSV]*

Then follows the first words pronounced by Jesus:

> *Now after John was arrested, Jesus came into Galilee,*
> *preaching the gospel of God, and saying,*
> *'The time is fulfilled, and the kingdom of God is at hand;*
> *repent, and believe in the Gospel.'*
> *St. Mark 1:14-15 [RSV]*

Jesus calls for man to be born again of the Holy Spirit in baptism, the sacrament celebrated by all of Christianity:

> *Jesus answered [Nicodemus], "Amen, amen, I say to thee,*
> *unless a man be born again of water and the Spirit,*
> *he cannot enter into the kingdom of God.*
> *That which is born of the flesh is flesh;*
> *and that which is born of the Spirit is spirit.*
> *Do not wonder that I said to thee, 'You must be born again.'*
> *The wind blows where it will, and thou hearest its sound*
> *but does not know where it comes from or where it goes.*
> *So is everyone who is born of the Spirit."*
> *...After these things Jesus and his disciples came into the*
> *land of Judea, and he stayed there with them and baptized.*
> *The Gospel of John 3:5-8, 22 [Douay-Rheims]*

Jesus gives us the **Beatitudes** on the Sermon on the Mount:

> *When he saw the crowds, he went up the mountain,*
> *and after he had sat down, his disciples came to him.*
> *He began to teach them, saying:*
>
> *"Blessed are the poor in spirit,*
> *for theirs is the kingdom of heaven.*
> *Blessed are they who mourn,*
> *for they will be comforted.*
> *Blessed are the meek,*
> *for they will inherit the land.*
> *Blessed are they who hunger and thirst for righteousness,*
> *for they will be satisfied.*
> *Blessed are the merciful,*
> *for they will be shown mercy.*
> *Blessed are the clean of heart,*
> *for they will see God.*
> *Blessed are the peacemakers,*
> *for they will be called children of God.*
> *Blessed are they who are persecuted*
> *for the sake of righteousness,*
> *for theirs is the kingdom of heaven."*
> *St. Matthew 5:1-10 [New American]*

Jesus continues, pointing out that he is here to fulfill, not to destroy the old law:

> *"Do not think that I have come to abolish the law or the prophets.*
> *I have come not to abolish but to fulfill.*
> *Amen, I say to you, until heaven and earth pass away,*
> *not the smallest letter or the smallest part of a letter*
> *will pass from the law, until all things have taken place.*
> *Therefore, whoever breaks one of the least of these commandments*
> *and teaches others to do so will be called*
> *least in the kingdom of heaven.*
> *But whoever obeys and teaches these commandments*
> *will be called greatest in the kingdom of heaven.*
> *St. Matthew 5:17-19 [New American]*

Jesus refers to himself as the Light of the World, gives the Simile of Light, and calls on us, his disciples, to be children of the light, thus becoming the Light of the World.

I am the Light of the World.
Whoever follows me will not walk in darkness,
but will have the light of life.
St. John 8:12 [New American]

"No one who lights a lamp hides it away or places it
(under a bushel basket), but on a lampstand
so that those who enter might see the light.
The lamp of the body is your eye. When your eye is sound,
then your whole body is filled with light,
but when it is bad, then your body is in darkness.
Take care, then, that the light in you not become darkness.
If your whole body is full of light,
and no part of it is in darkness,
then it will be as full of light as a lamp
illuminating you with its brightness."
St. Luke 11:33-36 [New American]

Jesus said to them,
"The light will be among you only a little while.
Walk while you have the light,
so that darkness may not overcome you.
Whoever walks in the dark does not know where he is going.
While you have the light, believe in the light,
so that you may become children of the light."
St. John 12:35-36 [New American]

You are the light of the world.
A city set on a mountain cannot be hidden.
Nor do they light a lamp and then put it under a bushel basket;
it is set on a lampstand,
where it gives light to all in the house.
Just so, your light must shine before others,
that they may see your good deeds
and glorify your heavenly Father.
St. Matthew 5:14-16 [New American]

Jesus performed many miracles, casting out devils, feeding thousands with a few loaves of bread, healing the sick, and raising the dead. Jesus often spoke in Parables, such as the Parable of the Sower:

> " *A sower went out to sow. And as he sowed, some seed fell along the path, and the birds came and devoured it. Other seed fell on rocky ground, where it had not much soil, and immediately it sprang up, since it had no depth of soil; and when the sun rose it was scorched, and since it had no root it withered away. Other seed fell among thorns and the thorns grew up and choked it, and it yielded no grain.   And other seeds fell into good soil and brought forth grain, growing up and increasing and yielding thirtyfold and sixtyfold and a hundredfold." And he said, "He who has ears to hear, let him hear."*
>
> *And when he was alone, those who were about him with the twelve asked him concerning the parables. And he said to them, "To you has been given the secret of the kingdom of God, but for those outside everything is in parables; so that they may indeed see but not perceive, and may indeed hear but not understand; lest they should turn again, and be forgiven." And he said to them, "Do you not understand this parable? How then will you understand all the parables? The sower sows the word. And these are the ones along the path, where the word is sown; when they hear, Satan immediately comes and takes away the word which is sown in them. And these in like manner are the ones sown upon rocky ground, who, when they hear the word, immediately receive it with joy; and they have no root in themselves, but endure for a while; then, when tribulation or persecution arises on account of the word, immediately they fall away. And others are the ones sown among thorns; they are those who hear the word, but the cares of the world, and the delight in riches, and the desire for other things, enter in and choke the word, and it proves unfruitful. But those that were sown upon the good soil are the ones who hear the word and accept it and bear fruit, thirtyfold and sixtyfold and a hundred-fold."*
>
> *St. Mark 4:3-20 [RSV]*

The Gospel of John explains the institution of the Eucharist, when Jesus calls himself the "Bread of Life" at Capernaum."

Jesus said to them, "I am the bread of life;
he who comes to me shall not hunger,
and he who believes in me shall never thirst.
But I said to you that you have seen me
and yet do not believe.
All that the Father gives me will come to me;
and him who comes to me I will not cast out.
For I have come down from heaven,
not to do my own will, but the will of him who sent me;
and this is the will of him who sent me,
that I should lose nothing of all that he has given me,
but raise it up at the last day.
For this is the will of my Father,
that every one who sees the Son and believes in him
should have eternal life;
and I will raise him up at the last day."
Gospel of John 6:35-40 [RSV]

It is in the raising of Lazarus that Jesus shows his humanity and Divinity all at once:

Now a certain man was ill, Lazarus of Bethany, the village of Mary and her sister Martha. It was Mary who anointed the Lord with ointment and wiped his feet with her hair, whose brother Lazarus was ill. So the sisters sent to him, saying, "Lord, he whom you love is ill." But when Jesus heard it he said, "This illness is not unto death; it is for the glory of God, so that the Son of God may be glorified by means of it."
Now Jesus loved Martha and her sister and Lazarus. So when he heard that he was ill, he stayed two days longer in the place where he was. Then after this he said to the disciples, "Let us go into Judea again." The disciples said to him, "Rabbi, the Jews were but now seeking to stone you, and are you going there again?"
Jesus answered, "Are there not twelve hours in the day?
If any one walks in the day, he does not stumble, because he sees the light of this world. But if any one walks in the night, he stumbles,

because the light is not in him."

Thus he spoke, and then he said to them, "Our friend Lazarus has fallen asleep, but I go to awake him out of sleep." The disciples said to him, "Lord, if he has fallen asleep, he will recover." Now Jesus had spoken of his death, but they thought that he meant taking rest in sleep. Then Jesus told them plainly, "Lazarus is dead; and for your sake I am glad that I was not there, so that you may believe. But let us go to him." Thomas, called the Twin, said to his fellow disciples, "Let us also go, that we may die with him."

Now when Jesus came, he found that Lazarus had already been in the tomb four days. Bethany was near Jerusalem, about two miles off, and many of the Jews had come to Martha and Mary to console them concerning their brother. When Martha heard that Jesus was coming, she went and met him, while Mary sat in the house. Martha said to Jesus, "Lord, if you had been here, my brother would not have died. And even now I know that whatever you ask from God, God will give you." Jesus said to her, "Your brother will rise again." Martha said to him, "I know that he will rise again in the resurrection at the last day."

Jesus said to her, "I am the resurrection and the life; he who believes in me, though he die, yet shall he live, and whoever lives and believes in me shall never die. Do you believe this?"

She said to him, "Yes, Lord; I believe that you are the Christ, the Son of God, he who is coming into the world."

When she had said this, she went and called her sister Mary, saying quietly, "The Teacher is here and is calling for you." And when she heard it, she rose quickly and went to him. Now Jesus had not yet come to the village, but was still in the place where Martha had met him. When the Jews who were with her in the house, consoling her, saw Mary rise quickly and go out, they followed her, supposing that she was going to the tomb to weep there.

Then Mary, when she came where Jesus was and saw him, fell at his feet, saying to him, "Lord, if you had been here, my brother would not have died." When Jesus saw her weeping, and the Jews who came with her also weeping, he was deeply moved in spirit and troubled; and he said, "Where have you laid him?" They said to him, "Lord, come and see."

Jesus wept.
So the Jews said, "See how he loved him!" But some of them said,
"Could not he who opened the eyes of the blind man have kept this
man from dying?"
Then Jesus, deeply moved again, came to the tomb; it was a cave, and
a stone lay upon it. Jesus said, "Take away the stone." Martha, the
sister of the dead man, said to him, "Lord, by this time there will be an
odor, for he has been dead four days." Jesus said to her, "Did I not tell
you that if you would believe you would see the glory of God?" So they
took away the stone. And Jesus lifted up his eyes and said, "Father, I
thank thee that thou hast heard me. I knew that thou hearest me al-
ways, but I have said this on account of the people standing by, that
they may believe that thou didst send me."
When he had said this, he cried with a loud voice,
"Lazarus, come out."
The dead man came out, his hands and feet bound with bandages,
and his face wrapped with a cloth.
Jesus said to them, "Unbind him, and let him go."
St. John 11:1-44 [RSV]

Jesus establishes Himself as an authority on Scripture. The Sadduccees, who observed only the Pentateuch and claim there is no mention of an after-life, pose the question of the widow who marries seven brothers after each dies - who will she end up with in heaven? Jesus responds Moses does speak of an afterlife:

The children of this world marry and are given in marriage;
but they that shall be accounted worthy of that world, and of the
resurrection from the dead, shall neither be married, nor take wives.
Neither can they die any more: for they are equal to the angels,
and are the children of God, being the children of the resurrection.
Now that the dead rise again, Moses also showed
at the bush[Exodus 3:6] when he called the Lord the
God of Abraham, and the God of Isaac, and the God of Jacob.
For he is not the God of the dead but of the living.
For all live to him.
St. Luke 20:34-38 [Douay-Rheims]

The religious authorities cannot accept Jesus, but rather plot his death.

At the Last Supper, Jesus celebrated the Passover with the Apostles, and chose this time to give his disciples the Bread of Life, the basis for the Sacrifice of the Mass and Holy Communion, celebrated by Catholics, Orthodox, and Christians throughout the world. The three synoptic gospels and St. Paul record this sacred moment:

> *Then he took the bread, said the blessing,*
> > *broke it, and gave it to them, saying,*
> > **"This is my body, which will be given for you;**
> > > **do this in memory of me."**
> > *And likewise the cup after they had eaten, saying,*
> > > **"This cup is the new covenant in my blood,**
> > > **which will be shed for you."**
> > > *St. Luke 22:19-20 [New American]*

> *The Lord Jesus, on the night he was betrayed, took bread,*
> > *and when he had given thanks, broke it and said,*
> > > **"This is my body which is for you.**
> > > **Do this in remembrance of me."**
> > *In the same way also the cup, after supper, saying,*
> > > **"This cup is the new covenant in my blood.**
> > > **Do this, as often as you drink it, in remembrance of me."**
> > > *1 Corinthians 11:23-25 [RSV]*

Mankind is redeemed when Jesus is crucified on the cross on Good Friday.

> *But Jesus cried out again in a loud voice,*
> > *and gave up his spirit.*
> *And behold, the veil of the sanctuary was torn in two*
> > *from top to bottom.*
> *The earth quaked, rocks were split, tombs were opened,*
> > *and the bodies of many saints who had fallen asleep were raised.*
> *And coming forth from their tombs after his resurrection,*
> > *they entered the holy city and appeared to many.*

The centurion and the men with him who were keeping watch over
Jesus feared greatly when they saw the earthquake
and all that was happening, and they said,
"Truly this was the Son of God!"
St. Matthew 27:50-54 [New American]

But on Easter Sunday, Jesus the Son of God rises from the dead:

"Then the angel said to the women in reply,
'Do not be afraid!
I know that you are seeking Jesus the crucified.
He is not here,
for he has been raised just as he said.
Come and see the place where he lay.
Then go quickly and tell his disciples,
" He has been raised from the dead.'"
St. Matthew 28:5-7 [New American]

"Behold, two men in dazzling garments appeared to them...
'Why do you seek the living one among the dead?
He is not here, but has been raised.
Remember what he said to you while he was still in Galilee,
that the Son of Man must be handed over to sinners
and be crucified, and rise on the third day."
St. Luke 24:4-7 [New American]

After Jesus rises from the dead, he appears to his disciples and
teaches them, telling them to spread his word:

"Go ye therefore and teach all nations, baptizing them in the
name of the Father and of the Son and of the Holy Ghost:
teaching them to observe all things whatsoever I have
commanded you; and lo, I am with you always, even unto the
end of the world."
St. Matthew 28:19-20 [King James]

Jesus said to them again,
"Peace be with you.
As the Father has sent me,
even so I send you."
          St. John 20:21 [RSV]

Jesus singles out Peter to feed his lambs and tend his sheep:

When they had finished breakfast, Jesus said to Simon Peter,
"Simon, son of John, do you love me more than these?"
He said to him,
"Yes, Lord, you know that I love you."
He said to him,
*   "Feed my lambs."*
A second time he said to him,
"Simon, son of John, do you love me?"
He said to him,
"Yes, Lord, you know that I love you."
He said to him,
*   "Tend my sheep."*
He said to him the third time,"Do you love me?"
Peter was grieved because he said to him the third time,
*   "Do you love me?"*
And he said to him,
*   "Lord, you know everything; you know that I love you."*
Jesus said to him,
*   "Feed my sheep."*
       St. John 21:15-17[RSV]

Jesus then joins his Father in Heaven:

And the Lord Jesus, after he had spoken to them,
*   was taken up into heaven,*
*   and sitteth on the right hand of God.*
       St. Mark 16:19 [Douay-Rheims]

St. Paul tells how mankind can reach heaven and salvation in the afterlife:

Brethren, my heart's desire and prayer to God for them
    is that they may be saved.
I bear them witness that they have a zeal for God,
    but it is not enlightened.
For, being ignorant of the righteousness that comes from God,
    and seeking to establish their own,
      they did not submit to God's righteousness.
For Christ is the end of the law,
    that every one who has faith may be justified.
Moses writes that the man who practices the righteousness
    which is based on the law shall live by it.
But the righteousness based on faith says,
Do not say in your heart,
    "Who will ascend into heaven?"
      (that is, to bring Christ down)
        or
    "Who will descend into the abyss?"
      (that is, to bring Christ up from the dead).
But what does it say? The word is near you, on your lips and
in your heart (that is, the word of faith which we preach);
because, if you confess with your lips that
    Jesus is Lord
    and believe in your heart
      that God raised him from the dead,
        you will be saved.
For man believes with his heart and so is justified,
    and he confesses with his lips and so is saved.
The scripture says,
    "No one who believes in him will be put to shame."
For there is no distinction between Jew and Greek; the same Lord is
Lord of all and bestows his riches upon all who call upon him. For,
"every one who calls upon the name of the Lord will be saved."
    St. Paul to the Romans 10:1-13 [RSV]

James tells us we must have "active faith" to obtain salvation in the afterlife:

What good is it, my brothers,
if a man says he has faith but has not works:
Can his faith save him?
If a brother or sister has nothing to wear and has no food for
the day, and one of you says to them,
'Go in peace, be warmed and filled,'
without giving them the things needed for the body,
what does it profit?
So faith by itself, if it has no works, is dead.
But someone will say, "You have faith and I have works."
Show me your faith apart from your works,
and I by my works will show you my faith.
You believe that God is one; you do well.
Even the demons believe - and shudder.
Do you want to be shown, you foolish fellow,
that faith apart from works is barren?
Was not Abraham our father justified by works,
when he offered his son Isaac upon the altar?
You see that faith was active along with his works,
and faith was completed by works,
and the scripture was fulfilled which says,
Abraham believed God, and it was reckoned to him as
righteousness; and he was called the friend of God.
You see that a man is justified by works
and not by faith alone.
And in the same way was not also Rahab the harlot
justified by works when she received the messengers
and sent them out another way?
For as the body apart from the spirit is dead,
so faith apart from works is dead.
James 2:14-26 [Revised Standard Version]

With the creation of the state of Israel as the Jewish homeland on May 14, 1948, and especially now with the new Millenium, intense interest is being generated in **Bible prophecy**.

Are these the beginning of the end times?

The Bible speaks of tribulation and the reign but eventual defeat of satan, the Second Coming of Jesus, the new Jerusalem, a time of peace, and the Last Judgement. Here is a passage from the Book of Daniel:

> *"My lord, what follows this?"*
> *"Go, Daniel," he said, "because the words are to be kept*
>   *secret and sealed until the end time.*
> *Many shall be refined, purified, and tested,*
>   *but the wicked shall prove wicked;*
>   *none of them shall have understanding,*
>   *but the wise shall have it.*
> *From the time that the daily sacrifice is abolished*
>   *and the horrible abomination is set up,*
> *there shall be one thousand two hundred and ninety days.*
> *Blessed is the man who has patience and perseveres*
>   *until one thousand three hundred and thirty five days.*
> *Go, take your rest, you shall rise for your reward*
>   *at the end of the days."*
>   *Daniel 12:8-13 [New American]*

All three synoptic gospels, Matthew, Mark, and Luke, discuss the end times:

> *As he sat on the Mount of Olives,*
>   *the disciples came to him privately, saying,*
> *"Tell us, when will this be, and what will be the sign of your coming*
>   *and of the close of the age?"*
> *And Jesus answered them, "Take heed that no one leads you astray.*
> *For many will come in my name, saying,*
>   *'I am the Christ,' and they will lead many astray.*
> *And you will hear of wars and rumors of wars;*
>   *see that you are not alarmed; for this must take place,*
>   *but the end is not yet.*

For nation will rise against nation, and kingdom against kingdom,
and there will be famines and earthquakes in various places:
>	*all this is but the beginning of the birth-pangs.*
"Then they will deliver you up to tribulation, and put you to death;
>	*and you will be hated by all nations for my name's sake.*
And then many will fall away,
>	*and betray one another, and hate one another.*
And many false prophets will arise and lead many astray.
And because wickedness is multiplied,
>	*most men's love will grow cold.*
But he who endures to the end will be saved.
And this gospel of the kingdom will be preached throughout the
>	*whole world, as a testimony to all nations;*
>		*and then the end will come.*
"So when you see the desolating sacrilege
>	*spoken of by the prophet Daniel,*
>		*standing in the holy place (let the reader understand),*
>	*then let those who are in Judea flee to the mountains;*
>	*let him who is on the housetop not go down to take what is in*
>	*his house; and let him who is in the field not turn back to take*
>	*his mantle.*
And alas for those who are with child and for those who give suck in
>	*those days!*
Pray that your flight may not be in winter or on a sabbath.
For then there will be great tribulation, such as has not been from
>	*the beginning of the world until now, no, and never will be.*
And if those days had not been shortened
>	*no human being would be saved;*
>	*but for the sake of the elect those days will be shortened.*
Then if any one says to you, 'Lo, here is the Christ!' or 'There he is!'
>	*do not believe it.*
For false Christs and false prophets will arise and show great signs
>	*and wonders, so as to lead astray, if possible, even the elect.*
Lo, I have told you beforehand.
So, if they say to you, 'Lo, he is in the wilderness,' do not go out;
>	*if they say, 'Lo, he is in the inner rooms,' do not believe it.*

For as the lightning comes from the east
and shines as far as the west,
so will be the coming of the Son of man.
Wherever the body is, there the eagles will be gathered together.
"Immediately after the tribulation of those days
the sun will be darkened,
and the moon will not give its light,
and the stars will fall from heaven,
and the powers of the heavens will be shaken;
then will appear the sign of the Son of man in heaven,
and then all the tribes of the earth will mourn,
and they will see the Son of man coming on the clouds
of heaven with power and great glory;
and he will send out his angels with a loud trumpet call,
and they will gather his elect from the four winds,
from one end of heaven to the other.
"From the fig tree learn its lesson:
as soon as its branch becomes tender and puts forth its
leaves, you know that summer is near.
So also, when you see all these things,
you know that he is near, at the very gates.
Truly, I say to you, this generation will not pass away
till all these things take place.
Heaven and earth will pass away,
but my words will not pass away.
"But of that day and hour no one knows,
not even the angels of heaven,
nor the Son, but the Father only.
St. Matthew 24:3-36 [RSV]

But in those days, after that tribulation,
the sun will be darkened,
and the moon will not give its light,
and the stars will be falling from heaven,
and the powers in heaven will be shaken.

And then they will see the Son of man coming in clouds
*   with great power and glory.*
And then he will send out the angels,
*   and gather his elect from the four winds,*
*   from the ends of the earth to the ends of heaven.*
From the fig tree learn its lesson: as soon as its branch
*   becomes tender and puts forth its leaves,*
*   you know that summer is near.*
So also, when you see these things taking place,
*   you know that he is near, at the very gates.*
Truly I say to you, this generation will not pass away
*   before all these things take place.*
Heaven and earth will pass away,
*   but my words will not pass away.*
But of that day or that hour no one knows,
*   not even the angels in heaven,*
*   nor the Son, but only the Father.*
*   St. Mark 13:24-32 [Revised Standard Version]*

And here will be signs in the sun and moon and stars,
*   and upon the earth distress of nations,*
*   in perplexity at the roaring of the sea and the waves,*
*   men fainting in fear and with foreboding*
*   of what is coming on the world,*
*   for the powers of heaven will be shaken.*
And then they will see the Son of Man coming in a cloud
*   with power and great glory.*
Now when these signs begin to take place,
*   **look up** and raise your heads*
*   because your redemption is drawing near.*
*   St. Luke 21:25-28 [RSV]*

Some Christians from some Protestant faiths believe an event called the Rapture will be separate from the coming of the Son of Man, based on the following passages of St. Paul:

Behold, I shew you a mystery.
We shall not all sleep,
but we shall all be changed,
in a moment, in the twinkling of an eye, at the last trumpet.
For the trumpet shall sound, and the dead shall be raised
incorruptible, and we shall be changed.
1 St. Paul to the Corinthians 15:51-52 [King James]

For since we believe that Jesus died and rose again,
even so, through Jesus, God will bring with him
those who have fallen asleep.
For this we declare to you by the word of the Lord,
that we who are alive
who are left until the coming of the Lord,
shall not precede those who have fallen asleep.
For the Lord himself will descend from heaven
with a cry of command, with the archangel's call,
and with the sound of the trumpet of God.
And the dead in Christ will rise first;
then we who are alive, who are left, shall be caught up
together with them in the clouds to meet the Lord in the air;
and so we shall always be with the Lord.
1 St. Paul to the Thessalonians 4:13-17 [RSV]

St. Peter urges us to be obedient, and warns us not to listen to "scoffers", but reaffirms that the Parousia (the Second Coming) will take place:

Therefore, gird up your minds, be sober,
set your hope fully upon the grace that is coming to you
at the revelation of Jesus Christ.
As obedient children, do not be conformed
to the passions of your former ignorance,
but as he who called you is holy,
be holy yourselves in all your conduct;
since it is written, "You shall be holy, for I am holy."
1 Peter 1:13-16 [RSV]

But, of this one thing be not ignorant, my beloved,
that one day with the Lord is as a thousand years,
and a thousand years as one day.
The Lord delayeth not his promise, as some imagine,
but dealeth patiently for your sake,
not willing that any should perish
but that all should turn to penance [repentance*].
But the day of the Lord will come as a thief:
in which the heavens shall pass away with great violence,
and the elements shall be melted with heat, and the earth,
and the works which are in it, shall be burnt up.
2 Peter 3:8-10 [Douay-Rheims, *RSV]

The Book of Revelation, or Apocalypse of John, ends the New Testament,and is one of the most difficult books of the Bible to understand. The Book of Revelation speaks of the end times, the final battle between good and evil, when the reign of God in heaven will prevail on earth, the coming of a new Jerusalem, the Last Judgement, and a time of peace.

One of Michelangelo's most famous paintings, found in the Sistine Chapel in Rome, captures one of the most memorable passages (Chapter 20:11-15) from the Book of Revelation, The Last Judgement.

Then I saw a great white throne and him who sat on it;
from his presence earth and sky fled away
and no place was found for them.
And I saw the dead, great and small, standing before the throne,
and books were opened.
Also another book was opened, which is **the book of life.**
And the dead were judged by what was written in the books, by what they had done. And the sea gave up the dead in it, Death and Hades gave up the dead in them, and all were judged by what they had done. Then Death and Hades were thrown into the lake of fire.
This is the second death, the lake of fire;
and if anyone's name was not found written in the book of life,
he was thrown into the lake of fire.
Revelation 20:11-15 [RSV]

The **History** of the development of the Bible is important, as the Bible is the foundation of our Western civilization and our source of ethics.

The Bible portrays the undying love God our Creator shows for humanity. The Bible tells of God giving his Son Jesus to save mankind. The Bible serves as a guide for a happy life on earth.

The authors of the Bible are God himself hand in hand with the writers of the Books of the Bible, as the writers received Divine inspiration [2 Peter 1:21].

The **Old Testament** for Christianity is Hebrew Scripture!

It is no wonder Pope John Paul II and the Second Vatican Council call Judaism the origin of Christianity!

Hebrew Scripture (Tanakh) contains 24 books, divided into the *Teachings (Torah),* the *Prophets (Neviim),* and *Holy Writings (Ketuvim).* The *Torah* is the Pentateuch, the Books of Moses, and includes Genesis, Exodus, Leviticus, Numbers, and Deuteronomy. The *Prophets* include the Books of Joshua, Judges, Samuel, Kings, Isaiah, Jeremiah, Ezekiel, and the Twelve Prophets. The *Holy Writings* include Psalms, Proverbs, Job, The Song of Songs, Ruth, Lamentations, Ecclesiastes, Esther, Daniel, Ezra-Nehemiah, and Chronicles.

The Tanakh at one time contained 22 books, to match the letters of the Hebrew alphabet, as Judges and Ruth were combined into one, as well as Jeremiah and Lamentations. These are all written in Hebrew.

Aramaic was the common language at the time of Jesus in Israel, ever since the fifth century before Christ (BC), when the Jewish people returned home following the Babylonian exile. Jesus and his Apostles spoke in Aramaic. Parts of the Book of Daniel, Tobias (Tobit), and Judith were written in Aramaic. Early Aramaic translations of the Bible were known as Targums, and have been found in the Dead Sea Scrolls in Cave 11, such as the Book of Job. The Maronite Catholic Church in Lebanon still celebrates part of the daily Mass in Aramaic.

In 1947, a Bedouin shepherd named Muhammad ed-Dib, while searching for a stray goat in the Judean Desert near the Dead Sea, accidentally discovered a cave containing ancient scrolls preserved in a jar. Thus began the greatest discovery of ancient manuscripts in the twentieth century, the Dead Sea Scrolls.

The **Dead Sea Scrolls** have been found in 9 of 11 caves excavated near the Qumran site. Dr James VanderKam, in his 1994 book *The Dead Sea Scrolls Today,* points out every book of the Old Testament has been found in the Dead Sea Scrolls except for the Book of Esther and the Book of Nehemiah. An intact Scroll of Isaiah was found, completely identical to our present book in the Bible, and is roughly 1000 years older than any previous manuscript! While the controversy of the Dead Sea Scrolls are a story in themselves on human nature, their discovery is certainly confirmatory of Hebrew Scripture, and help to clarify Judaism as the origin of Christianity.

It is thought the Dead Sea Scrolls originally were the work of a highly spiritual monastic sect of Judaism known as the Essenes, who broke off from everyday society, and shunned material pleasures. They regarded the soul as immortal, and left everything in the hands of God. The War Scroll of the Essenes describes a final battle at the End of Days, between good and evil, between the Sons of Light and the Sons of Darkness. It is when "God fortifies the hearts of the sons of Light" that "in the seventh lot, the mighty hand of God shall bring down" satan and the Sons of Darkness. Also five of the caves bore documents describing a New Jerusalem.

While the dates of the Dead Sea Scrolls are controversial and range from about 250 BC until the time of Jesus, some of the last persons mentioned include the Queen of Judea, John Hyrcanus, and Emilius, all who lived in the First Century BC. Dr. VanderKam points out **no one** from the first century AD is mentioned in the Dead Sea Scrolls.

While a monastic Jewish sect would hardly include Christian writings even if they existed, it is important to note that New Testament writings **followed** the time of the Dead Sea Scrolls.

However, Dr. VanderKam does discuss possible influences of the Essenes during this transitional and turbulent time in history upon the New Testament. One does wonder about the influences of the Essenes on St. John the Baptist, a monastic from the Judean Desert, who heralded the coming of the Messiah, Jesus! Did the War Scroll influence the Book of Revelation?

In addition, the Dead Sea Scrolls include 3 books written in Hebrew, which are part of the Apocrypha or Deuterocanonical Books - Tobias (or Tobit), Sirach, and the Letter of Jeremiah, as well as Psalm 151 of David.

The First Century Jewish historian Josephus Flavius also had this to say in Book XVIII, Chapter III in his work, *The Antiquities of the Jews:*

"Now there was about this time **Jesus**, a wise man, if it be lawful to call him a man; for he was a doer of wonderful works, a teacher of such men as receive the truth with pleasure. He drew over to him many of the Jews and many of the Gentiles. **He was the Christ**. And when Pilate, at the suggestion of the principal men amongst us, had condemned him to the cross, those that loved him at the first did not forsake him; for he appeared to them alive again the third day; as the divine prophets had foretold these and ten thousand other wonderful things concerning him. And the tribe of Christians, so named from him, are not extinct at this day."

The **Greek Septuagint** was the translation of Hebrew Scripture by Jewish scholars in Alexandria, Egypt, begun in the third century BC. Since early Christians spoke Greek, it became adopted as the form of the Old Testament for Christianity. In this translation, the books are in a new order, and the Hebrew books of Samuel, Kings, Chronicles, and Ezra-Nehemiah were split into 2 parts, and the Book of the Twelve Prophets was split into 12 parts, giving a total of **39** books. In addition, seven books, the "Deuterocanonical" books, were included, for a total of 46 books. Also, 1 and 2 Esdras, Psalm 151, and the Prayer of Manasseh were in the Greek Septuagint. 3 and 4 Maccabees were present in some ancient Greek texts, but not in others. The Greek Septuagint was in circulation at the time of Christ and was not only widely read by Jews but also by Gentiles and early Christians. In fact , the majority of Old Testament quotations in the Greek New Testament are based on the Greek Septuagint Old Testament.

The **Apocrypha** are the books of the Old Testament that were included in the Septuagint Greek translation written in Egypt, but were later excluded from Hebrew canon. At the turn of the first century, some thirty years after the destruction of Jerusalem, the rabbinical school at Jamnia held a famous synod in 96 A. D., at which the rabbis arbitrarily redefined the canon of the Old Testament.

The Council of Jamnia used four criteria to determine which books should be retained as ancient Hebrew Scripture, and which should be removed. Their first criterion was that the book had to conform to the Pentateuch; it could not have been written after the time of Ezra (c. 400 BC); it had to be written in Hebrew; and it had to be written in Palestine.

Ten books did not meet these criteria, and are known as the Apocrypha. Baruch, which includes the Epistle of Jeremiah, was not of Palestinian origin. Ecclesiasticus (Sirach) and First Maccabees were written after the time of Ezra. Tobit, along with parts of Daniel and Esther, were originally composed in Aramaic and also probably outside of Palestine. The Book of Judith was probably written in Aramaic, and Wisdom and Second Maccabees were written in Greek. Also, 1 and 2 Esdras (3 and 4 Ezra), the Prayer of Manasseh, Psalm 151, and the variably present 3 and 4 Maccabees, were also struck from the Hebrew canon.

The **Deuterocanonical Books** are **seven** of the ten books of the Greek Septuagint Old Testament Apocrypha that were included in the original Catholic Bible. The deuterocanonical books are Tobit or Tobias, Judith, Wisdom of Solomon, Sirach or Ecclesiasticus; Baruch, with the Letter of Jeremiah as Chapter Six; and 1 Maccabees and 2 Maccabees; as well as six sections in the Book of Esther and three stories in Daniel (the Song of the Three Young Men, Susanna, and Bel and the Dragon). 1 and 2 Esdras (3 and 4 Ezra), Psalm 151, the Prayer of Manasseh, and the variably present 3 and 4 Maccabees did not become part of the Catholic Bible. Thus, there are **46** books in the Catholic Old Testament.

The Catholic Old Testament ends with the First and Second Books of Maccabees, which were written in the second century B. C. and are of important historical and theological value.

1 Maccabees describes the persecution of the Jews by the ruler of Syria Antiochus IV in 167 BC. The priest Mattathias opposed Antiochus, and his third son Judas the Maccabee (meaning "hammer") led a revolt against the Syrians and recaptured the Jerusalem Temple in 164 BC. The Maccabees restored Jewish worship in the temple. Even though there was only one day of oil to keep the holy lamps of the Temple burning, the holy lamps miraculously burned for a full eight days. This is commemorated in the eight-day Jewish celebration of Hanukkah, which occurs near Christmas.

Maccabees 2 was written only in Greek, and thus would not be in the Dead Sea Scrolls. It is an important book, as it refers to the resurrection of life (chapter 7), the ability of the living to pray for the dead (chapter 12), and the intercession of the saints for those still on earth (chapter 15).

The **New Testament** portrays the Life and Ministry of **Jesus,** and His teachings of Christianity. Considering the impact of his Life and Teaching, it is remarkable the ministry of Jesus lasted such a short time!

The length of the Ministry of Jesus is a matter of debate among Biblical scholars. We know that the Gospel of John refers explicity to three passovers. The first Passover finds Jesus in Jerusalem [John 2:13-14]; the second Passover occurs near the time of the multiplication of the loaves [John 6:4-9], and the third passover occurs at the time of the Passion and Crucifixion of Jesus [John 11:55-57]. Three passovers would make two years. John 5:1 refers to "a feast of the Jews" - if this is also a passover, four passovers would make three years. Add to this the months of his ministry from his Baptism by John to the first Passover, and the ministry of Jesus lasted two or three years and some months.

All of Christianity, Catholics, Orthodox, and Protestants, accept Jesus as our Saviour. He is the Christ, the Messiah, Immanuel, the Son of God who became man for the Salvation of mankind. The word Christ is the Greek *Christos* for the Hebrew word Messiah, or anointed one. All of Christianity has the New Testament, as well as the Old Testament from Hebrew Scripture. The **27** Books of the New Testament of the Catholic, Eastern Orthodox, the King James and all Protestant Bibles are exactly the same!

The 27 Books of the New Testament include the 4 Gospels of Matthew, Mark, Luke, and John; the Acts of the Apostles by St. Luke; 14 Epistles of St. Paul - to the Romans, Corinthians (I and II), Galatians, Ephesians, Philippians, Colossians, Thessalonians (I and II), Timothy (I and II), Titus, Philemon, and the Hebrews; the 7 Universal Letters, written by the Apostles Peter (2), James (1), John (3); and Jude [the Apostle Judas, son of James, or Jude Thaddeus] (1); and the Apocalypse or Revelation of John. The New Testament originally was written in Greek. The New Testament Canon, or chosen Books of the New Testament, was formalized in **393** by St. Augustine and the Council of Hippo.

The Four **Gospels** describe the Life and Teachings of Jesus, and his Passion, Crucifixion, and Resurrection from the dead.

There are three stages in the formation of the Gospels: the actual teachings of Jesus; the oral tradition of the Apostles and the disciples; and the written word.

Jesus appeared for forty days after his Resurrection, teaching the Apostles, until his Ascension into heaven.

> *In the first book, Theophilus, I dealt with all that Jesus did and*
> *taught, until the day he was taken up, after giving instructions*
> *through the holy Spirit to the apostles whom he had chosen.*
> *He presented himself alive to them by many proofs*
> *after he had suffered, appearing to them during forty days*
> *and speaking about the kingdom of God.*
> *Acts of the Apostles 1:1-3 [New American]*

The Holy Spirit then appeared on the Pentecost, 10 days after the Ascension of Jesus, to the Apostles and disciples. Thus the oral tradition of the Apostles was established in the period from the time of Jesus (~33 AD) to the written Gospels (~70 to 90 AD).

The Gospel of St. Matthew is the first and most quoted of the four Gospels, and is noted for identifying Jesus as the long-awaited Messiah foretold in the Old Testament. It is now thought the Gospel of St. Mark, the close disciple of St. Peter, was actually the first composed Gospel, written after St. Peter's martyrdom in 64 AD, but before the destruction of the Jerusalem Temple in 70 AD. Written in Rome, the concise, narrative Gospel of St. Mark is primarily directed to the Gentiles. It is now thought the Gospel of Mark served as a source to the well-written Gospels of St. Matthew and Luke, both completed about 80 to 85 AD. The Gospel of St. John was written about 90 AD.

The Acts of the Apostles written by St. Luke portrays the time following the death of Jesus about 33 AD. Following the coming of the Holy Spirit on Pentecost, the twelve Apostles and St. Paul began their work as evangelists, spreading Christianity throughout Asia Minor and the Mediterranean world. St. Luke portrays the early missions of the Apostles, focusing primarily on Peter and Paul.

St. Peter was the leader of the Twelve Apostles. As the rock upon which he would build his Church, Jesus gave Peter keys to the kingdom of Heaven:

> *And I say also unto thee, that "thou art Peter,*
> *and upon this rock I will build my Church,*
> *and the gates of hell shall not prevail against it."*
> *And I will give unto thee the keys of the kingdom of heaven;*
> *and whatsoever thou shalt bind on earth*
> *shall be bound in heaven,*
> *and whatever thou shalt loose on earth*
> *shall be loosed in heaven.*
> *Matthew 16:18-19 [King James Version]*

Jesus, after predicting Peter's denial, called upon him to 'strengthen the faith of thy brethren' [Luke 22:32], and, in the Gospel of John, Jesus calls Peter to 'feed my lambs' [John 21:15-17]. He was an early witness of the Resurrection [1Cor 15:5], and with James and John was present for the Transfiguration of Jesus [Matthew 17:1-8].

St. Peter spread the faith both to Christian Jews and the Gentiles. After leading the Christian Jews in Jerusalem, he travelled to Antioch, then settled in Rome, serving as its first Bishop. The Papacy begins with St. Peter. St. Peter is credited with two epistles becoming part of the New Testament. He was crucified upside-down, martyred by Nero in 64 AD, and is buried under St. Peter's Basilica in Rome.

St. Paul experienced a dramatic conversion to Christianity. Independent, well-educated, and outspoken, St. Paul was different from the Twelve Apostles in that he knew only the risen Christ. In contrast to Matthew, who traces the lineage of Jesus through the Old Testament, and sees Jesus as the long-awaited Messiah of Israel, St. Paul, struck down on the road to Damascus, saw Jesus as the Saviour of all humanity.

The first writings in the New Testament were actually by Paul, from about 51 to 67 AD. St. Paul is given credit for fourteen epistles, being the letters he wrote to the Christian communities he had established in his travels spreading the Word of Christ. His first two letters were to the Thessalonians in 51 AD.

Paul made great headway with the Gentiles, as he pointed out that salvation came through faith in Christ and not by observance of Jewish law. They could become Christians without first adopting Judaism. This concept was controversial in early Christianity, as the traditional Apostles held that one must observe the laws of Moses and that Jesus was the long-awaited Messiah.

Chapter 15 of Acts of the Apostles finds Paul successful in winning over the Apostles to this point of view at the meeting at Jerusalem.

St. Paul was just as passionate spreading Christianity as he was persecuting Christians prior to his conversion. His direct and confrontational manner placed him frequently in jail, and, in fact, his letters to the Ephesians, Philippians, Colossians, and Philemon were all written in jail. The Acts of the Apostles ends with Paul's imprisonment in Rome for two years.

Early Christianity, from the time of the Resurrection of Jesus, was spread by word of mouth. The written word by Paul (and subsequently Mark and the other writers) became increasingly important as Christian persecution by Nero and the Romans came into full force.

Paul was beheaded along the Ostian Way in 68 AD, prior to the Roman destruction of the Jerusalem temple in 70 AD. Paul's concept of Christianity as autonomous became prevalent once Roman persecution of Jews began.

Early Christianity, in spite of persecution, flourished, primarily in five centers: Rome, Constantinople, Alexandria, Antioch, and Jerusalem. The five centers became *patriarchates*, when Constantine recognized Christianity in the Roman Empire in 313. All were followers of Jesus Christ from the time of the Apostles, and considered themselves one holy, catholic and apostolic Church. Each developed and retained their ancient and distinctive liturgies, rites, and customs. The Greek Septuagint and New Testament were in common use to all.

The five Patriarchates were led by five Patriarchs, with the Pope, the Bishop of Rome, as the representative of Peter, acknowledged as presiding "with love," as a *first among equals.* In response to theological challenges to early Christian beliefs, they met in seven councils. The Nicene Creed originated at the Council of Nicaea in 325, and was expanded to quote John 15:26, *the Holy Spirit proceeding from the Father"* at the Council of Constantinople in 381. The seven Councils are still recognized today by all of the early Christian Churches.

The distances of geography and the barriers of language, however, led to an inability to communicate on several theological issues, and a schism developed between East and West. The self-governing Eastern Christian Churches, with their own patriarch, then became known as the Eastern Orthodox Churches, such as the Greek Orthodox Church.

Eastern rite Catholics include the Maronite Church of Lebanon, the one Eastern Church that remained in communion with Rome, and Eastern churches, such as the Greek Byzantine Catholic Church, that re-established ties to Rome.

There is now a spirit of reconciliation among the early Christian Churches.

St. Jerome's Latin Vulgate Bible was the standard Bible in Western civilization for over 1000 years. St. Jerome was a well-educated linguist in Latin and Greek, who began an intense study of Hebrew and Scripture. Pope Damascus I commissioned him to translate the Greek Septuagint text into Latin. St. Jerome, seeing the difference in books between the Greek Septuagint text and the Hebrew canon redefined by the Pharisees in A. D. 96, called these books "the Apocrypha," or "hidden or secret books". After over 20 years work, he completed the translation of both the Old and New Testaments in the year **405**. The St. Jerome Latin Vulgate Bible became the standard Bible for Western Europe until the sixteenth century, and for the Roman Catholic Church until the present!

Martin Luther was a Catholic priest who completed a translation from the original sources into German in 1534. Also in 1534 King Henry VIII , seeking to wed Anne Boleyn and being denied an annulment of his marriage to Catherine of Aragon, rejected the authority of the Pope and had Parliament declare the King as head of the Church of England. Martin Luther also challenged the Catholic Church and began the Reformation. While he included the Apocrypha in a separate section, Martin Luther called the books "good for reading," but not part of inspired Scripture. His version, and all subsequent Protestant versions of the Bible, have 39 books to the Old Testament, just as the Hebrew canon.

In response to the Reformation, Pope Paul III commissioned the Council of Trent to address the problems within the Church and began the Counter-Reformation of the Roman Catholic Church in 1546. The Council instituted much-needed reforms within the Church. The Council confirmed the importance of **Scripture** and the historical **Tradition** of the Catholic Church, established with the oral tradition of the Apostles. The Council of Trent reaffirmed the original Scriptural canon, accepted by St. Augustine and the Council of Hippo in **393**, which includes **46** books of the Septuagint Greek Biblical text of the Old Testament. The Roman Catholic Church asserted its right both to determine the canon and its right to interpret Holy Scripture.

The **Douay-Rheims Bible** was the first English translation of the St. Jerome Latin Vulgate Bible approved by the Catholic Church. Dr. Gregory Martin of Oxford began the translation of the New Testament at the English College of Douay, and because of political upheaval, completed the work at the English College of Rheims, France in 1582. The Old Testament was completed after the return to Douay, France in 1609. This was a pure translation from the Latin: where there was a question of meaning, the original Latin word was inserted rather than the expression of the time! During the Catholic persecution in England, Bishop Richard Challoner translated the Douay-Rheims Bible into pure English from 1749-1752. This has served as the primary translation for Catholics until 1970.

King James I as head of the Church of England in 1604 commissioned a group of scholars to establish an authoritative translation of the Bible. Influenced by early English translations such as John Wycliffe (1384), William Tyndale (1526) , Miles Coverdale (1535), Thomas Matthew (1537), the Geneva Bible, the Douay-Rheims Bible, and Martin Luther, they completed the Authorized version of the King James Bible in 1611. The King James Bible originally included the Apocrypha but in a separate section.   One of the masterpieces of the English language, the original King James Bible is still in use today.

The **Revised Standard Version (RSV)** of the Protestant King James Bible is perhaps one of the most accurate translations of the Bible, due to improvement in scholarly translation of ancient Hebrew and Greek texts. A Catholic edition, which includes the seven deuterocanonical books in the original order, also has been published, known as the St. Ignatius Bible. Influenced by a movement for Christian unity and approved for both Catholics and Protestants, the RSV translation was completed in 1952, to be enjoyed by **all** of Christianity!

The **New American** Bible is the first completely American translation of the Bible for Catholics. The Catholic Biblical Association, sponsored by the U. S. Catholic Bishops' Committee of the Confraternity of Christian Doctrine, first published the New American Bible in 1970. Noted for its ease of readability and up-to-date translation, this was the first Bible I ever read.

It is important to read a Bible that is a true translation, and not one of the bibles that gives its own interpretation. While there are subtle differences in words among the major bibles that we have quoted in this book, the meaning is essentially the same! (See page 195 for an example).

The division among religions is man-made!

It is important for **all** of Christianity to unite and find common ground in these troubled times! In his 1995 encyclical *Et Unum Sint*, Pope John Paul II echoes the call of Pope John XXIII and the Second Vatican Council by calling for unity of all of Christianity. All of Christianity accepts Jesus Christ as our Savior! All of Christianity accepts the Bible as the Word of God. Christianity respects life and the Natural Law.

It is important to remember that all are seeking the truth. There is One Truth! **The Word of God is the Word of God!** Whichever your favorite Bible may be, reading Scripture is a great source of prayer, inspiration, and peace. God gives us the Bible to serve as a source of wisdom and comfort and to guide us on the road of life.

CHAPTER 5
THE ROSARY AND THE APPARITIONS OF MARY

Sally and Tom called me about a pilgrimage to Medjugorje, the week following Easter of 1996. In addition to reading the Bible, I began reading all about the apparitions of Mary. Mary in her apparitions guides mankind and leads us to her son Jesus. The rosary traces key events in the life of Jesus in the Bible.
The foundation of the Rosary is Biblical scripture!

The New Testament Gospel of Luke introduces Mary, in the Annunciation:
In the sixth month the angel Gabriel was sent from God to a city of Galilee named Nazareth, to a virgin betrothed to a man whose name was Joseph, of the house of David; and the virgin's name was Mary. And he came to her and said,
"Hail, full of grace, the Lord is with you!"
But she was greatly troubled at the saying, and considered in her mind what sort of greeting this might be.
And the angel said to her,
"Do not be afraid, Mary, for you have found favor with God. And behold, you will conceive in your womb and bear a son, and you shall call his name Jesus.
He will be great, and will be called the Son of the Most High; and the Lord God will give to him the throne of his father David, and he will reign over the house of Jacob forever; and of his kingdom there will be no end."
And Mary said to the angel,
"How shall this be, since I have no husband?"
And the angel said to her,
"The Holy Spirit will come upon you, and the power of the Most High will overshadow you; therefore the child to be born will be called holy, the Son of God.
And behold, your kinswoman Elizabeth in her old age has also conceived a son; and this is the sixth month with her who was called barren. For with God nothing will be impossible."
And Mary said, "Behold, I am the handmaid of the Lord; let it be [done] to me according to your word."
And the angel departed from her.
St. Luke 1:26-38 [RSV]

Mary visits her cousin Elizabeth, as Luke continues the story of the visitation:

> *In those days Mary arose and went with haste into the hill country,*
> *to a city of Judah, and she entered into the house of*
> *Zechariah and greeted Elizabeth.*
> *And when Elizabeth heard the greeting of Mary, the babe leaped*
> *in her womb; and Elizabeth was filled with the Holy Spirit and*
> *she exclaimed with a loud cry,*
> ## *"Blessed are you among women,*
> ## *and blessed is the fruit of your womb!*
> *And why is this granted me, that the mother of my Lord should*
> *come to me? For behold, when the voice of your greeting came to*
> *my ears, the babe in my womb leaped for joy.*
> *And blessed is she who believed that there would be a fulfillment*
> *of what was spoken to her from the Lord."*
> *St. Luke 1:39-45 [RSV]*

These two passages from the Bible give us the origin of the prayer, the Hail Mary:

> Hail Mary, full of grace, the Lord is with you;
> Blessed are you among women,
> and blessed is the fruit of your womb, Jesus.
> Holy Mary, Mother of God, pray for us sinners,
> Now and at the hour of our death, Amen

St. Luke continues with the Nativity in Chapter Two:

> *And Joseph too went up from Galilee from the town of*
> *Nazareth to Judea, to the city of David that is called Bethlehem...*
> *to be enrolled with Mary, his betrothed, who was with child.*
> *While they were there, the time came for her to have her*
> *child, and she gave birth to her firstborn son.*
> *She wrapped him in swaddling clothes*
> *and laid him in a manger,*
> *because there was no room for them in the inn.*
> *St. Luke 2:4-7 [New American]*

Luke continues in Chapter Two with the Presentation of Jesus in the temple:

> *And when the time came for their purification according to the law of Moses, they brought him up to Jerusalem to present him to the Lord (as it is written in the law of the Lord, "Every male that opens the womb shall be called holy to the Lord") and to offer a sacrifice according to what is said in the law of the Lord, "a pair of turtle doves, or two young pigeons."*
>
> *St. Luke 2:22-24 [RSV]*

Luke continues with Joseph and Mary fulfilling Jewish custom:

> *And the child grew and became strong, filled with wisdom; and the favor of God was upon him. Now his parents went to Jerusalem every year at the feast of the Passover. And when he was twelve years old, they went up according to custom; and when the feast was ended, as they were returning, the boy Jesus stayed behind in Jerusalem. His parents did not know it, but supposing him to be in the company they went a day's journey, and they sought him among their kinsfolk and acquaintances; and when they did not find him, they returned to Jerusalem, seeking him. After three days they found him in the temple, sitting among the teachers, listening to them and asking them questions; and all who heard him were amazed at his understanding and his answers. And when they saw him they were astonished; and his mother said to him,*
> *"Son, why have you treated us so? Behold, your father and I have been looking for you anxiously."*
> *And he said to them, "How is it that you sought me? Did you not know that I must be in my Father's house?" And they did not understand the saying which he spoke to them. And he went down with them and came to Nazareth, and was obedient to them; and his mother kept all these things in her heart.*
> *And Jesus increased in wisdom and in stature, and in favor with God and man.*
>
> *St. Luke 2:40-52 [RSV]*

These five events recalling the conception, the birth, and the childhood of Jesus (the Annunciation, the Visitation, the Nativity, the Presentation, and the Finding of the child Jesus in the temple) are remembered when one prays the **Joyful** mysteries of the Rosary.

The **Sorrowful** mysteries of the Rosary recall the passion and death of Jesus. The first Sorrowful mystery recalls the agony of Jesus in the garden:

> *And they went to a place which was called Gethsemane;*
> *and he said to his disciples, "Sit here, while I pray."*
> *And he took with him Peter and James and John, and began to be*
> *greatly distressed and troubled. And he said to them,*
> *"My soul is very sorrowful, even to death; remain here, and watch."*
> *And going a little farther, he fell on the ground and prayed that, if it*
> *were possible, the hour might pass from him.*
> *And he said, "Abba, Father, all things are possible to thee;*
> *remove this cup from me; yet not what I will, but what thou*
> *wilt."*
> *And he came and found them sleeping, and he said to Peter,*
> *"Simon, are you asleep? Could you not watch one hour?*
> *Watch and pray that you may not enter into temptation;*
> *the spirit indeed is willing, but the flesh is weak."*
> *And again he went away and prayed, saying the same words.*
> *And again he came and found them sleeping, for their eyes were*
> *very heavy; and they did not know what to answer him.*
> *And he came the third time, and said to them,*
> *"Are you still sleeping and taking your rest?*
> *It is enough;*
> *the hour has come;*
> *the Son of man is betrayed into the hands of sinners.*
> *Rise, let us be going; see, my betrayer is at hand."*
> *St. Mark 14:32-42 [RSV]*

Jesus then suffered the Scourging at the pillar and the Crowning of thorns by Pontius Pilate, remembered in the second and third Sorrowful mysteries of the Rosary:

"Then Pilate took Jesus and had him scourged.
And the soldiers wove a crown out of thorns and placed it
      on his head, and clothed him in a purple cloak,
      and they came to him and said, "Hail, King of the Jews!"
And they struck him repeatedly.
Once more Pilate went out and said to them,
"Look, I am bringing him out to you,
      so that you may know that I find no guilt in him."
So Jesus came out, wearing the crown of thorns and the
purple cloak. And he said to them, "Behold, the man!"
When the chief priests and the guards saw him they cried out,
      "Crucify him, crucify him!"
             St. John 19:1-6 [New American]

The fourth Sorrowful mystery recalls Jesus carrying His cross:

As they led him away they took hold of a certain Simon,
a Cyrenian, who was coming in from the country; and after
laying the cross on him, they made him carry it behind Jesus.
A large crowd of people followed Jesus,
      including many women who mourned and lamented him.
           St. Luke 23:26-27[New American]

The fifth Sorrowful mystery recalls the Crucifixion of Jesus:
And when they came to a place called Golgotha (which means the
place of a skull), they offered him wine to drink, mingled with gall;
but when he tasted it, he would not drink it.   And when they had
crucified him, they divided his garments among them by casting lots;
then they sat down and kept watch over him there.   And over his
head they put the charge against him, which read,
      "This is Jesus the King of the Jews."
Then two robbers were crucified with him, one on the right and one
on the left. And those who passed by derided him, wagging their
heads and saying,
"You who would destroy the temple and build it in three days, save
yourself! If you are the Son of God, come down from the cross."

So also the chief priests, with the scribes and elders, mocked him, saying, "He saved others; he cannot save himself. He is the King of Israel; let him come down now from the cross, and we will believe in him. He trusts in God; let God deliver him now, if he desires him; for he said, 'I am the Son of God.'" And the robbers who were crucified with him also reviled him in the same way.
Now from the sixth hour there was darkness over all the land until the ninth hour.
And about the ninth hour Jesus cried with a loud voice,

> *"Eli, Eli, lama sabach-thani?" that is,*
> *"My God, my God, why hast thou forsaken me?"*

And some of the bystanders hearing it said, "This man is calling Elijah." And one of them at once ran and took a sponge, filled it with vinegar, and put it on a reed, and gave it to him to drink. But the others said, "Wait, let us see whether Elijah will come to save him."

> *And Jesus cried again with a loud voice*
> *and yielded up his spirit.*

And behold, the curtain of the temple was torn in two, from top to bottom; and the earth shook, and the rocks were split; the tombs also were opened, and many bodies of the saints who had fallen asleep were raised, and coming out of the tombs after his resurrection they went into the holy city and appeared to many. When the centurion and those who were with him, keeping watch over Jesus, saw the earthquake and what took place, they were filled with awe, and said,

> *"Truly this was the Son of God!"*
> *St. Matthew 27:33-54 [RSV]*

The **Glorious** mysteries of the Rosary give us great hope for the future. The first Glorious mystery is the Resurrection of Jesus:

When the sabbath was over, Mary Magdalene,
> *Mary, the mother of James, and Salome bought spices*
> *so that they might go and anoint him.*
Very early when the sun had risen, on the first day of the week, they came to the tomb. They were saying to one another,

"Who will roll back the stone for us from the entrance to the tomb?"
When they looked up, they saw that the stone
had been rolled back; it was very large.
On entering the tomb they saw a young man sitting on the
right side, clothed in a white robe, and they were utterly
amazed. He said to them, "Do not be amazed!
You seek Jesus of Nazareth, the crucified.
He has been raised; he is not here.
Behold the place where they laid him.
But go and tell his disciples and Peter, 'He is going
before you to Galilee;
there you will see him, as he told you.'"
Then they went out and fled from the tomb,
seized with trembling and bewilderment.
They said nothing to anyone, for they were afraid.
St. Mark 16:1-8 [New American]

St. Mark continues in Chapter Sixteen and recounts the Ascension of our Lord, remembered in the second Glorious mystery of the Rosary:

"So then the Lord Jesus, after he spoke to them, was taken up
into heaven and took his seat at the right hand of God.
But they went forth and preached everywhere,
while the Lord worked with them
and confirmed the word through accompanying signs."
St. Mark 16:19-20 [New American]

The second chapter of St. Luke in the Bible, The Acts of the Apostles, continues his presentation of Biblical history as he describes how the salvation promised to Israel in the Old Testament has been fulfilled by Jesus and has now, under the guidance of the Holy Spirit and through the apostles, been extended to the Gentiles.

St. Luke relates The Descent of the Holy Spirit upon the apostles in The Acts of the Apostles, and this event is remembered in the third Glorious mystery of the Rosary.

"When the time for Pentecost was fulfilled,
*   they were all in one place together.*
And suddenly there came from the sky a noise like a strong
driving wind, and it filled the entire house in which they were.
Then there appeared to them tongues as of fire,
*   which parted and came to rest on each one of them.*
And they were all filled with the holy Spirit and
*   began to speak in different tongues,*
*   as the Spirit enabled them to proclaim."*
*   Acts of the Apostles 2:1-4 [New American]*

A critical role for Mary is portrayed in the last book of the Bible, the Apocalypse, or Revelation of John, and is recalled in the fourth and fifth Glorious mysteries of the Rosary, the Assumption of Mary and the Coronation of Mary in Heaven.

"A great sign appeared in the sky,
*   a woman clothed with the sun,*
*   with the moon under her feet,*
*   and on her head a crown of twelve stars.*
She was with child and wailed aloud
*   in pain as she labored to give birth.*
Then another sign appeared in the sky;
*   it was a huge red dragon,*
*   with seven heads and ten horns,*
*   and on its heads were seven diadems.*
Its tail swept away a third of the stars in the sky
*   and hurled them down to the earth.*
Then the dragon stood before the woman about to give birth,
*   to devour her child when she gave birth.*
She gave birth to a son, a male child,
*   destined to rule all the nations with an iron rod.*
Her child was caught up to God and his throne.
* The woman herself fled into the desert,*
*   where she had a place prepared by God, that there*
she might be taken care of for twelve hundred and sixty days.
*   Revelation 12:1-6 [New American]*

Mary was involved in the life of her Son Jesus throughout His ministry. The last recorded words of Mary in the Bible were at the wedding in Cana:

> *On the third day there was a marriage at Cana in Galilee, and the mother of Jesus was there; Jesus also was invited to the marriage, with his disciples. When the wine failed, the mother of Jesus said to him, "They have no wine."*
> *And Jesus said to her,*
> *"O woman, what have you to do with me?*
> *My hour has not yet come."*
> *His mother said to the servants, "Do whatever he tells you." Now six stone jars were standing there, for the Jewish rites of purification, each holding twenty or thirty gallons. Jesus said to them, "Fill the jars with water." And they filled them up to the brim. He said to them, "Now draw some out, and take it to the steward of the feast." So they took it. When the steward of the feast tasted the water now become wine, and did not know where it came from (though the servants who had drawn the water knew), the steward of the feast called the bridegroom and said to him, "Every man serves the good wine first; and when men have drunk freely, then the poor wine; but you have kept the good wine until now."*
> *St. John 2:1-10 [RSV]*

Just as at the wedding feast of Cana, Catholics approach Mary to intercede for them with Her Son Jesus.

Just before his death, Jesus gave His mother to His disciple John:

> *When Jesus saw his mother, and the disciple whom he loved standing near, he said to his mother, "Woman, behold, your son!" Then he said to the disciple, "Behold, your mother!" And from that hour the disciple took her to his own home.*
> *St. John 19:26-27 [RSV]*

Mary was part of the first community in Jerusalem at the time of the Pentecost:

> *All these devoted themselves to prayer, together with some women, and Mary the mother of Jesus, and his brothers.*
> *Acts 1:14 [New American]*

Throughout history the faithful have experienced apparitions of Mary. Each of these apparitions report miraculous events such as healings, messages from Heaven, and supernatural intervention, but never so frequently as these latter times of the twentieth century. Many apparitions, such as Prouille, Lourdes, Fatima, and now Medjugorje confirm the importance of the **Rosary**. Credit must be given to St. Dominic at Prouille for spreading the Rosary devotion.

It is important to remember that an apparition is a **subjective** event experienced by a person, and thus is subject to many variables, such as cultural and intellectual background, emotional stability, and inherited traditions.

A word of caution is important before we begin our recounting of the major Marian apparitions. Apparitions are subjective human experiences from a supernatural source, in this case, Mary, the Mother of Jesus. The Catholic Church exercises great prudence and caution in the investigation of an apparition, and does not thoroughly render judgment until a particular apparition is over. Several criteria must be met prior to approval or disapproval. When the Church does approve an apparition, it cannot prove the person actually had a vision of the heavenly person. It can merely state evidence suggests an appariton may well have happened and that there is nothing contrary to the beliefs of the Catholic Church.

You may be Catholic or Christian and you are not required to believe in any of the approved apparitions!

It is wise to heed the words of Jesus when assessing these modern apparitions:

> *"Beware of false prophets,*
> *who come to you in sheep's clothing*
> *but inwardly are ravenous wolves.*
> *You will know them by their fruits.*
> *Are grapes gathered from thorns, or figs from thistles?*
> *So, every sound tree bears good fruit,*
> *but the bad tree bears evil fruit.*
> *A sound tree cannot bear evil fruit,*
> *nor can a bad tree bear good fruit.*
> *Every tree that does not bear good fruit is cut down*
> *and thrown into the fire.*
> *Thus you will know them by their fruits.*
> *Matthew 7:15-20 [RSV]*

We recount some of the approved Marian apparitions throughout history.

The adjoining page is a rosary on a postcard of Mary mailed from Medjugorje. The card arrived in the United States fresh with tears! With the Rosary Cross you make the **Sign of the Cross**, and say the **Apostles' Creed**. Then one says an Our Father and three Hail Marys and the Glory Prayer following the Cross.

That leaves five large single beads (**Our Father**), each followed by a group of ten small blue beads (**Hail Mary**). After every group of Hail Marys, one says the **Glory Prayer.** An Our Father and ten Hail Marys and the Glory Prayer make one mystery of the Rosary.

	Joyful	**Sorrowful**	**Glorious**
1	The Annunciation	The Agony in the Garden	The Resurrection of Jesus
2	The Visitation	The Scourging at the Pillar	The Ascension of Jesus
3	The Nativity	The Crowning of Thorns	The Descent of the Holy Spirit upon the Apostles
4	The Presentation	The Carrying of the Cross	The Assumption of Mary
5	Finding in the Temple	The Crucifixion of Jesus	The Coronation of Mary

Sign of the Cross

In the name of the Father, and of the Son, and of the Holy Spirit, Amen.

Apostles' Creed   I believe in God, the Father Almighty, Creator of Heaven and earth; and in Jesus Christ, His only Son, our Lord; who was conceived by the Holy Spirit, born of the Virgin Mary, suffered under Pontius Pilate, was crucified; died, and was buried. He descended to the dead, the third day he arose again from the dead; He ascended into heaven, sitteth at the right hand of God the Father Almighty; from thence He shall come to judge the living and the dead.

I believe in the Holy Spirit, the Holy Catholic Church, the Communion of Saints, the forgiveness of sins, the resurrection of the body, and life everlasting, Amen.

Our Father

Our Father, who art in heaven, hallowed be thy name, thy kingdom come, thy will be done, on earth as it is in heaven. Give us this day our daily bread, and forgive us our trespasses as we forgive those who trespass against us. And lead us not into temptation, but deliver us from evil, Amen.

Hail Mary

Hail Mary, full of grace, the Lord is with thee, blessed art thou among women, and blessed is the fruit of thy womb Jesus.

Holy Mary, Mother of God, pray for us sinners, now and at the hour of our death, Amen.

Glory Prayer   Glory be to the Father, and to the Son, and to the Holy Spirit, as it was in the beginning, is now, and ever shall be, world without end, Amen.

Ave Maria

Saragossa, Spain (40 AD)

The first apparition of Mary is thought to have occurred to St. James the apostle in 40 AD. Following the ministry of Jesus, His apostle, James, began to spread His message as far as the northern village of Saragossa, Spain. When St. James was deep in prayer, tradition holds that Mary appeared to him and gave him a small wooden statue of herself and a jasper column and instructed him to build a church in her honor. James built a small chapel in Mary's honor, the first church dedicated to the virgin Mary. When James returned to Jerusalem, he was executed by Herod in 44 AD, the first apostle to be martyred for his faith. His disciples returned his body for final burial in Spain. A cathedral in honor of St. James was built over the burial site, when this site was rediscovered eight centuries later by a hermit who noticed an unusual star formation over a country field, now called Compostella, or starry field.

Prouille, France (1208)

There have been attempts to trace the origin of the Rosary to the ancient prayer or worry beads of Middle East and Asia, although these beads largely have 33 beads. Others point to prayer beads as a means to count the 150 Psalms. But it was St. Dominic who truly spread devotion to the **Rosary**.

In 1208 Domingo de Guzman was a Spanish preacher who went to southern France to preserve the faith against the Albigensian heresy. While he was praying for three days in a chapel in Prouille, Dominic saw Mary give him the Rosary and taught him how to pray the Rosary.

Mary gave 15 promises to St. Dominic for those Christians who recite the rosary. She offered the rosary for all people as a source of grace and means of protection and strength against sin. The rosary will bring virtue and good works to fluorish, and obtain the abundant mercy of God. She promised that whoever shall recite the rosary devoutly, applying himself to the consideration of its sacred mysteries, shall never be conquered by misfortune. Whoever shall have a true devotion for the rosary shall not die without the sacraments of the Church. Those who are faithful to recite the rosary shall have during their life and at their death the light of God and the plentitude of His graces. "You shall obtain all you ask of me by the recitation of the rosary." She calls all who recite the rosary "her sons, and brothers of my only son, Jesus Christ."

St. Dominic founded the Dominican Friars, and established monasteries all over the world. The heresy ended during his lifetime. The most famous Dominican was St. Thomas Aquinas (1224-1274), one of greatest theologians of the Catholic Church, the author of *Summa Theologica*.

Aylesford, England (1251)

Simon Stock had an apparition of Mary on July 16, 1251. He had become a member of the religious order of Our Lady of Mount Carmel while on a pilgrimage to the Holy Land. Friar Stock was given the brown scapular, to be worn as a "pledge of peace and special protection until the end of time. Those who die devotedly clothed with this scapular shall be preserved from eternal fire." The scapular was one of the most widely used religious symbols among Catholics until its disappearance in the 1960s, the time when religion left our daily lives and the American scene.

Guadalupe, Mexico (1531)

The conversion of the Americas to the Christian faith was hastened by the apparition of Mary to the poor Aztec Indian, Juan Diego, in 1531. At daybreak, on Saturday, December 9, 1531, Juan Diego was walking from his village of Tolpetlac, five miles outside of Mexico City, to attend a Franciscan mass. As he ran by the west side of a hill named Tepeyac, on which once stood a temple to the Mother goddess of the Aztecs, he suddenly heard a throng of songbirds burst into harmony. The music stopped as suddenly as it had begun. A beautiful girl surrounded by the golden beams of the sun was calling him by name, "Juan Diego!" The girl said:

"Dear little son, I love you. I want you to know who I am. I am the ever-virgin Mary, Mother of the true God who gives life and maintains it in existence. He created all things. He is in all places. He is Lord of heaven and earth. I desire a teocali (temple or church) at this place where I will show my compassion to your people and to all people who sincerely ask my help in their work and in their sorrows. I am your merciful Mother, the Mother of all who live united in this land, and of all mankind, of all those who love me, of those who cry to me, of those who have confidence in me. Here I will hear their weeping and their sorrows, and I will console them and they will be at peace. So run now to Tenochtitlan (Mexico City) and tell the Lord Bishop all that you have seen and heard."

Juan Diego went to the palace of the Bishop-elect, Don Fray Juan de Zumarraga, a Franciscan, and after much difficulty, was granted an audience with the Bishop-elect. The Bishop-elect said that he would consider the request of the

Lady and that he was welcome to come visit again. Dismayed, Juan returned to the hill and found Mary waiting for him. He asked her to send someone more suitable to deliver her message "for I am a nobody."

She said, "Listen, little son. There are many I could send. But you are the one I have chosen for this task. So, tomorrow morning, go back to the Bishop. Tell him it is the Virgin Mary who sends you, and repeat to him my great desire for a church in this place." So, Sunday morning Juan Diego called again on the Bishop for the second time. The Bishop told him to ask for a sign. Juan Diego reported this to Mary, and she told him to return the following morning for the sign.

However, when Juan Diego returned home he found his uncle sick and dying. He stayed there for two days and realizing he was going to die, he woke up early Tuesday morning, December 12th, to fetch a priest to give his uncle a last blessing. Juan had to pass Tepeyac hill to get to the priest. He went around the east side of Tepeyac hill to avoid possibly seeing the Lady and the possible delay. It didn't work. He saw her descending the hill to intercept his route.

She said, "Least of my sons, what is the matter?"

Juan was embarrassed. "My Lady, why are you up so early? Are you well? Forgive me. My uncle is dying and desires me to find a priest for the Last Sacraments. It was no heedless promise I made to you yesterday morning. But my uncle fell ill."

Mary said, "My little son. Do not be distressed and afraid. Am I not here who am your Mother? Are you not under my shadow and protection? Your uncle will not die at this time. This very moment his health is restored. There is no reason now for the errand you set out on, and you can peacefully attend to mine. Go up to the top of the hill; cut the flowers that are growing there and bring them to me."

Flowers in December? Impossible, thought Juan Diego. But he was obedient, and sure enough found Castilian roses on the hilltop. As he cut them, he decided the best way to protect them against the cold was to cradle them in his *tilma* --a long, cloth cape worn by the Aztecs, and often looped up as a carryall. He ran back to Mary and she rearranged the roses and tied the lower corners of the *tilma* behind his neck so that nothing will spill, and said, "You see, little son, this is the sign I am sending to the Bishop. Tell him that now he has his sign, he should build the temple I desire in this place. Do not let anyone but him see what you are carrying. Hold both sides until you are in his presence and tell him how I intercepted you on your way to fetch a priest to give the Last Sacraments to your uncle, how I assured you he was perfectly healed and sent you up to cut these roses, and myself arranged them like this. Remember, little son, that you are my trusted ambassador, and this time the Bishop will believe all that you tell him." This was the last known time Juan Diego ever saw the virgin Mary.

Juan called for the third time on the Bishop and explained all that had past. Then Juan put up both hands and untied the corners of crude cloth behind his neck. The looped-up fold of the tilma fell; the flowers he thought were the precious sign tumbled out on the floor.

The Bishop rose from his chair and knelt at Juan's feet as well as every-one else in the room. Millions of people have knelt before the tilma since, in awe and gratitude as profound as the ones who saw it first. For on the tilma was a picture of the Blessed virgin Mary just as described by Juan Diego.

While Juan was calling on the Bishop, the dying uncle suddenly found his room filled with a soft light. A luminous young woman filled with love was stand-ing there and told him he would get well. She told him that she had sent his nephew, Juan, to the Bishop with a picture of herself and said, "Call me and call my image Santa Maria de Guadalupe".

The image has been extensively studied using modern sophisticated techniques and its longevity and method of production are impossible to explain. You can still see the tilma in the cathedral today in Mexico City.

Paris, France (1830)

Catherine Laboure was a Sister of Charity nun and was stationed at the Paris seminary at 140 rue du Bac. During the night of July 18, 1830 Sister Catherine was awakened by a beautiful child of four or five years of age. He urged her to come to the chapel, and she followed. At midnight, the child said, "Here is the Blessed Virgin, and Mary appeared and warned her that grave misfortune would soon fall upon France, and again in forty years. Shortly there-after, the French Revolution of 1830 broke out. And, in 1870 the Franco-Prus-sian War ensued.

On November 27, 1830 Mary appeared again to Sister Catherine. She was dressed in a shining white robe and was standing on a globe, her feet crushing the serpent. Mary said, "The globe that you see represents the entire world, especially France and each person in particular." The globe disappeared and Mary extended her radiant hands saying, "Behold the symbol of graces I shed upon those who ask me for them." There now formed around Mary an oval-shaped frame which appeared the words, "O Mary, conceived without sin, pray for us who have recourse to you." Mary then told Sister Catherine, "Have a medal struck upon this model. All who wear it will receive great graces. Graces will be bestowed abundantly on those who have confidence." Suddenly, the medal seemed to turn, and Catherine saw the reverse side of the medal: the letter M was surmounted by a cross with a bar at its base. Beneath the M were two hearts, one encircled by a crown of thorns and the other pierced with a sword. Twelve stars encircled the border of this side. This is the origin of the Miraculous Medal, which Catholics wear for protection and as a source of grace.

LaSalette, France (1846)

Melanie Mathieu, age 14, and Maximin Giraud, age 11, were herding cattle on a mountain meadow in LaSalette, France on September 19, 1846, a time of social disruption after the French Revolution. People were working on Sundays and not attending church at the time. Once there had prevailed a Christian view of life and an awareness of God, but during this time Christian attitudes had given way to self-indulgence, greed, and a worldly spirit. Suddenly, Melanie saw a large circle of brilliant light, vibrant in outshining the sun. She called Maximin and they observed that the luminous circle was opening. Gradually they could see a sorrowful woman, weeping. The beautiful Lady expressed her sorrow to the children that people were working on Sunday and not attending Sunday mass. She said she could no longer restrain "the hand of her Son." She predicted a great famine, and urged the children to pray. She stood still for a moment then rose in the air. Her figure and the circle of light grew more luminous, and then disappeared.

The potato famine of 1846 took place, and the wheat and corn shortage were so severe that more than a million people in Europe died of starvation. A spring discovered at the appearance site became noted for its healing waters, and many documented miracles took place. There was a return to the faith and unnecessary work ceased on Sunday. Within five years, the Catholic church approved the apparition.

Lourdes, France (1858)

On February 11, 1858 in the grotto at Massabieille near Lourdes, France an 14 year old girl named Bernadette Soubirous describes in her own words her first apparition of Mary.

"Suddenly I heard a great noise, like the sound of a storm. I looked to the right, to the left, under the trees of the river, but nothing moved. I thought I was mistaken. . . . Then I heard a fresh noise like the first. I was frightened and stood straight up. I lost all power of speech and thought when, turning my head toward the grotto, I saw at one of the openings of the rock a rosebush, one only, moving as if it were very windy. Almost at the same time there came out of the interior of the grotto a golden colored cloud, and soon after a Lady, young and beautiful, exceedingly beautiful, the like of whom I had never seen, came and placed herself at the entrance of the opening above the rosebush. She looked at me immediately, smiled at me and signaled to me to advance, as if she had been my Mother. All fear had left me but I seemed to know no longer where I was. I rubbed my eyes, I shut them, I opened them; but the Lady was still there continuing to smile at me and making me understand that I was not mistaken. Without thinking of what I was doing, I took my Rosary in my hands and went on my knees. The Lady made a sign of approval with her head and herself took into her hands a Rosary which hung on her right arm. . . The Lady let me pray all alone; she passed the beads of her **Rosary** between her fingers but she said nothing; only at the end of each decade did she say the "Gloria" with me."

Mary appeared 17 more times to Bernadette. On the eighth apparition, February 24, 1858, she called for "Penitence, Penitence, Penitence." Catholics say the following prayer of penitence, the Act of Contrition, privately or after Confession.

Act of Contrition:

O My God, I am heartily sorry for having offended you, and I detest of all my sins, because I dread the loss of heaven and the pains of hell, but most of all, because they have offended you, My God, who are all good and deserving of all my love. I firmly resolve with the help of thy grace, to confess my sins, to do penance, and to amend my life, Amen.

On February 25, the ninth apparition, Mary instructed Bernadette to scratch gravel off the ground.   At the site, she discovered a spring, with a pool forming.   The following day, the pool was overflowing, and water was dripping over the rock, and forming a stream.   During the sixteenth apparition, March 25, 1858, the Feast of the Annunciation, the Lady revealed her identity: "I am the Immaculate Conception."   This doctrine of Pius IX had been made known only four years previously, and was generally unknown by the populace.

Lourdes has become one of the major pilgrimage sites in Europe and is noted for the thousands of miracles that have occurred at the healing spring in the grotto of Massabieille.

Knock, Ireland (1879)

The faithful of Ireland were rewarded, when, on August 21, 1879, by the humble church in Knock, County Mayo, Ireland, the night became lit with a brilliant light.   Passers-by saw Mary in the center with St. Joseph on her right and St. John the Evangelist on the left.   They were suspended in space and looking towards Heaven praying in silence.   An altar with a large cross and a lamb at the foot of the cross were also visible, surrounded by angels.   Although words were never spoken, the apparition of Knock is notable for the large number of people that were present.   Innumerable cures have occurred at Knock since.

Fatima, Portugal (1917)

In the spring of 1916, Lucia, age 9, Francisco, age 8, and Jacinta, age 6, were tending their families' flock of sheep at Chousa Velha when a strong wind shook the trees and then a light appeared. As the light drew near they saw a young man in a shining, flowing robe. "Fear not, I am the Angel of peace. Pray with me." He taught them the following prayer: "My God, I believe, I adore, I hope and I love you! I ask pardon of You for those who do not believe, do not adore, do not hope and do not love you." He then said, "Pray this way. The Hearts of Jesus and Mary are attentive to the words of your prayers." He appeared a few weeks later and urged them to pray and sacrifice. His third and last visit occurred in the fall of that year and he gave Lucia communion, and to Francisco and Jacinta, who had not yet made their first communion, he offered a chalice for them to drink.

On May 13, 1917, the children, now a year older, were tending their sheep, when they were startled by a flash of light. Fearing a storm, they ran under a holm oak, or *carrasqueira* . A second flash of light was even brighter, and frightened, they ran again, until they suddenly stopped in amazement in front of a small evergreen called the *azinheira.* For there stood "the most beautiful Lady they had ever seen."

In Lucia's own words, "She was a Lady dressed all in white, more brilliant than the sun, shedding rays of light clearer and stronger than a crystal glass filled with crystalline water and pierced by the burning rays of the sun." She held a rosary in her right hand.

"Do not be afraid. I will not harm you."

They felt peaceful in her presence, and Lucia asked her where she was from.

"I am from Heaven."

The three children asked if they would also be going to Heaven one day, and she said yes, but with gentle reproach, Francisco would first have to say many rosaries. She asked them to return to the same spot on the same day for the next six months and then she would identify herself. She then asked them a difficult question:

"Do you wish to offer yourselves to God to endure all the sufferings He may send you in reparation for sins and for the conversion of sinners?"

With childlike faith they heroically said yes.

"Then you will have much to suffer. But the grace of God will strengthen you and be your comfort."

She then opened her hands and from her palms came two streams of light which in Lucia's words, "made us see ourselves in God more clearly in that light than in the best of mirrors." The children then prayed in her presence, and then she said,

"Say the Rosary every day, to obtain peace for the world, and the end of the war."

She then glided towards the east and disappeared in the sunlight.

On June 13, 1917, Mary gave the children a prayer to say after each decade of the Rosary:

"Oh, my Jesus, forgive us our sins. Save us from the fire of hell and lead all souls to Heaven, especially those who have most need of Your Mercy."

She then spoke to Lucia: "I will come soon for Jacinta and Francisco. You will remain on the earth for a long time. God wishes to guide you to make me known and loved, to establish throughout the world devotion to my Immaculate Heart. I promise salvation to those who embrace devotion to my Immaculate Heart."

During the third apparition on July 13, 1917, Mary revealed the three secrets of Fatima. She opened her hands and the rays of light pierced the very heart of the earth, and the children were given the first secret, a vision of hell, described in Lucia's own words: "a sea of fire; and plunged in this fire were the demons and the souls, as if they were red-hot coals, transparent and black or bronze-colored, with human forms, which floated about in the conflagration, borne by the flames which issued from it with clouds of smoke, falling on all sides as sparks fall in great flagrations--without weight or equilibrium, among shrieks and groans of sorrow and despair which horrified and caused us to shudder with fear. The devils were distinguished by horrible and loathsome forms of animals frightful and unknown, but transparent like black coals that have turned red-hot."

She then gave them the second secret:

"You have seen hell, where the souls of sinners go. To save them God wishes to establish in the world the devotion to my Immaculate Heart. If people do as I shall ask, many souls will be converted and there will be peace. This war (World War I) is going to end, but if people do not cease offending God, not much time will elapse and during the Pontificate of Pius XI another and more terrible war will begin. When you shall see a night illumined by an unknown light, know that this is the great sign from God that the chastisement of the world for its many transgressions is at hand through war, famine, persecution of the Church and of the Holy Father."

"To prevent this, I shall come to ask for the consecration of Russia to my Immaculate Heart and the Communion of reparation on the First Saturdays. If my requests are heard, Russia will be converted and there will be peace. If not, she will spread her errors throughout the entire world, provoking wars and persecution of the Church. The good will suffer martyrdom; the Holy Father will suffer much; different nations will be annihilated."

"In the end my Immaculate Heart will triumph. The Holy Father will consecrate Russia to me, and it will be converted and a period of peace will be granted the world."

She then revealed a third and final secret which has never been revealed. The Lady disappeared. The crowd remained in silence, sensing the solemnity of the occasion, when nothing less than the fate of the entire human race may be at stake. On the night of January 25, 1938, the strange illumination of light appeared, serving as a harbinger of World War II, which began later that year.

On August 13, 1917, the children were kidnapped by the chief magistrate of the county, Arthur Santos, in an effort to quell the growing publicity of Fatima. However, his effort backfired, as this only infuriated the crowd that had gathered for the event. Our Lady appeared privately to the children later in the week.

A crowd of 30,000 gathered on September 13, 1917, and they were astonished when a luminous globe of light suddenly appeared in the cloudless sky. Our Lady asked the children:
"Continue to say the Rosary to bring about the end of the war."
Then she said she would identify herself and perform a miracle in October.

The night of October 12, 1917 a terrible storm and winds descended on Fatima and the surrounding areas. Nonetheless, 70,000 brave souls withstood the onslaught to be present for the day of the miracle. The Lady appeared in the rain on October 13, 1917 over the azinheira.

"I have come to tell you to build a chapel here in my honor. I am the Lady of the **Rosary**."

Her face became graver as she continued,
"Let them offend our God no more, for He is already much offended."

The three children then saw a vision of the Holy Family: Mary was standing by St. Joseph who was holding the child Jesus.

Then the crowd of 70,000 saw the miracle of the sun, as described by William Thomas Walsh in his 1954 book *Our Lady of Fatima* :
"The sun stood forth in the clear zenith like a great silver disk which, though bright as any sun they had ever seen, they could look straight at without blinking, and with a unique and delightful satisfaction. This lasted but a moment. While they gazed, the huge ball began to "dance"--that was the word all the beholders applied to it. Now it was whirling rapidly like a gigantic fire-wheel. After doing this for some time, it stopped. Then it rotated again, with dizzy, sickening speed. Finally there appeared on the rim a border of crimson, which flung across the sky, as from a vortex, blood-red streamers of flame, reflecting to the earth, to the trees and shrubs, to the upturned faces and the clothes all sorts of brilliant colors

in succession: green, red, orange, blue, violet, the whole spectrum in fact. Madly gyrating in this manner three times, the fiery orb seemed to tremble, to shudder, and then to plunge precipitately, in a mighty zigzag, toward the crowd, causing widespread panic. This had lasted about ten minutes, perhaps. Then all saw the sun begin to climb, in the same zigzag manner, to where it had appeared before. It became tranquil, then dazzling. No one could look at it any longer. It was the sun of every day."

The great influenza epidemic of 1918 struck Europe and the entire world, and afflicted the two youngest children. Francisco received his first Communion April 3, 1919, and died the following day. Jacinta died February 20, 1920

Lucia joined the Sisters of St. Dorothy at Vilar, near Porto and became Sister Maria of the Sorrows. There, on December 10, 1925, Mary appeared to Lucia and further explained the Communion of reparation of the First Saturdays: "Look, my daughter, at my Heart wounded... with the thorns of ungrateful men... You, at least, try to console me, and announce that I promise to assist at the hour of death, with the graces necessary for salvation, all those who, on the first Saturdays of five consecutive months, confess, receive Holy Communion, recite the Rosary, and keep me company for a quarter of an hour meditating on its mysteries with the intention of offering me reparation."

Beauraing, Belgium (1932)

Mary appeared on 33 occasions in Beauraing, Belgium from November 29, 1932 to January 3, 1933 to five children, Gilberte (13), Fernande (15), and Albert (11) Voisin, and Andree (14) and Gilberte (9) Degeimbre. Mary appeared with a heart of gold and identified herself as the Immaculate Virgin. She appeared by a hawthorn tree and many cures took place there.

Banneux, Belgium (1933)

Mary appeared 8 times to Mariette Beco, age 12, in Banneux, Belgium from January 15 to March 2, 1933. On January 19, 1933, she identified herself as the Virgin of the Poor. She blessed a spring which was to be reserved for all nations to relieve the sick. The healing spring of Banneux has cured pilgrims from all over the world.

This ends our accounting of the major Marian apparitions approved by the Catholic Church. These were brief events in critical times for mankind, which played an important role in the history of Christianity. For example, her one appearance in 1208 to St. Dominic established the rosary, stopped the spread of heresy in Europe, and preserved Christianity in southern Europe. Mary's brief appearance at Guadalupe led to the massive conversion of Latin America from primitive Indian religions to Christianity. The incredible events at Fatima are just beginning to be realized. How could little children in a rural town in the hills of Portugal predict the rise and fall of Russia in the Twentieth Century!

Medjugorje, Bosnia-Hercegovina

Because Mary is reported to appear in Medjugorje on a daily basis from 1981 right up to the present day, formal investigation and approval by the Catholic Church cannot take place until an apparition has been completed. All who write about Medjugorje, including this author, submit to the final judgement of the Church concerning the apparitions of Medjugorje. Thus the apparitions of Medjugorje at present do not have formal approval by the Catholic Church.

Judging by its fruits, 25 million pilgrims to this little village in the mountains of Hercegovina return inspired and renewed in their faith. Pope John Paul II as an individual has been very supportive of Medjugorje, as he has called people of all faiths: *"Let them come to Medjugorje! Let them pray there...*(National Catholic Register, June 14, 1987).

Medjugorje is a village of 400 families, nestled between two mountain ranges in Hercegovina, and surrounded by grape vineyards. It is about a three-hour bus ride through Dalmatia (the original home of the Dalmatian), now known as Croatia, from Split on the Adriatic Sea. Key places in Medjugorje are St. James Catholic Church in the center of the valley; Mount Krisevac, or Cross Mountain, on the top of which was erected a large cross in 1933, in memory of the death of Jesus 1900 years earlier; and Apparition Hill on Mount Podbrdo.

June 24, 1981, the feast day of St. John the Baptist (who heralded the First coming of the Messiah), was a holiday in Medjugorje and no one worked in the fields. Two young girls, Ivanka Ivankovich, age 15, and Mirjana Dragicevic, age 16, were walking by Mount Podbrdo, near Bijakovici, a cluster of homes about a 15-minute walk from Medjugorje. Ivanka turned and saw a brilliant light, and in the light she saw a beautiful woman holding her baby. She turned to Mirjana and said, "I think that Our Lady is on the hill."

At first Mirjana would not look, and began walking back to the village. But Mirjana described a strange feeling inside her, that made her want to return, and she went back to where Ivanka stood. Ivanka said, "Look now, please." Mirjana looked and saw a woman in a long, grey dress with a child in her arms.

Another girl named Milka Pavlovic, age 13, also came and saw. Ivan came by carrying apples, and also saw the woman surrounded by the brilliant light. They were joined by Vicka Ivankovic, age 17, who described the woman as having dark hair and a pale white complexion, and she was holding an infant in her arms. When she beckoned them to come up the hill, they were frozen in fear. They became afraid and ran away.

When they went home and told their families, they were scolded and ridiculed. Vicka's grandmother suggested they go back up the hill the next day and throw holy water at the apparition, and that would tell whether it was truly a heavenly spirit.

The next evening, June 25, 1981, Vicka, Ivanka, and Mirjana felt an urging to return to the mountain. When they stopped to get Milka, she was away with her mother, so they invited her sister Marija Pavlovic, age 17, to join them. Ivan Dragicevic, age 16, who had run away the day before, decided to go, and Mirjana brought Jakov Colo, age 10, with them. They again saw great flashes of light, and were afraid. Then the beautiful woman appeared, this time without the child and beckoned to them. This time they ran up the hill, and began to pray. By all accounts, her first words were "**Praised be Jesus.**" Vicka stood, and sprinkled holy water on the Lady in the sign of the cross, and said "If you are Our Lady, then remain with us. If you are not, then go away." The woman smiled at this, and said:

> **Do not be afraid, dear angels.**
> **I am the Mother of God**
> **I am the Queen of Peace**
> **I am the Mother of all the people.**

The children asked her why she had come.
I have come to tell you that God exists, and He loves you.

When the children asked for a sign for those who could not see her, she said,
> **Blessed are those who have not seen and who believe.**

On the way down the mountain, after the apparition is over, Marija walked off the path to where she saw a shining bare cross, and sees the Blessed Mother, who is sobbing.

Peace, Peace, Peace! Be reconciled! Only Peace.
Make your peace with God and among yourselves.
For that, it is necessary
to believe, to pray, to fast, to go to confession..

The six of them, Ivanka Ivankovic, Mirjana Dragicevic, Vicka Ivankovic, Marija Pavlovic, Ivan Dragicevic,and Jakov Colo have become known and would remain the six visionaries of Medjugorje.

Medjugorje was still under Communist rule at the time, and the authorities were opposed to the apparition. They turned to the pastor of St. James Catholic Church, Father Jozo Zovko, to handle the situation. Father Jozo was at first skeptical of the apparitions. One week after the apparitions began, the police decided to arrest the visionaries. Father Jozo was praying alone in the Church. He suddenly heard the words *"Go out now and protect the children."* Stunned by the clearly audible message, he ran and opened the back door of the Church, and saw the children running towards him begging for help and crying. He hid them inside the Church. When the authorities came, they asked Father Jozo quickly, "Have you seen those children?" He answered, "yes." Before the police asked where, they charged off in the direction of Apparition Hill (Mount Podbrdo). That day the apparition took place in the Church, and Father Jozo saw as well. From then on, he became the leading defender of the apparitions, and was ultimately jailed for 18 months at hard labor for refusing to close the Church or put a stop to the apparitions.

For the first three years of the daily apparitions, the messages of Mary were directed to the visionaries themselves and to St. James Parish. Her message is one of love and peace: peace in your heart, peace in your family, peace in your community, peace in the world. Mary loves all of us as her children, and she wants to save all of us, and bring us all back to God.

The message of Mary is to bring love and forgiveness for mankind through peace, conversion, fasting, penance, and prayer.   We can bring peace through the corporal and spiritual works of mercy.

The Corporal Works of Mercy		The Spiritual Works of Mercy	
1	Feed the Hungry	1	Admonish sinners
2	Give drink to the thirsty	2	Instruct the uninformed
3	Clothe the naked	3	Counsel the doubtful
4	Shelter the homeless	4	Comfort the sorrowful
5	Comfort the imprisoned	5	Be patient with those in error
6	Visit the sick	6	Forgive offenses
7	Bury the dead	7	Pray for the living and the dead

Forgiveness is the key to peace. Conversion means total commitment to God and His commandments, and the avoidance of sin. Mary asks us to fast on Wednesdays and Fridays, as self-denial helps one in self-control. She asks us to offer penance for our sins, and for Catholics to go to confession at least once a month. She asks us to pray with the heart by daily reading of Holy Scripture. Her favorite prayer is the Rosary. She also wants us to attend Church and receive her Son Jesus in our hearts through communion. She calls all people, for we are all children of God. She wants us to be messengers of love and mercy, and spread the Word of God.

Why is she appearing?

Has the time come for the whole world to finally listen, and live in harmony with our Creator? Mary has given the visionaries Mirjana, Ivanka, and Jakov 10 secrets each on future events of mankind. Mirjana received all 10 secrets by December 24, 1982 and now sees Mary on her birthday and the second of every month. Ivanka received all 10 secrets by May 7, 1985, and now sees Mary yearly on June 25. Jakov just received the tenth secret on September 12, 1998, and was told he will see Mary Christmas Day. Ivan, Vicka, and Marija have nine secrets each and still see Mary daily. The events will begin to occur when all six visionaries have all ten secrets.

The message of Mary is one of light and hope! How peaceful this world would be if we are merciful and forgive offenses and show love and respect to others! Essential to her message are that these 10 events may be mitigated if mankind has a change of heart.

Mirjana has said the first two secrets will be warnings to the world--events that will occur before a visible sign is given to humanity. These will happen in her lifetime. Ten days before the first secret and the second secret she will notify her priest who will pray and fast for seven days and then he will announce these to the world. The ninth and tenth secrets are serious, and concern chastisement for the sins of the world.

Are these the beginning of the end times?

The visionaries of Medjugorje have undergone the most extensive medical and psychologic testing modern science has to offer, only to be found completely normal. They have been videotaped during an apparition and has been noted by a French scientific team that all six visionaries focused on a single reference point.

From March 1, 1984 through January 8, 1987 messages were given on a weekly basis to the parishioners of St. James Church in Medjugorje for the direction of their spiritual life. Beginning on January 8, 1987 Mary began giving monthly messages to the world through Marija on the 25th of every month.

Only a few listened to her message.

On June 25, 1991, ten years from when Mary first identified herself, Croatia and Slovenia declared independence from the former country of Yugoslavia, precipitating civil war. Serbia mobilized the former Yugoslav army, and invaded within 48 hours. We have seen night after night in our homes the horrible atrocities, ethnic cleansing, and near-destruction of that beautiful and scenic country. We saw Sarajevo, once the proud host of the 1984 Olympic games, become world-famous for its endless bread lines. It was not until U. S. Air Force pilot Scott O'Grady was shot down over Bosnia in 1995 and rescued six days later by the Marines that the U. S. became involved. Bombing of Serb positions ended the war within three months. The formal signing of the Dayton Peace Accords took place in Paris on December 14, 1995.   60,000 U. N. and now U. S. troops occupy the country to maintain a fragile peace.

On the fifth day of the apparitions, Mary was asked how long would she appear:

As long as you will want me to, my angels.

June 29, 1981

Here are some of the key messages of Mary. She sees herself as our Mother and affectionately calls us her "little children."

A great struggle is about to unfold,
a struggle between my Son and satan.
Human souls are at stake.   *August 2, 1981*

I have come to call the world to conversion
for the last time.
After that, I will not appear any more on this earth.
May 2, 1982

At the moment of death, we are conscious
of the separation of the body and soul.
One is born only once.
The body, drawn from the earth, decomposes after death.
Man receives a transfigured body.
Whoever has done very much evil during his life
can go straight to heaven if he confesses,
is sorry for what he has done,
and receives communion at the end of his life.
July 24, 1982

To be very happy, live a simple, humble life;
pray a great deal,
and do not delve into your problems
but let God solve them.
Date unknown

This century is under the power of the Devil,
but when the secrets confided to you come to pass,
his power will be destroyed.
Even now he is beginning to lose his power
and has become aggressive.
He is destroying marriages, creating division
among priests and
is responsible for obsessions and murder.
You must protect yourselves against these things
through fasting and prayer,
especially community prayer.
Sometime in 1982

In Purgatory there are different levels; the lowest is close to
　　Hell and the highest gradually draws near to Heaven.
It is not on All Souls Day, but at Christmas,
　　that the greatest number of souls leave Purgatory.
There are in Purgatory, souls who pray ardently to God,
　　but for whom no relative or friend prays on earth.
God makes them benefit from the prayers of other people.
It happens that God permits them to manifest themselves in
different ways, close to their relatives on earth,
in order to remind men of the existence of Purgatory and to
solicit their prayers to come close to God who is just, but good.
　　The majority of people go to Purgatory.
　　Many go to Hell.
　　A small number go directly to Heaven.
　　　　　　January 10, 1983

Messages beginning in 1984 were intended and spread to the whole world.

Dear children!
　　I, your mother, love you all.
　　I love you even when you are far from me and my son.
　　　　　　May 24, 1984

Dear children!
Today I wish to tell you:
　　always pray before your work
　　 and end your work with prayer.
If you do that God will bless you and your work.
These days you have been praying too little
　　and working too much.
Pray therefore. In prayer you will find rest.
　　Thank you for your response to my call.
　　　　　　July 5, 1984

I request the families of the parish to pray the family rosary.
　　　　　　September 27, 1984

Dear children! Today I want to call you to pray, pray, pray!
In prayer you will come to know the greatest joy
      and the way out of every situation that has no way out.
March 28, 1985

**I wish to give you messages as it has never been
in history from the beginning of the world.**
April 4, 1985

Dear children!
      I love this parish and I protect it with my mantle
from every work of Satan. Pray that Satan flees from the parish
and from every individual that comes to this parish.
In that way you will hear every call
      and answer it with your life.
July 11, 1985

Dear children!
 Again I call you to prayer with the heart.
If you pray with the heart, dear children,
      the ice of your brother's hearts will melt
        and every barrier shall disappear.
Conversion will be easy for all those who want to receive it.
It is a gift you have to obtain by prayer for your neighbor.
January 23, 1986

Children, darkness reigns over the whole world.
People are attracted by many things and they forget
      about the more important . . .
Many people now live without faith;
      some don't even want to hear about Jesus,
      but they still want peace and satisfaction!
Children, here is the reason why I need your prayer:
      prayer is the only way to save the human race.
July 30, 1987

From today on I would like to start a New Year,
    the Year of the Young People.
During this year, pray for the young people; talk with them.
Young people find themselves now in a very difficult situation.
    Help each other. I think of you in a special way.
Young people have a role to play in the Church now.
    Pray, dear children.
        August 15, 1988

Today I invite you to give thanks to God for all the gifts
    you have discovered in the course of your life
        and even for the least gift you have received.
I give thanks with you and want all of you to experience
    the joy of these gifts, and
        I want God to be everything for each one of you.
And then you can grow continuously on the way of holiness.
        September 25, 1989

    I invite you to **pray with the heart** in order that your prayer may be a conversation with God. I desire each one of you spend more time with God. Satan is strong and wants to destroy and deceive you in many ways.   *September 25, 1989*

The United States attacked Iraq January 17, 1991 for its invasion of Kuwait.

    Today, like never before, I invite you to prayer.
Your prayer should be a prayer for peace.
Satan is strong and wishes not only to destroy human life but
    also nature and the planet on which you live.
Therefore pray that you can protect yourselves through prayer and
    the blessing of God's peace.
God sent me to you so that I can help you.
If you wish to, grasp for the rosary.
The Rosary can do miracles in the world and in your lives.
I bless you and I stay among you as long as it is God's will.
        January 25, 1991

Dear children!
Today I invite you to decide for God,
    because distance from God
        is the fruit of the lack of peace in your heart.
God is only peace;
    therefore approach Him through your personal prayer
and then live peace in your hearts, and in this way
    peace will flow from your heart
        like a river into the whole world.
            February 25, 1991

The Civil War in Yugoslavia began on June 25, 1991 when Slovenia and Croatia declared their independence from Yugoslavia.

Dear children,
Today I invite you to pray for peace.
At this time, peace is threatened in a special way and I am
seeking from you to renew fasting and prayer in your families.
I desire you to grasp the seriousness of the situation and that
much of what will happen depends on your prayers,
    and you are praying a little bit!
Dear children, I am with you and I am inviting you to pray and
    fast seriously as in the first days of my coming.
Thank you for having responded to my call.
            July 25, 1991

14,000 United Nation Peacekeepers were deployed in January 1992 when a cease fire is negotiated between Croatian and Serbian forces in Croatia. Serbian "ethnic cleansing" extends to Bosnia and detention camps are discovered in Bosnia.

Dear children,
Today as never before I invite you to live my messages
    and to put them into practice in your life.
I have come to you to help you and therefore I invite you to change
your life because you have taken a path of misery, a path of ruin.

When I told you, 'Convert, pray, fast, be reconciled,' you took these messages superficially. You started to live them and then you stopped, because it was difficult for you.

No, dear children, when something is good, you have to persevere in the good, and not think, 'God does not see me, He is not listening, He is not helping.'

And so you have gone away from God and from me
       because of your miserable interest.

I wanted to create of you an oasis of peace, love and goodness.

God wanted you with your love and with His help to do miracles and thus give an example.

Therefore, here is what I say to you, 'Satan is playing with you and with your souls and I cannot help you because you are far from my heart.

Therefore, pray, live my messages and then you will see the miracles of God's love in your everyday life.

March 25, 1992

In the spring of 1993, the United Nations designated six "safe areas" for starving Muslims and war victims in Bosnia: Sarajevo, Bihac, Goradze, Srebrenica, Tuzla, and Zepa. However, attacks on these safe areas continued.

Dear children,

Today I call you to accept and live my messages with
       seriousness.

These are the days you need to decide for God,
       for peace and for the good.

May every hatred and jealousy disappear from your life
       and your thoughts, and may there only dwell love for
              God and for your neighbor.

Only thus shall you be able to discern the signs of this time.

I am with you, and I guide you into a new time,
       a time which God gives you as grace,
       so that you may get to know him more.

Thank you for having responded to my call.

January 25, 1993

The war between Bosnia and Serbia escalated in 1994 when 68 civilians were massacred in the Sarajevo marketplace when Bosnian Serbs launched a mortar attack into the Sarajevo bread lines in February. Further episodes of Serbian ethnic cleansing were reported in Banja Luka, and the Bosnian Serbs began intense shelling of the United Nation safe areas. The United Nations estimated in December of 1994 that more than 200,000 people were killed and 2.7 million people have become homeless since the Bosnian War began in 1991.

> **Dear Children, today I thank you for your prayers.**
> **You all have helped me so that this war may finish as soon as possible.**
> **I am close to you and I pray for each one of you and I beg you pray, pray, pray. Only through prayer can we defeat evil and protect all that Satan wants to destroy in your life.**
> **I am your Mother; as I love you all the same;**
> **as I intercede for you before God.**
> *February 25, 1994*

It was not until the summer of 1995, in response to the Scott O'Grady episode and the Bosnian Serbs again shelling the Sarajevo marketplace, that NATO began an extensive bombing of Bosnian Serb targets. Cease-fire occurred in October 1995, and the Dayton Peace Accord was signed in Paris December 14, 1995.

> **Dear Children;**
> **Today I also rejoice with you and I bring you little Jesus so that He may bless you. I invite you so that your life may be united with Him. Jesus is the King of Peace and only He can give you the peace that you seek. I am with you and I present you to Jesus in a special way now in this new time in which one should decide for Him.**
> **This time is the time of grace.**
> *December 25, 1995*

In April of 1996 I went with the Joseph Helow family from Jacksonville, Florida for a trip to Medjugorje. The trip to Medjugorje took 26 hours with no sleep. This trip changed my whole life. I am able to find peace and love when

I follow the messages of Mary, and live the way of Jesus. As my friend Tony put it, a trip to Medjugorje is such a profound experience one shares with others that you become "friends for life."

I believe Mary is appearing in Medjugorje.

It is impossible for me to ever convey the experience of Medjugorje.

You can only experience this for yourself!

Dear children,
pray in order to understand that you all, through your life and
example, collaborate in the work of salvation.
I wish that all people convert
and see me and my son Jesus in you.
I will intercede for you and help you to become the light.
In helping the other, your soul will also find salvation.
May 25, 1996

Dear children,
I invite you to reflect about your future.
You are creating a new world without God, and that is why you are
unsatisfied and without joy in the heart. This time is my time and
that is why, little children, I invite you again to pray.
When you find unity with God, you will feel hunger for the word of
God and your heart will overflow with joy.
You will witness God's love wherever you go.
I bless you and I repeat to you that I am with you to help you.
January 25, 1997

Dear children!
Today I invite you in a special way to open yourselves to God
the Creator and become active. I invite you, little children, to see at
this time who needs your spiritual or material help.
By your example, little children, you will be the extended hands of
God, which humanity is seeking.
Only in this way will you understand, that you are called
to witness and become joyful carriers of God's word and of his love.
February 25, 1997

Dear children,
Today, in a special way, I invite you to take the cross in the hands and to meditate on the wounds of Jesus.
Ask of Jesus to heal your wounds, which you, dear children, during your life sustained because of your sins or the sins of your parents. Only in this way, dear children, you will understand that the world is in need of healing of faith in God the Creator.
By Jesus' passion and death on the cross, you will understand that only through prayer you, too, can become true apostles of faith; when, in simplicity and prayer, you live faith which is a gift.

March 25, 1997

Dear children,
God gives me this time as a gift to you, so that I may instruct and lead you on the path of salvation.
Now you do not comprehend this grace, but soon a time will come when you will lament for these messages.
That is why, live all of the words which I have given you through this time of grace and renew prayer, until prayer becomes a joy for you. Especially, I call all those who have consecrated themselves to my Immaculate Heart to become an example to others. I call all priests and religious brothers and sisters to pray the rosary and teach others to pray. The rosary is especially dear to me. Through the rosary open your heart to me and I am able to help you.

August 25, 1997

Today I invite you to comprehend your Christian vocation. Little children, I led and am leading you through this time of grace, that you may become conscious of your Christian vocation. Holy martyrs died witnessing: I am a Christian and love God over everything. Today also I invite you to rejoice and be joyful Christians, responsible and conscious that God called you in a special way to be joyfully extended hands toward those who do not believe, and that through the example of your life, they may receive faith and love for God. Therefore, pray, pray, pray that your heart may open and be sensitive for the word of God.

November 25, 1997

Today I call you, through prayer, to open yourselves to God as a flower opens itself to the rays of the morning sun. I am with you and I intercede before God for each of you so that your heart receives the gift of conversion. Only in this way, will you comprehend the importance of grace in these times and God will become nearer to you.
April 25, 1998

Today I invite you, through prayer, to be with Jesus so that through personal experience of prayer you may be able to discover the beauty of God's creatures. You cannot speak or witness about prayer, if you do not pray. That is why, in the silence of the heart, remain with Jesus , so that He may change and transform you with His love. This, little children, is a time of grace for you.
Make good use of it for your personal conversion, because
when you have God, you have everything. *July 25, 1998*

Kosovo is a Muslim state of primarily Greek Orthodox Serbia, and has ethnic and religious ties to primarily Muslim Albania.

In a dispute over refugees from Kosovo, **NATO**, the North Atlantic Treaty Organization, began the bombing of Serbia on March 24, 1999, attacking a sovereign European country for the first time in the alliance's history.

Also today I call you to prayer. Little children, be joyful carriers of peace and love in this peaceless world. By fasting and prayer, witness that you are mine and that you live my messages. Pray and seek! I am praying and interceding for you before God that you convert; that your life and behavior always be Christian. Thank you for having responded to my call. *April 25, 1999*

Our two youngest daughters Elizabeth Anne and Madeleine Mary, both college students, and I took a trip to Rome and Medjugorje on August 4, 1997. We stayed in the Sisters of the Atonement Convent near St. Peters Square in Rome. On Wednesday August 6 we were fortunate enough to have a general audience with the Pope. When he came in the auditorium there was great excitement. In spite of his poor health, his smile lit up the room! The elderly Pope was leaving soon for Sarajevo on a mission of healing - what a man of courage!

They especially enjoyed the paintings of Michelangelo and Raphael. Favorites were *The Last Judgment* and the Ceiling of the Sistine Chapel, by Michelangelo, and *The Transfiguration,* by Raphael in St. Peter's Basilica.

Saturday, August 9, we flew to Split, and took the 3-hour bus ride to Medjugorje. We were meeting a group sponsored by Caritas of Birmingham. After going to church on Sunday, Elizabeth Anne, Madeleine, and I agreed that everything we did would be voluntary.

That Sunday evening, August 10, Madeleine wanted to walk up Apparition Hill with me. She had a remarkable experience. She went off by herself on Apparition Hill and was watching the sunset. As she saw the setting sun beginning to drift over the horizon, she saw the sun actually drift *upwards* at sunset! She ran over to me and I saw it as well. We prayed the Rosary together and asked for guidance during the week. She couldn't wait to get back and tell Elizabeth Anne. Madeleine and Elizabeth Anne have been roommates since age one and were always very close.

On Monday Madeleine wanted to join the group and go up Apparition Hill as well as Don, who was my new roommate. Elizabeth Anne didn't want to go so I stayed behind with her. Before the group left Madeleine ran upstairs and begged us both to go. Finally, Elizabeth Anne agreed to go. We went up Apparition Hill and everyone said the Rosary but Elizabeth Anne and Madeleine. They didn't speak one word. While they did walk up the mountain they did not want to walk over to Apparition Hill and stayed behind. I went over to Apparition Hill with the group and prayed. I walked back to where the girls were sitting and to my amazement they were saying the Rosary with an emaciated, homeless man who was gestering to them silently with a Rosary in his hand. I couldn't believe my eyes. Being typical modern youth, they were often skeptical of religious ideas; however, they are very generous and compassionate. And, I suspect they didn't want to let this poor, homeless man down.

On Tuesday morning all the young people of the group were going up Cross Mountain at 5:00 in the morning and Elizabeth Anne and Madeleine joined them, as did Don my roommate. Going up Cross Mountain they have the 14 stations of the cross, a reminder of the passion and death of our Savior Jesus Christ. The person who said the station was supposed to give the prayer for the next station to someone they thought needed prayer. Someone in the group handed the prayers to Elizabeth Anne and she burst into tears. After she read the prayers she saw the sun spin with a green haze over it.

Wednesday, August 13, was a day of fasting. Elizabeth wanted to go up that evening on Apparition Hill, just as Madeleine had on Sunday. So, around 6:30 that evening we arrived on Apparition Hill and Elizabeth watched the sun. I advised her to leave her mind open and to pray and see what thoughts entered her mind. She came back to me about 15 minutes later and said she didn't see anything but that she wanted to talk with me.

Tears came to her eyes, and for the next hour she poured out all the hurt and anger that she experienced during her teenage years. We were both overwhelmed with all the honesty, and we held each other and forgave each other.

It was then she felt a tap on her shoulder--it was the same homeless man who had said the Rosary with her on Monday! He had all his possessions in a grocery bag, and he reached in his grocery bag and gave Elizabeth Anne a candy bar to make her feel better. We both were deeply moved. Elizabeth Anne exclaimed, "This man has nothing and he is happy. We have everything in America and we are never satisfied." She took the man and we walked back to the home we were staying in and she gave Ivo, the homeless man, her meal.

That evening we went to an Apparition at the Blue Cross. I knelt down and opened my heart and mind when Mary was said to appear. I felt that my role was to become a messenger of love to all around me.

On Thursday, August 14, Madeleine wanted to have a long talk with me just as Elizabeth Anne and I had done the night before. However, we got into an argument and she ran off into the grape vineyards and got lost. She was there crying and was lost for over a half hour. She began to pray and ask God if He would just send someone to keep her company. No one came. She then cried out that she was all alone. It was then she heard the voice of Jesus, *"How do you think I feel!"*

Madeleine and I finally caught up with each other and she was also able to express everything that had upset her throughout her childhood. Love overcame anger and hurt, as we had an emotional reunion.

Thursday evening Elizabeth Anne and Don, who had become friends, and Madeleine and a family from San Diego went to confession at the Church. Friday was August 15, the Feast of the Assumption, and we all went to Mass and Communion together.

Our trip to Medjugorje was most meaningful, and has had a profound effect on each of us. Elizabeth Anne is now a missionary in St. Anthony's Children Orphanage in Kingston, Jamaica. Madeleine has become quite a student of the Bible, and is the peacemaker of our family.

Chapter 6
THE CULTURE OF LIFE

I pledge allegiance to the flag
Of the United States of America.
And to the Republic for which it stands,
One nation, under God, indivisible,
With liberty and justice for all.

Our country was founded on the Biblical ethic, where society is in harmony with God our Creator. In the Declaration of Independence, Thomas Jefferson speaks of God our Creator and the Natural Law. Inherent in this concept is a respect for life, where all members of the human race are treated with dignity and respect. The United States prospered in the Culture of Life.

When in the course of human events, it becomes necessary for one people to dissolve the political bands which have connected them with another, and to assume among the powers of the earth, the separate and equal station to which the Laws of Nature and Nature's God entitles them...
We hold these truths to be self-evident, that all men are created equal, that they are endowed by their Creator with certain unalienable rights, that among these are Life, Liberty, and the pursuit of happiness.
The Declaration of Independence
July 4, 1776

We are a religious people whose institutions presuppose a Supreme Being. The fact that the founding fathers were devoted in their belief that there was a God and that the unalienable rights of man were rooted in God and his Natural Law is clearly evidenced in their writings, from the Mayflower Compact to the Constitution itself. This background is evidenced today in our public life through the continuance in our oaths of office from the Presidency to the alderman of the final supplication, "So help me God". Likewise all of our coins and dollar bills have the inscription "In God we Trust."

James Madison, the Father of the Constitution, also recognized the history of man as inseparable from the history of religion. One of the great dilemmas faced by our Founding Fathers was to ensure freedom of religion. All too often in

Europe, government-prescribed religion resulted in religious persecution, such as with the Church of England, and the Spanish Inquisition. The Founders knew that only a few years after the Book of Common Prayer became the only accepted form of religious services in the established Church of England, an Act of Uniformity was passed to compel all Englishmen to attend those services and to make it a criminal offense to conduct or attend religious gatherings of any other kind. James Madison and others felt the need to protect future Americans from speaking only the religious thoughts that government wanted them to speak and to pray only to the God that the government wanted them to pray to. Thus, he introduced the First Amendment of the Bill of Rights of the US Constitution.

Congress shall make no law respecting an establishment of religion, or prohibiting the free exercise thereof; or abridging the freedom of speech, or of the press; or the right of the people peaceably to assemble, and to petition the government for a redress of grievances.

Amendment I
Constitution of the United States

At the same time Thomas Jefferson and James Madison were Christians and wanted to be free to practice their form of Christianity. And obviously, they never once felt the need to extend the restriction on establishment of a state religion to school prayer! Free religious expression was essential to American life! And children have prayed daily in American public schools for nearly two hundred years, until 1963.

We have staked the whole future of the American civilization not upon the bowers of government, far from it. We have staked the future of all our political institutions upon the capacity of each and all of us to govern ourselves according to the Ten Commandments of God.

James Madison
Father of the Constitution

A review of Hebrew scripture, the King James Bible, and the St. Joseph Catholic Bible finds the text of the Ten Commandments to be the same!

We know that there are only Ten Commandments from three passages in the Bible, Exodus 34:28, Deuteronomy 4:13, and Deuteronomy 10:4.

> **He proclaimed to you his covenant, which he**
> **commanded you to keep; the Ten Commandments,**
> **which he wrote on two tablets of stone.**
> ***Deuteronomy 4:13 [New American]***

The selection of wording from the first paragraph of Chapter 20 in Exodus constitutes the difference in the Ten Commandments of the three major religions in the United States:

I am the Lord thy God, who have brought thee out of the land of Mizrahim, out of the house of bondage. Thou shalt not have any other gods besides me.
Thou shalt not make for thyself any graven image (carved idol)...
Exodus 20:1-4

Thus, the Hebrew Ten Commandments chose the following wording for the First and Second Commandments:

HEBREW

1 **I am the Lord thy God who have brought thee out of the house of bondage.**
2 **Thou shalt have no other gods besides me**
3 **Thou shalt not take the name of the Lord thy God in vain.**
4 **Remember the Sabbath Day to keep it holy.**
5 **Honor thy Father and Mother.**
6 **Thou shalt not murder.**
7 **Thou shalt not commit adultery.**
8 **Thou shalt not steal.**
9 **Thou shalt not bear false witness against thy neighbor.**
10 **Thou shalt not covet.**

Whereas, some Protestant churches chose the following wording from the first paragraph for their First and Second Commandments:

PROTESTANT

1   I am the Lord thy God and thou shalt not have other gods besides me.
2   Thou shalt not make for thyself any graven image.
3   Thou shalt not take the name of the Lord thy God in vain.
4   Remember the Lord's Day to keep it holy.
5   Honor thy Father and Mother.
6   Thou shalt not kill.
7   Thou shalt not commit adultery.
8   Thou shalt not steal.
9   Thou shalt not bear false witness against thy neighbor.
10   Thou shalt not covet.

The Catholic Church was influenced by St. Augustine in the 4th century. While this is debatable, it is thought St. Augustine did not make explicit the sentence from Chapter 20 in Exodus concerning "graven images or carved idols," as worshipping and sacrificing animals to golden idols was a thing of the past. It is thought he was more concerned with "sins of the flesh" , so he expanded the concept "Thou shalt not covet" by adopting the rendition of the Ten Commandments found in Deuteronomy (Chapter 5:21) for the Catholic form of the Ten Commandments:

CATHOLIC

1   I am the Lord thy God and thou shalt not have strange gods before me.
2   Thou shalt not take the name of the Lord in vain.
3   Remember to keep holy the Lord's Day.
4   Honor thy Father and Mother.
5   Thou shalt not kill.
6   Thou shalt not commit adultery.
7   Thou shalt not steal.
8   Thou shalt not bear false witness against thy neighbor.
9   Thou shalt not covet thy neighbor's wife.
10   Thou shalt not covet thy neighbor's goods.

The commandment, **"Thou shalt not kill"** rings out clearly in all 3 major religions!

So then, how did we end up with abortion and the recent discussions on physician-assisted suicide in America? How have we lost 40,000,000 unborn Americans in the U.S.A.?

Every physician on graduation from medical school must take the Hippocratic Oath. We are taught above all to respect life, and **never** do harm to anyone. Furthermore, the Hippocratic Oath expressly forbids a physician from performing an abortion or assisting in anyone's death:

THE HIPPOCRATIC OATH

I swear by Apollo the Physician...the following oath: to consider dear to me as my parents him who taught me this art; to live in common with him and if necessary to share my goods with him; to look upon his children as my own brothers, to teach them this art if they so desire without fee or written promise; to impart to my sons and the sons of the master who taught me and the disciples who have enrolled themselves and have agreed to the rules of the profession, but to these alone, the precepts and the instruction.

I will prescribe regimen for the good of my patients according to my ability and my judgement and never do harm to anyone. To please no one will I prescribe a deadly drug, nor give advice which may cause his death. Nor will I give a woman a pessary to procure abortion. But I will preserve the purity of my life and my art.

I will not cut for stone, even for patients in whom the disease is manifest; I will leave this operation to be performed by practitioners. In every house where I come I will enter only for the good of my patients, keeping myself far from all intentional ill-doing and all seduction, and especially from the pleasures of love with women or with men, be they free or slaves. All that may come to my knowledge in the exercise of my profession or outside of my profession or in daily commerce with men, which ought not be spread abroad, I will keep secret and never reveal. If I keep this oath faithfully, may I enjoy my life and practice my art, respected by all men and in all times; but if I swerve from it or violate it, may the reverse be my lot.

Physicians are guided by principles of medical ethics. While the primary textbook on the subject contains many volumes, a very brief review of medical ethics should be helpful to the reader to understand the guiding principles of physicians in their practice of medicine.

First, the foundation of the principles of medical ethics must have **moral justification** and a **moral code.** The tradition of American medicine is founded upon the Judeo-Christian ethic and the traditions of our Greco-Roman heritage. This explains why Western medicine has long upheld the primary concept of the sanctity of life.

Second, physicians must show **respect for autonomy** of the patient. Individual self-determination is highly valued in our American tradition, and rightly so! Patients should have the right to accept or refuse treatment, or allow the natural course of events take place.

The third principle is **beneficence** .   Beneficence refers to the traditional role of the physician, the Good Samaritan performing an act of mercy and charity, in coming to the aid of the injured, the sick, and the dying. To relieve suffering is an essential aspect of the compassionate physician.

Elizabeth Kubler-Ross pointed out in her book *On Death and Dying* (MacMillan , New York, 1969) the stages of the dying process. A fundamental concept in hospice care holds that even in the midst of tragic terminal illness, there is value in "suffering through" the dying process. This allows the patient to go through the different stages - the isolation and denial, the anger, "bargaining," the depression, and finally the acceptance of death. This also allows the family time to adjust to losing their loved one. Human nature being what it is, it gives everyone time to resolve any differences that may have built up through the years. It is a time for the physician to provide modern pain management to relieve the suffering of his patient.

The fourth principle is *nonmaleficence.*   Nonmaleficence is the warning, **"Never do harm to anyone."** This speaks for itself!

The fifth principle of medical ethics is **justice**. The physician must be just to his patient and give the patient proper access to health care. This principle has come under ferocious attack by the Federal Government, the Corporate world, and the insurance industry in their efforts at cost-containment. "Bottom-line health care" puts the profit margin as the ultimate principle instead of patient care and proper access to medical care. There are many responsible insurance companies, there are many demanding patients, there are many over-cautious physicians who order too many tests because they fear lawsuits. There are also managed-care health plans that want the physician to provide the most expedient and least expensive health care possible.

The sixth principle of medical ethics is the physician must serve as **advocate** for the patient, and respect *the doctor-patient relationship*. He must ensure privacy, give informed consent, and be truthful with the patient. He must fulfill his traditional role as the healer and protector of the patient's life.

Finally the seventh principle of medical ethics is the physician must be diligent in developing a **virtuous character.** He must be *compassionate* with his patients, he must be *prudent,* he must be *trustworthy* and have moral *integrity.*

These seven principles of medical ethics play an important part in our daily practice of medicine, especially in life-and-death decisions and on modern issues.

Briefly, let us take a look at *respect for autonomy.* Proponents for euthanasia place this as the highest guiding principle, even over respect for the sanctity of life. They argue that the patient should have a right to choose death rather than face a horrible and painful terminal illness. The problem with this is that if self-determination is the sole guiding principle, then why withhold the right to choose death for anyone! We must respect autonomy as long as we live in harmony with moral law and the sanctity of life.

Proponents for abortion believe that the mother should have a choice if she wants to keep her baby, that it is for us to respect her rights and autonomy. I have two problems with this - first, this completely disregards the primary principle of the sanctity of life, and second, what about the respect for the autonomy of the baby!

If the physician is to become the minister of death, this will forever destroy the very essence of our role as protector and physician advocate, and will destroy whatever trust patients have left for us! How will you know if your doctor has your best interest at heart?!

Shortly after he was named the 1994 Time's Man of the Year, Pope John Paul II published his treatise *Evangelium Vitae* , or *The Gospel of Life* (Times Books, Random House, New York, March 25, 1995). The treatise itself received worldwide media attention, and actually ended up on the cover of the April 10, 1995 issue of Newsweek Magazine. His encyclical letter received the support of other religious leaders, most notably the Reverend Billy Graham.

In his treatise, the Pope stated that *"Society must respect, defend and promote the dignity of every human person at every moment and in every condition of that person's life."* He supported natural family planning, organ donation, and the right to a natural death, allowing modern pain management. He stated that society best prospers in a spirit of mutual respect, in a "Culture of Life." The Pope specifically condemned abortion, euthanasia, and exploitation of the embryo and called countries allowing such practices "cultures of Death." Furthermore, while the Pope did not specifically condemn capital punishment, he states his opposition except in cases of "absolute necessity."

In a scriptural-based letter with over 300 biblical references, Pope John Paul II refers to God as the very origin of life, as first noted in ancient Hebrew Scripture, in the Book of Genesis:

> **Then God said: "Let us make man in our image, after our likeness."**
> **Genesis 1:26 [King James]**

Pope John Paul then refers to the passage where God tells Noah he will demand an accounting of human life:

> **And from man in regard to his fellow man**
> **I will demand an accounting for human life.**
> **If anyone sheds the blood of man,**
> **by man shall his blood be shed;**
> **For in the image of God**
> **has man been made.**
> **Be fertile, then, and multiply;**
> **abound on earth and subdue it."**
> **Genesis 9:5-7[New American]**

We are given the Ten Commandments in the Book of Exodus. The Book of Leviticus calls us to love our neighbor:

> **You shall not take vengeance or bear any grudge**
> **against the sons of your own people, but**
> **You shall love your neighbor as yourself.**
> **I am the Lord.**
> **Leviticus 19:18 [RSV]**

The Pope sadly noted that "Choices once unanimously considered criminal and rejected by the common moral sense are now becoming socially acceptable. The end result of this is tragic: not only is the destruction of so many human lives extremely grave and disturbing, but no less grave and disturbing is the fact that *conscience* itself, darkened as it were by such widespread conditioning, is finding it increasingly difficult to distinguish between good and evil in what concerns the basic value of human life."

The Pope stated "the very nature of the medical profession is distorted and contradicted and the dignity of those who practice it is being degraded." This rang loud and clear with me, as we have just discussed in our brief review of medical ethics.

The Pope pointed out that "a life, which would require greater acceptance, love and care is considered useless, or an intolerable burden and is therefore rejected in one way or another. A person who, because of illness, handicap, or more simply, just by existing compromises the life-style of those who are more favored, such as the unborn or elderly, tends to be looked upon as an enemy to be resisted or eliminated." He spoke of the "war of the powerful against the weak" in the name of *efficiency* and *choice.*

He voiced his concern about the false sense of freedom which is now being propagated. "This notion of freedom which exalts the isolated individual in an absolute way gives no place to community, or openness or consideration to others. This completely individualistic concept of freedom ends up by being the freedom of the strong against the weak, who have no choice but to submit." This is obvious in abortion, where the unborn have no choice at all.

"There is even a more profound aspect which needs to be emphasized: freedom negates and destroys itself and becomes a factor leading to the destruction of others, when it no longer recognizes and respects its essential *link with the truth.*

When freedom, out of a desire to emancipate itself from all forms of tradition and authority, shuts out even the most obvious evidence of an objective and universal truth, which is the foundation of personal and social life, then the person ends up by no longer taking as the sole and indisputable point of reference for his own choices the truth about good and evil, but only his subjective and changeable opinion or, indeed, his selfish interest and whim."

The Pope expressed grave concern about modern man's desire to live in a secular world, forgetting our Creator. Modern society pushes the exaltation of the creature, such that man should be concerned only with his personal self-gratification, his own pleasure, materialism, choice, and rights. Instead of living in harmony with God and your fellow man, *everyone* is a god, consumed in their own self-interest. The problem with this is that society becomes a mass of individuals living side by side. Everyone else becomes the enemy which one has to defend himself. This can only lead to self-destruction.

Everyone wants their own way, and "do their own thing." Mothers or fathers just walk out of marriages so they can be "free" - the children or mate have no vote, and are rejected and victimized. And when someone doesn't get his or her own way, all hell breaks loose. This is why we are now faced with all of our modern social horrors: divorce, domestic violence, child abuse, rampant teenage drug abuse, elder neglect, riots, homosexuality and AIDS, suicide and homicide, and the list goes on. This year, even with managed care, emergency physicians throughout the United States will handle nearly 100,000,000 visits to our Emergency Departments, a reflection of this disturbing trend in our society.

To quote the Pope, "When the sense of God the Creator is lost, there is also a tendency to lose the sense of man, of his dignity, and his life." We become just another organism, just another thing. Life, instead of a special gift of God, becomes just biologic activity, which may then be regulated by the State. It is in fact recognizing that God is Our Creator and that life is a gift from God that makes us special, and in fact gives us our freedom!

The Pope further points out that the role of government is to *serve* mankind and society. However, practices such as abortion and euthanasia have actually given the government *control* over life, setting a dangerous precedent for them to have control over **your life.**

The Pope calls human life a treasure, as noted in his concluding remarks:
Life is a gift from our Creator and it is a treasure to be given the utmost respect and dignity...

Truly great must be the value of human life if the Son of God has taken it up and made it the instrument of the salvation of all humanity...

Consistent with Sacred Scripture, I confirm that the direct and voluntary killing of an innocent human being is always gravely immoral.

Pope John Paul II

Euthanasia. The issue of physician-assisted suicide was thrust into the national spotlight largely because of Dr. Jack Kevorkian, a retired pathologist from Michigan who assisted over 50 people in committing suicide in recent years. He was charged with second-degree murder on March 26, 1999 for *actively* rendering a lethal injection to a patient with Lou Gehrig's disease. The Hemlock Society in Oregon was successful in obtaining passage of a referendum on physician-assisted suicide in the state of Oregon, the only state thus far that this has occurred. Euthanasia became legal in the Netherlands in 1984; however, this has led to widespread abuse, and in a formal investigation in 1991, the Dutch government discovered 1,000 of 3,300 cases of euthanasia involved incompetent patients who of course could not give consent of their own free will! Of course, we are all familiar with the euthanasia practices of the Nazi regime!

Fortunately, the United States Supreme Court on June 26, 1997 supported the sanctity of life and the traditional role of physician as healer and protector of life and unanimously upheld States' rights to ban physician-assisted suicide. In two cases, one from the state of Washington, *Washington v. Glucksberg* (117 U.S. 2302), and one from the state of New York, *Vacco v. Quill* (117 U.S. 2293), the Supreme Court upheld the right of the State to protect vulnerable groups such as the poor, the elderly, and the disabled from abuse, neglect, and mistreatment. The Supreme Court in *Washington v. Glucksberg* "recognized the real risk of subtle coercion in undue influence in the end of life situations...The risk of harm is greatest for the many individuals in our society whose autonomy and well being are already compromised by poverty, lack of access to good medical care, advanced age, or membership in a stigmatized social group."

The Supreme Court in *Vacco v. Quill* upheld the right of the states "to prohibit intentional killing and preserving life; preventing suicide; maintaining physicians' role as their patients' healers; protecting vulnerable people from indifference, prejudice, and psychological and financial pressure to end their lives; and avoiding a possible slide towards euthanasia."

Abortion. What happened then on the abortion issue, and the death of 40 million American unborn since 1973?

We have to go back to January 22, 1973, to the Supreme Court decisions on *Roe v. Wade* (410 U.S. 113) and its companion decision *Doe v. Bolton* (410 U.S. 179). To quote the text from *Roe v. Wade,* "Jane Roe, a single woman who was residing in Dallas County, Texas, instituted this federal action in March

1970 against the District Attorney of Dallas County. Roe alleged that she was unmarried and pregnant; that she wished to terminate her pregnancy by an abortion "performed by a competent, licensed physician, under safe clinical conditions"; that she was unable to get a "legal" abortion in Texas because her life did not appear to be threatened by the continuation of her pregnancy; and that she could not afford to travel to another jurisdiction in order to secure a legal abortion under safe conditions.

Roe claimed that the Texas statutes were unconstitutionally vague and that they abridged her right of personal privacy. By an amendment to her complaint Roe purported in addition to sue 'on behalf of herself and all other women' similarly situated."

The ruling was complicated by being consolidated with two other cases, both of which were dismissed. It is very confusing how two of the three cases were dismissed, but *Roe v. Wade* was allowed to continue! In its opinion written by Justice Harry Blackmun, the Supreme Court supported the Texas District Court when it held the fundamental right of single women and married persons to choose whether to have children as protected by the Ninth and Fourteenth Amendment, within the first trimester of pregnancy.

While *Roe v. Wade* concerned only the first trimester, it was actually the companion ruling, *Doe v. Bolton*, that allowed abortion almost under any circumstances and at any time. However, evidence, as later discussed in this chapter, shows that *Doe v. Bolton* was based on fabrication! This companion decision by the U. S. Supreme Court, along with the Dred Scott decision on slavery, school prayer, and the flag-burning decision, remain the most controversial decisions in American history! Americans are completely divided over the abortion issue.

The Fourteenth Amendment refers to our civil rights.
Who represented the civil rights of the unborn in these two cases!

After reviewing these Supreme Court cases, while it is obvious our Justices are brilliant men, they have reached a point where they discuss purely legal issues. I find it frightening that not one reference to any moral code, religious or spiritual belief, or human emotion, such as the maternal instinct, was ever mentioned in these two cases!

Both Justice Byron White and Justice William Rehnquist dissented on both cases. Justice Rehnquist wrote the dissenting opinion on *Roe v. Wade*. Here is the dissenting opinion of Justice Byron White on *Doe v. Bolton*, the case based on fabrication that allows partial-birth abortion:

"At the heart of the controversy in these cases are those recurring pregnancies that pose no danger whatsoever to the life or health of the mother but are, nevertheless, unwanted for any one or more of a variety of reasons--convenience, family planning, economics, dislike of children, the embarrassment of illegitimacy, etc. The common claim before us is that, for any one of such reasons, or for no reason at all, and without asserting or claiming any threat to life or health, any woman is entitled to an abortion at her request if she is able to find a medical advisor willing to undertake the procedure."

"The Court, for the most part, sustains this position: during the period prior to the time the fetus becomes viable, the Constitution of the United States values the convenience, whim, or caprice of the putative mother more than the life or potential life of the fetus; the Constitution, therefore, guarantees the right to an abortion as against any state law or policy seeking to protect the fetus from an abortion not prompted by more compelling reasons of the mother."

"With all due respect, I dissent. I find nothing in the language or history of the Constitution to support the Court's judgment. The Court simply fashions and announces a new constitutional right for pregnant mothers [410 U.S. 222] and, with scarcely any reason or authority for its action, invests that right with sufficient substance to override most existing state abortion statutes. The upshot is that the people and the legislatures of the 50 States are constitutionally dissentitled to weigh the relative importance of the continued existence and development of the fetus, on the one hand, against a spectrum of possible impacts on the mother, on the other hand.

As an exercise of raw judicial power, the Court perhaps has authority to do what it does today; but, in my view, its judgement is an improvident and extravagant exercise of the power of judicial review that the Constitution extends to this Court."

"The Court apparently values the convenience of the pregnant mother more than the continued existence and development of the life or potential life that she carries. Whether or not I might agree with that marshaling of values, I can in no event join the Court's judgment because I find no constitutional warrant for imposing such an order of priorities on the people and legislatures of the States, in a sensitive area such as this, involving as it does issues over which reasonable men may easily and heatedly differ. I cannot accept the Court's exercise of its clear power of choice by interposing a constitutional barrier to state efforts to protect human life and by investing mothers and doctors with the

189

constitutionally protected right to exterminate it. This issue, for the most part, should be left with the people and to the political processes the people have devised to govern their affairs."

Justice Byron R. White
U. S. Supreme Court Justice

The *Doe v. Bolton* case, which basically allows abortion on demand, partial-birth abortion, and abortion for any reason at any time, is especially troubling. According to the woman in question, Sandra Cano, the case is based on lies.

In 1970 Sandra Cano (then Sandra Besing) found herself pregnant and alone. Her husband was in jail and two of her children had been taken from her by County welfare workers. She went to the legal aid clinic in Atlanta, looking for help in divorcing her husband and regaining custody of her children. What she received instead was an interview with a female attorney who was an abortion activist. It is reported Sandra Cano felt that she was pressured to have an abortion, and was actually scheduled for an abortion by these activists. She became Mary Doe, the plaintiff in *Doe v. Bolton*. She never spoke in Court!

Just three days before she was scheduled to abort, Sandra Cano fled to Oklahoma to live with her grandmother. Her baby, Melissa, was born November 6, 1970, and placed for adoption.

From the U. S. Supreme Court record itself, it states (II,2): "On March 25, 1970, she applied to the Abortion Committee of Grady Memorial Hospital, Atlanta, for a therapeutic abortion under 26-1202. Her application was denied 16 days later, on April 10, when she was eight weeks pregnant, on the ground that her situation was not one described in 26-1202(a)."

Grady Memorial Hospital is the public hospital cited, but that hospital has no records of ever treating Mrs. Cano or reviewing her case. Grady's records division wrote and said, "Grady Health System is unable to locate" any records despite spending 32 hours searching under every possible name and variation.

Can unjust judges be your allies,
those who create burdens in the name of law,
Those who conspire against the just
and condemn the innocent to death?
Psalm 94:20-21[New American]

The official unveiling and dedication of the National Memorial for the Unborn took place in Chattanooga, Tennessee, March 23, 1997. At the site the two principals in the above two cases, Norma McCorvey (Roe in *Roe v. Wade*) and Sandra Cano (Doe in *Doe v. Bolton*), have bronze plaques present which read:

"I am Norma McCorvey. I became known as Jane Roe on January 22, 1973 when the U.S. Supreme Court released the Roe v. Wade decision which created a woman's "right to abortion". I am now a child of God, a new creature in Christ; I am forgiven and redeemed. Today I publicly recant my involvement in the tragedy of abortion. I humbly ask forgiveness of the millions of women and unborn babies who have experienced the violence of abortion. In this place of healing, the National Memorial for the Unborn, I stand with those who honor the worth of every unborn child as created in the image of God. I will strive, in the name of Jesus, to end this holocaust.
Norma McCorvey

"I am Sandra Cano. I became known as Mary Doe when the U.S. Supreme Court released Roe v. Wade's companion decision, Doe v. Bolton, which allowed abortion for virtually any reason. I am against abortion; I never sought an abortion; I have never had an abortion. Abortion is murder. For over twenty years, and against my will, my name has been synonomous with abortion. The Doe v. Bolton case is based on deceit and fraud. I stand today in this place of healing, the National Memorial for the Unborn, and pledge to the memory of these innocent children, that as long as I have breath, I will strive to see abortion ended in America.
Sandra Cano

All you have to see is the film of an abortion taking place and see the destruction of recognizable, living tissue to know this is completely wrong. Partial birth abortion is especially abhorrent - in this late second and third trimester abortion, the abortionist turns the unborn child into the breech position and pulls the child from the mother until the head is all but delivered. The abortionist then forces scissors into the base of the skull and inserts a catheter to suction out the child's brain.

We had a lecture on Pro-Life at our Medical University of South Carolina Intensive Review in Emergency Medicine Board Review Course in September

1998. Dr. Christine Tullius gave a very powerful lecture. Some had to leave the room because the description of an abortion was so upsetting.

There are Biblical references from the Old Testament, Hebrew Scripture, that refers to God's divine plan, that each life has a purpose, even *before* being born, even *before* the moment of conception!
Job speaks in a soliloquy:

> **Did not He who made me in the womb make him also?**
> **And did not one and the same form me in the womb?**
> **Job 31:15 [Douay-Rheims]**

David prays to God, in the Book of Psalms:

> **You formed my inmost being;**
> **you knit me in my mother's womb.**
> **I praise you, so wonderfully you made me;**
> **wonderful are your works!**
> **My very self you knew;**
> **my bones were not hidden from you,**
> **When I was being made in secret,**
> **fashioned as in the depths of the earth.**
> **Your eyes foresaw my actions;**
> **in your book all are written down;**
> **my days were shaped, before one came to be.**
> **Psalms 139:13-16**
> **New American**

God speaks to Jeremiah in the Old Testament:

> **Before I formed thee in the womb I knew you;**
> **and before thou camest forth out of the womb I**
> **sanctified thee, and ordained thee a prophet unto the nations.**
> **Jeremiah 1:5 [King James Version]**

Medical science has rapidly progressed in the past 30 years. Our second son Stephen was born premature at 4 pounds, 8 ounces in 1968, and they were barely capable of saving his life. After 4 weeks in the Hospital, he did come home, but in such a weakened state, he died a crib death at 3 months of age.

Now with Neonatal Intensive Care Units, they are saving babies who weigh *less* than one pound (450 grams)! At the Neonatal Intensive Care Unit at Memorial Medical Center in Savannah, Georgia, Angela, a pediatric neonatal nurse, confirmed they just sent home a baby who was born **13 ounces!** Now, if you can save a baby at 13 ounces, there is **no** justification for partial-birth abortion!

An embryo is an individual, no matter how small. While the embryo receives cells from the mother and the father, it is neither the mother nor the father.

The embryo is a new human life which is genetically distinct and which has energy and a direction of its own from the moment of conception.

Mother Teresa said it all, in her acceptance speech for the Nobel Prize:

I feel the greatest destroyer of peace today is abortion,
because it is a direct war, a direct killing
- direct murder by the mother herself. ...
Because if a mother can kill her own child -what is left for me
to kill you and you kill me -there is nothing in between."
Mother Teresa
December 11, 1979

Mother Teresa practiced what she preached:

Unborn children are among the poorest of the poor.
They are so close to God.
I always ask doctors at hospitals in India never to kill an unborn child.
If there is no one who wants it, I'll take it.
Mother Teresa
A Simple Path, 1995

In his 1995 Encyclical, Pope John Paul II called for humility and repentance for those women who have had an abortion, that "the Father of Mercy is ready to give forgiveness and peace," and pointed out those women may become "the most eloquent defenders of everyone's right to life.

The Natural Law. It is natural for a man and woman to be together. This is recorded in Genesis, the first book of the Old Testament, when God blessed man and woman and called them to be "fruitful and multiply."

> *And God created man to his own image,*
> *to the image of God he created him.*
> *Male and female he created them.*
> *And God blessed them, saying, Increase and multiply...*
> *Genesis 1:27-28 [Douay-Rheims]*

And God created woman in Chapter Two of Genesis:

> *And the Lord God said: it is not good for man to be alone:*
> *let us make him a help like unto himself...*
> *Then the Lord God cast a deep sleep upon Adam:*
> *and when he was fast asleep, he took one of his ribs,*
> *and filled up flesh for it.*
> *And the Lord God built the rib which he took from Adam*
> *into a woman, and brought her to Adam.*
> *And Adam said:*
> *This now is bone of my bones, and flesh of my flesh;*
> *she shall be called woman,*
> *because she was taken out of man.*
> *Wherefore a man shall leave father and mother,*
> *and shall cleave to his wife,*
> *and they shall be two in one flesh.*
> *Genesis 2:18, 21-24 [Douay-Rheims]*

The natural law puts man and woman together for mutual comfort and for the procreation of the human race. Religion has always protected the sanctity of marriage and the family, because both life and love come from God our Creator. Marriage is the institution of our Creator and blessed in the ceremony of our Churches to realize in man his design for love. By means of the reciprocal personal gift of self, proper and exclusive to them, husband and wife, in the communion of their beings, give each other love and cooperate with God in the generation and education of new life.

Children are the fruit and the bond of a marriage.

The Old Testament books of Ruth and Tobias (Tobit) bear witness to an elevated sense of marriage and to the fidelity and tenderness of spouses. Even though the Old Testament does not explicitly reject the polygamy of patriarchs and kings, the prophets such as Isaiah (Chapter 54) and Jeremiah (chapter 31) referred to God's covenant with Israel as an image of exclusive and faithful married love. Ezekiel (chapter 16) and Hosea (chapters 1-3) speak of the faithless spouse. The prophet Malachi clearly speaks out against divorce.

> *You ask, "Why does he not?"*
> *Because the LORD was witness to the covenant between you*
> *and the wife of your youth, to whom you have been faithless,*
> *though she is your companion and your wife by covenant.*
> *Has not the one God made and sustained for us the spirit of*
> *life? And what does he desire? Godly offspring.*
> *So take heed to yourselves,*
> > *and let none be faithless to the wife of his youth.*
> *"For I hate divorce,*
> > *says the LORD the God of Israel, and covering one's*
> > *garment with violence, says the LORD of hosts.*
> *So take heed to yourselves and do not be faithless."*
> > *Malachi 2:14-16 [RSV]*

In order to restore marriage to its original state as in Genesis, where "two become one flesh,"Jesus confirms the concept of exclusive and faithful married love in the Gospel of St. Matthew, and adds the concept of the indissolubility of the marriage bond between man and woman:

> *Answering, he said to them:*
> *Have ye not read that he who made man from the beginning*
> > *made them male and female?*
> *And he said: For this cause shall a man leave father and*
> > *mother and shall cleave to his wife:*
> > > *and they two shall be in one flesh.*
> *What therefore God hath joined together, let no man put asunder.*
> > *Matthew 19:4-6 [Douay-Rheims, 1582]*

Here is Jesus in 4 major English translations of the Bible!

Everyone that putteth away his wife and marrieth another
committeth adultery; and he that marrieth her
that is put away from her husband committeth adultery.
Luke 16:18 [Douay-Rheims, 1582]
Whosoever putteth away his wife, and marrieth another,
committeth adultery: and whosoever marrieth her
that is put away from her husband committeth adultery.
Luke 16:18 [King James, 1611]
Everyone who divorces his wife and marries another
commits adultery, and he who marries a woman
divorced from her husband commits adultery.
Luke 16:18 {RSV, 1946]
Everyone who divorces his wife and marries another
commits adultery, and the one who marries a woman
divorced from her husband commits adultery.
Luke 16:18 [New American, 1970]

We must accept the fact that a natural family is a natural family, and all the divorce laws in the universe will not change that fact. To a child, his mother is always his mother, and his father is always his father. These are the two individuals that he trusts first and foremost in his life. When one leaves, it is devastating. If you cannot trust your own parents, who can you trust?! Children are torn between their parents, and struggle with their own sense of direction.

There were unhappy marriages in the 1950s. It is just that Mom and Dad stayed together for the children and did not disrupt the home.

One cannot describe the pain and agony of divorce, especially when children are involved. Living through a divorce has long-term effects on all concerned for years to come. If it is impossible to save the home, a unique solution, particularly with large families, is to have the children stay at home, and the parents switch! While family dysfunction persists, there is still a framework. At least the children are still able to have Mom and Dad in their home, each parent has a chance to be with every child, and all the children bond with each other. There is still a family, for relationships to grow in the years ahead.

Love, patience, and forgiveness can bring healing.

196

Homosexuality is unnatural and has always been considered taboo. God warns Moses and the priests in the Old Testament Book of Leviticus:

Ye shall not lie with a male as with a woman;
it is an abomination."
Leviticus 18:22 [RSV]

St. Paul in a Letter to the Romans in the New Testament admonishes:

"They exchanged the truth of God for a lie and revered and
worshipped the creature rather than the creator
who is blessed forever. Amen.
Therefore, God handed them over to degrading passions.
Their females exchanged natural relations for unnatural,
and the males likewise gave up natural relations
with females and burned with lust for one another.
Males did shameful things with males and thus received
in their own persons the due penalty for their perversity."
St. Paul to the Romans 1:25-27 [New American]

Is this a sign of the decline and fall of the United States of America?

Responding to legal pressure , the American Psychiatry Association, at their national meeting on December 15, 1973, declared homosexuality was no longer a mental illness, deleting the term "sexual orientation disturbance" from the list of mental illnesses.

Physicians and psychiatrists should act to all people and all patients in a loving and compassionate manner. This is especially true of the tragedy of homosexuality, the leading cause of AIDS. In Emergency Medicine we are faced every day with AIDS patients, and they are generally quite appreciative of our efforts.

It is natural for a man and woman to be together. The survival of the human race depends on it!

Human Cloning.   And finally, we cannot end this chapter without comment on human cloning. These are my own opinions, unless otherwise stated.

We as physicians fall between the scientists and the philosophers, as we receive a Medical Degree in the the Art and Science of Medicine. It is important to note that the word *Art* precedes the word science, although we certainly have become inundated with science in the past 25 years.

February 24, 1997 was the day of announcement of the scientific break-through of the Roslin Institute near Edinburgh, Scotland, when scientists published an article in *Nature* entitled "Viable offspring derived from fetal and adult mammalian cells." By nuclear transfer from an adult sheep mammary cell to an enucleated egg and then implantation in a surrogate mother, they were able to clone Dolly, an identical lamb.

They had one success in 277 attempts.

World-wide reaction was immediate and swift as fears of human cloning surfaced. The relationship of man to woman and marriage would be forever altered. If human cloning was perfected, the male would become reproductively obsolete.

Cloning negates the whole advantage of sexual dimorphism in evolution.

The United States and twenty European nations banned or restricted research on human cloning. The U. S. National Bioethics Advisory Commission Report recommended a five year ban on human cloning reseach. Nobel peace-prize winner Joseph Rotblat compared the breakthrough with the creation of the atomic bomb. 87% of Americans think cloning should be banned in a poll on ABC Television "Nightline."   Talk-show hosts asked, "Will there ever be another ewe?"

The Vatican issued a statement that "the creation of life outside of marriage went against God's plan. A person has a right to be born in a human way and not in the laboratory." The Southern Baptist Convention stated that any scientific discovery that touches upon human creation is also a matter of morality and spirituality, and voted on March 6, 1997 to call upon Congress and all nations of the world to "make human cloning unlawful and...to prevent the cloning of any human being."

Historically, Hebrew Scripture, which is the same as the Old Testament of the Christian and Catholic Bibles tells us human life and death are in the hands of God alone in his power, as noted in Pope John Paul's encyclical letter. We are planned by God, and the soul, the "breath of life," is given via the natural law.

God speaks to Moses in the Book of Deuteronomy :

> *"Learn then that I, I alone, am God,*
> *and there is no god besides me.*
> *It is I who bring both death and life."*
> *Deuteronomy 32:39*
> *New American Edition*

Job exclaims:

> *In his hand is the life of every living thing*
> *and the breath of all mankind.*
> *Job 12:10 [RSV]*

The scientific breakthrough ignited a fierce debate over ethical issues, including discussion of the soul in the lay media, such as Time Magazine.

Will the clone of a human being have a soul? Or will it be a mass of biologic material with human intelligence? What is the relation of the body and the soul?

Isaiah, Ezekiel, and Daniel spoke of the resurrection of the body in the Old Testament. Plato felt the soul was imprisoned in the body, until death, when it became free for all eternity. Aristotle believed there was a fundamental unity between the body and soul. The common conception of the soul being distracted, tempted, and tormented by the flesh was given a twist by the poet Andrew Marvell in his 1681 poem, *A Dialogue between the Soul and the Body:*

A Dialogue Between the Soul and the Body

Soul   *O who shall, from this dungeon, raise*
A soul enslav'd so many ways?
With bolts of bones, that fetter'd stands
In feet, and manacled in hands;
Here blinded with an eye, and there
Deaf with the drumming of an ear;
A soul hung up, as 'twere, in chains
Of nerves, and arteries, and veins;
Tortur'd, besides each other part,
In a vain head, and double heart.

Body

                    O who shall me deliver whole
                    From bonds of this tyrannic soul?
                    Which, stretch'd upright, impales me so
                    That mine own precipice I go:
                    And warms and moves this needless frame,
                    (A fever could but do the same)
                    And, wanting where its spite to try,
                    Has made me live to let me die.
                    A body that could never rest,
                    Since this ill spirit it possest.

Soul

What magic could me thus confine
Within another's grief to pine?
Where whatsoever it complain,
I feel, that cannot feel, the pain;
And all my care itself employs;
That to preserve which me destroys;
Constrain'd not only to endure
Diseases, but, what's worse, the cure;
And ready off the port to gain,
And shipwreck'd into health again.

Body

                    But physic yet could never reach
                    The maladies thou me dost teach
                    Whom first the cramp of hope does tear,
                    And then the palsy shakes of fear;
                    The pestilence of love does heat,
                    Or hatred's hidden ulcer eat;
                    Joy's cheerful madness does perplex,
                    Or sorrow's other madness vex;
                    Which knowledge forces me to know,
                    And memory will not forego.
                    What but a soul could have the wit
                    To build me up for sin so fit?
                    So architects do square and hew
                    Green trees that in the forest grew.
                    Andrew Marvell

Humanity has always been fascinated by the concept of transferring life by means other than the natural law, typified by Mary Shelley's haunting 1818 novel, *Frankenstein or, The Modern Prometheus.* Should mankind proceed, will the first human clone protest as did Adam, before he repented in Milton's *Paradise Lost :*

> *"Did I request thee, Maker, from my clay*
>   *To mold me Man,*
>   *did I solicit thee*
>   *From darkness to promote me?"*
> **John Milton**
> **Paradise Lost, X,743-745**

Mary Shelley begins her book with the above quote. As with the tormented and tragic monster of Dr. Frankenstein, will the clone be more human than his vain and foolish creator?

How tragic for the clone! He will never be unique, he will never have a sense of individuality, he will never be truly independent of his creator.

Undue power would be given to the person or agency requesting the clone.

What about an unsuccessful clone? Dolly was one out of 277 tries. What possible misadventure would be created? Who would be responsible? Suppose the misadventure procreates?!

The beauty and special gift of a couple having a precious baby will no longer be a unique experience for humanity to treasure.

From a humanitarian point of view, I suggest to the scientists that we must first take care of those humans that already occupy this planet. Perhaps they will be kind enough to donate monies allocated for cloning to feed the hundreds of millions that go to bed hungry each night, and shelter the homeless, before they resume their research on cloning.

CHAPTER 7
SAVE OUR NATION

And where the Spirit of the Lord is, there is freedom.
2 Corinthians 3:17

America is troubled. We are losing our direction. I see it every day in Emergency Medicine.   Teenagers and young adults especially do not know what is important, what is right or wrong, and they are lost for answers. Judging by what is coming out of Washington these days, neither do some adults. Family disintegration and divorce often leave the young without moral values. Children and the elderly suffer from neglect and abuse.   Rampant teenage drug abuse, suicide, and homicide are taking our productive citizens of tomorrow.

Love and mutual respect often lose out in human relationships.

I believe America is in the fourth quarter, and we have just had the two-minute warning.   It is almost as if America has collectively developed Alzheimer's disease, for we have forgotten our rich national heritage. We have discussed how we have ended up the way things are today.   1963 was the turning point. We literally need resuscitation before we have a cardiac arrest!

What about Bible prophecy?

Are the warnings from the visionaries of Medjugorje truly private revelations from Mary? Will grave events happen in Mirjana's lifetime as reported? Will mankind continue on its present path of instant gratification and self-destruction?

We only have to look at nature to see this destructive path. We have had a hole in the ozone since 1985, and nations *still* produce freon!

Look at global warming.   Even though we have just had the hottest summer ever, we continue to burn fossil fuels at unprecedented rates.

Look at the loss of natural species in the animal and plant kingdoms! Are we next?

What can we do to save our Nation?

It is time to wake up and turn things around! With the help of God we must first change ourselves and our relations to others, and then we must restore the founding principles of our Nation, and restore trust and hope to America and the American family. Here are ten ideas I believe will put America once again on the right path.

1   Trust in the Lord and Read Scripture

While over 90% of Americans believe in God, how many really have faith to trust in him on a daily basis?   W. Somerset Maugham in his 1944 book describes the road in life to goodness as a razor's edge. We need guidance in the many crises we face in life. We need to have faith in our God to lead us.   If you could listen to Don relate his near-death experience, and look in his eyes, you would know how deeply he believed when he told me to "Trust in the Lord."

All too often we turn to things of this world to satisfy that yearning for fulfillment, that thirst in our souls. But whether it is intellectual pursuits, a love affair, money, power, or sex, it all leaves us unfulfilled, empty, and often worse off than when we started. The youth pursue drugs, sex, and rock 'n' roll. They end up hurt, empty, jaded, depressed, or in a drug treatment center

And never before has a generation been raised without the basics. The young learn that hedonism is unfulfilling, that living for good times and the weekend does not last. After living for thrill after thrill, they become bored and restless. An uneasiness takes over their lives, or they may become depressed. Teenagers and young adults are searching for answers, and they are not finding the answers in our society today.

That is why the young are especially vulnerable to evil as never before. They are looking for answers, but they are surrounded by evil. Television is beyond repair, satan and evil fill the music and album covers, and the book stores are filled with subjects such as fortune telling, seances, and the occult. They may try a tattoo. Many are being led astray! If only the young would read Scripture, the Book of Leviticus clearly speaks out against such things:

> *Do not lacerate your bodies for the dead,*
> *and do not tattoo yourselves...*
> *Do not go to mediums or consult fortune tellers,*
> *for you will be defiled by them.*
> *I, the LORD, am your God.*
> *Leviticus 19:28, 31 [New American]*

Today we forget about satan. Many believe he does not exist. Billy Graham in his book on *Angels* reminds us of the story of Lucifer, the angel of the morning, the morning star. He was an angel as great as Michael the Archangel, who decided that instead of worshipping God the Creator, he wished to be worshipped and rebelled against God the Creator. A third of the angels rebelled with him, but they were driven from heaven by Michael and the host of angels loyal to God and cast into hell. Lucifer, the morning star, became satan, the fallen angel, with his hoard of demons.

God created man - we are His chosen creation to fill heaven!

Lucifer is the Temptor, represented by the lowly serpent, who began his campaign of hatred against mankind in the Garden of Eden, when he tempted our first parents, Adam and Eve. Satan and his demons wage unrelentless war against mankind, and until this warfare ends in the Final Battle, man will be plagued with temptation, confusion, doubt, weakness and sin.

The Bible points out the passage on the King of Babylon in the Book of Isaiah refers to Lucifer on a spiritual plane:

> *How art thou fallen from heaven,*
> *O Lucifer, who didst rise in the morning!*
> *How art thou fallen to the earth,*
> >*that didst wound the nations?*
> *And thou saidst in thy heart:*
> >*"I will ascend into heaven,*
> >*I will exalt my throne above the stars of God;*
> >*I will sit in the mountain of the covenant,*
> >>*in the sides of the North.*
> >*I will ascend above the height of the clouds;*
> >*I will be like the Most High!"*
> *But yet thou shalt be brought down to hell,*
> >*into the depth of the pit!*
> >>*Isaiah 14:12-15 [Douay-Rheims]*

St. Paul warns the devil may masquerade as an angel of light.

> *And no wonder, for even Satan disguises himself as an angel of light.*
> >*So it is not strange if his servants also disguise*
> >>*themselves as servants of righteousness.*
> >*Their end will correspond to their deeds.*
> >>*II St. Paul to the Corinthians 11:14-15[RSV]*

Mary of Medjugorje warns us we are in a time of spiritual warfare.

A great struggle is about to unfold.
A struggle between my Son and satan.
Human souls are at stake.
August 2, 1981.

But she was reported to tell us the power of satan will soon end.

God gave us free will. All too often we fall and wander away. But, I believe a yearning within us leads us back to God, as so eloquently put by the seventeenth-century English poet, George Herbert:

When God at first made man,
Having a glass of blessings standing by -
"Let us," said he, "pour on him all we can;
Let the world's riches, which dispersed lie,
Contract into a span."

So strength first made a way,
Then beauty flowed, then wisdom, honor, pleasure
When almost all was out, God made a stay,
Perceiving that, alone of all his treasure,
Rest in the bottom lay.

"For if I should," said he,
"Bestow this jewel also on my creature,
He would adore my gifts instead of me,
And rest in nature, not the God of nature:
So both should losers be.

"Yet let him keep the rest,
But keep them with repining restlessness;
Let him be rich and weary, that at least,
If goodness lead him not, yet weariness
May toss him to my breast."

George Herbert
The Pulley

Instead of having faith in the Lord, I always tried to do everything on my own strength. I lived a life without God, the secular way. How often I fell! And now I am left with a deep sadness, because of all my sins and because of the ones I have disappointed in life. I never read the Bible, and considered it irrelevant. But that was my loss, our loss. There is a sign on the way to Tybee Island - it has a picture of the Bible, with the inscription - "When all else fails, read the instructions." It is all there! Our world has been given the instructions from our Creator. All we have to do is read the instructions, and let Him lead us.

The Epistles of St. Peter tells us Scripture comes from the Holy Spirit and is sent from Heaven to the prophets to guide us to salvation. We are so fortunate to have Scripture, as even angels long to look!

> *It was revealed to them*
> *that they were serving not themselves but you,*
> *in the things which have now been announced to you*
> *by those who preached the Gospel to you*
> *through the Holy Spirit sent from heaven,*
> *things into which angels long to look.*
> *1 Peter 1:10-12 [RSV]*

> *For no prophecy ever came through human will;*
> *but rather human beings moved by the holy Spirit*
> *spoke under the influence of God.*
> *2 Peter 1:21 [New American]*

Here are two passages recommending we trust in the Lord.

> *The Lord is my shepherd;*
> *I shall not want.*
> *He maketh me to lie down*
> *in green pastures;*
> *He leadeth me beside the still waters.*
> *He restoreth my soul:*
> *He leadeth me in the paths of righteousness*
> *for his name's sake.*

Yea, though I walk
    through the valley of the shadow of death,
        I will fear no evil:
            for thou art with me;
    Thy rod and thy staff they comfort me.
Thou preparest a table before me
    in the presence of mine enemies;
Thou anointest my head with oil; my cup runneth over.
Surely goodness and mercy shall follow me
    all the days of my life
And I will dwell in the house of the Lord forever.
        Psalm 23:1-6 [Authorized King James Version]

Jesus speaks, after giving sight to the man born blind:

I am the good shepherd.
A good shepherd lays down his life for the sheep.
A hired man, who is not a shepherd
    and whose sheep are not his own,
        sees a wolf coming
        and leaves the sheep and runs away,
        and the wolf catches and scatters them.
        This is because he works for pay
        and has no concern for the sheep.
I am the good shepherd,
    and I know mine and mine know me,
        just as the Father knows me
        and I know the Father;
    and I will lay down my life for the sheep.
        John 10:11-16 [New American]

The spiritual goal in Buddhism is Nirvana, which is to want nothing. It is not easy in this time of instant gratification to put aside our desires, and to trust in the Lord and let God lead us. God loves us and will look after us. All we have to do is follow His way. And if we trust in the Lord and live his way, the **Holy Spirit** will dwell in us, and his **guardian angels** will protect us.

Jesus refers to the **Holy Spirit** at the Last Supper:

> *Whoever loves me will keep my word,*
> *and my Father will love him,*
> *and we will come to him, and make our dwelling with him.*
> *Whoever does not love me does not keep my words;*
> *yet the word that you hear is not mine*
> *but that of the Father who sent me.*
> *I have told you this while I am with you.*
> *The Advocate, the holy Spirit that the Father will send in my name -*
> *he will teach you everything*
> *and remind you of all that [I] told you.*
> *Peace I leave with you, my peace I give to you.*
> *John 14:23-27 [New American]*

At the Pentecost, the Apostles were filled with the Holy Spirit and began to proclaim the mighty works of God and spread his word. St. Peter instructs them:

> *"Repent and be baptized, every one of you,*
> *in the name of Jesus Christ*
> *for the forgiveness of your sins;*
> *and you will receive the gift of the holy Spirit."*
> *The Acts of the Apostles 2:38 [New American]*

St. Paul reminds us that our bodies are temples of the Holy Spirit:

> *Do you not know that your body*
> *is a temple of the holy Spirit within you...?*
> *1 Corinthians 6:19 [New American]*

St. Paul further cautions us not to disappoint the Holy Spirit!

> *And do not grieve the Holy Spirit of God,*
> *in whom you were sealed for the day of redemption.*
> *Ephesians 4:30 [RSV]*

The Holy Spirit guides our lives by giving us his Gifts and his Fruits when we are open to the Lord. The gifts of the Holy Spirit, as noted in the Greek Septuagint version of *Isaiah 11:2-3* are wisdom, counsel, understanding, knowledge, fortitude, piety, and fear [of separation] from the Lord. The seven gifts of the Holy Spirit are given in the Sacrament of Confirmation to young Catholic adults to reaffirm Baptism, so that they may too be filled with the Holy Spirit and be representatives of Christ.

The fruits of the Holy Spirit, as noted in *St. Paul to the Galatians 5:22-23* are charity, joy, peace, patience, kindness, generosity, faithfulness, gentleness, and chastity, or self-control.

God protects us with his guardian angels, especially when we trust in Him. Fr. Paul O'Sullivan in his book *All About the Angels* tells us our guardian angel is our best friend, and that we should treat him with respect, look to him for advice and protection, converse with him, and call upon him when in need. Angels appear throughout the Bible from the first Book of Genesis to the final Book of Revelations!

The very first appearance of an angel occurs in Chapter 3 of Genesis, when God places an angel to guard the Garden of Eden:

> **And he cast out Adam; and placed before the paradise of pleasure Cherubims, and a flaming sword, turning every way, to guard the way to the tree of life.**
> **Genesis 3:24 [Douay-Rheims]**

God tells Moses in the Book of Exodus:

> **"See, I am sending an angel before you,**
> **to guard you on the way and bring you**
> **to the place I have prepared.**
> **Be attentive to him and heed his voice.**
> **Do not rebel against him, for he will not forgive your sin.**
> **My authority resides in him.**
> **If you heed his voice and carry out all I tell you,**
> **I will be an enemy to your enemies, and a foe to your foes."**
> **Exodus 23:20-22 [New American]**

The Book of Psalms tells us that all who trust in the Lord have a guardian angel.

> *The angel of the LORD, who encamps with them,*
> *delivers all who fear God.*
> *Psalms 34:8 [New American]*

> *For He shall give His angels charge over thee.*
> *to keep thee in all thy ways. They shall bear thee up*
> *in their hands lest thou dash thy foot against a stone.*
> *Psalm 91:11-12 [King James]*

The Book of Daniel is replete with stories of angels, the most famous being Daniel in the Lion's Den. Thrown into the lion's den, Daniel trusted in God:

> *My God hath sent his angel and shut up the mouths of the lions*
> *and they have not hurt me!"*
> *Daniel 6:22 [Douay-Rheims]*

The Books of the Apocrypha are filled with beautiful stories of angels, such as the Book of Tobias or Tobit. This is from the Letter of Jeremiah (Baruch 6).

> *Rather, say in your hearts,*
> *"You, O Lord, are to be worshipped."*
> *For my angel is with you,*
> *and he is the custodian of your lives.*
> *Letter of Jeremiah [Baruch 6:5-6, Douay-Rheims]*

The three named Archangels are Michael, Gabriel, and Raphael. Michael is God's great warrior, who drove the evil ones from Heaven, and who will free earth and bring the peace of God in the Final Battle in Revelation. Here is a prayer to St. Michael the Archangel, important in these troubled times:

Prayer to St. Michael St. Michael, the Archangel, defend us in battle. Be our safeguard against the wickedness and snares of the devil. May God rebuke him we humbly pray; and do thou, O Prince of the Heavenly Host, by the power of God, thrust into hell satan and all the other evil spirits, who wander through the world seeking the ruin of souls. Amen.

Gabriel is the bearer of good news, the angel who announced to Mary she would be the Mother of Jesus. Raphael is the healer of the sick and protector of travelers. Raphael uses the name of Azarias, before he reveals his identity in the Book of Tobias:

> **I am the angel Raphael,**
>> **one of the seven, who stand before the Lord.**
>>> **Tobias 12:15   [Douay-Rheims]**

St. Augustine tells us that angels are spirits who serve as messengers of God. St. Thomas Aquinas believed the good idea that pops into your mind is from an angel, "by bringing within man's reach some truth which the angel himself contemplates."

My favorite quote about angels probably happens more than we realize.

> **Let brotherly love continue.**
> **Do not neglect to show hospitality to strangers,**
>> **for thereby some have entertained angels unawares.**
>>> **Hebrews 13:1-2 [RSV]**

In summary, give the Lord a chance and trust in Him.

Attending Mass or Church service brings peace to your soul . It removes you from the cares of our fast-paced world. When you receive Holy Communion, you receive Jesus in your heart. It is good to listen to your priest, minister, or rabbi. They have devoted their entire lives to studying the word of God and serving God on earth. Thus they have great insight into the Word of God, that they can pass on to you in Church service.

Read Scripture.

Open your heart and listen. Let Him "drive."   You will be pleasantly surprised!

2   Love one another.

Love means being there for someone you care about, no matter what.

> *But if you love, let these be your desires:*
> *To melt and be like a running brook*
> *that sings its melody to the night.*
> *To know the pain of too much tenderness.*
> *To be wounded by your own understanding of love...*
> **Kahlil Gibran**
> **The Prophet**

Love is the favorite subject of poets through the ages.

She Walks in Beauty

She walks in beauty, like the night
Of cloudless climes and starry skies,
And all that's best of dark and bright
Meet in her aspect and her eyes;
Thus mellowed to that tender light
Which heaven to gaudy day denies.

One shade the more, one ray the less,
Had half impaired the nameless grace
Which waves in every raven tress
Or softly lightens o'er her face,
Where thoughts serenely sweet express
How pure, how dear their dwelling-place.

And on that cheek and o'er that brow
So soft, so calm, yet eloquent,
the smiles that win, the tints that glow
But tell of days in goodness spent,
A mind at peace with all below
A heart whose love is innocent.

George Gordon, Lord Byron

The movie *Titanic* is a beautiful love story. Jack loved Rose. He even died for her. How beautiful to know that love is still alive today!

God loves us very much, and he wants us to love one another. In the Old Testament, God compares his love to that of a mother for her child.

> **Can a mother forget her infant,**
> **be without tenderness for the child of her womb?**
> **Even should she forget, I will never forget you.**
> **See, upon the palms of my hands,**
> **I have written your name.**
> **Isaiah 49:15-16 [New American]**

Jesus speaks simply in the Gospel of John:

> **This is my commandment:**
> **love one another as I love you.**
> **No one has greater love than this,**
> **to lay down one's life for one's friends.**
> **John 15:12-13 [New American]**

Jesus practiced what he preached! Jesus loved us. He became one of us, born on Christmas Day. He even died for us on Good Friday, on the Cross at Calvary. Jesus is the Savior of mankind. His resurrection from the dead on Easter Sunday showed us he is God, who became man to redeem all humanity.

Jesus gives us the Parable of the Good Samaritan as an example of love towards our neighbor:

> **And behold, a lawyer stood up to put him to the test, saying, "Teacher, what shall I do to inherit eternal life?" He said to him, "What is written in the law? How do you read?" And he answered,**
> **"You shall love the Lord your God with all your heart,**
> **and with all your soul, and with all your strength,**
> **and with all your mind; and your neighbor as yourself."**
> **And he said to him,**
> **"You have answered right; do this, and you will live."**

But he, desiring to justify himself, said to Jesus,
> *"And who is my neighbor?"*

Jesus replied,

"A man was going down from Jerusalem to Jericho,
> *and he fell among robbers, who stripped him*
> *and beat him, and departed, leaving him half dead.*

Now by chance a priest was going down that road; and
> *when he saw him he passed by on the other side.*

So likewise a Levite, when he came to the place and
> *saw him, passed by on the other side.*

But a Samaritan, as he journeyed, came to where he was;
> *and when he saw him, he had compassion,*
> *and went to him and bound up his wounds,*
> *pouring on oil and wine; then he set him on his*
> *own beast and brought him to an inn,*
> *and took care of him.*

And the next day he took out two denarii
> *and gave them to the innkeeper, saying,*

'Take care of him; and whatever more you spend, I will
repay you when I come back.'

Which of these three, do you think, proved neighbor to the
> *man who fell among the robbers?"*

He said, "The one who showed mercy on him."

And Jesus said to him,
> *"Go and do likewise."*

> *Luke 10:25-37 [RSV]*

We all want and need love. This is essential to the human race. We need to help each other, cooperate with each other, and think of the next person *before* we think of ourselves. This does not come naturally.

C. S. Lewis in his book *The Four Loves* describes four kinds of human love - affection, friendship, romantic love, and the love of God.

Storge, or affection, is the natural love a parent has for a child.

Eros is a physical love, romantic love, the love two have for each other. It is selfish, and seeks personal advantage and fulfillment.

Filia is the love of friendship, but it has conditions. It gives, but expects something equal in return.

Agape is true, unconditional love, a generosity of spirit which gives and expects nothing in return. It is the love God has for us.

One of the most beautiful passages from St. Paul in the Bible concerns this unconditional love:

> **If I speak in human and angelic tongues**
> **but do not have love,**
> **I am a resounding gong or a clashing symbol.**
> **And if I have the gift of prophecy**
> **and comprehend all mysteries and all knowledge;**
> **if I have all faith so as to move mountains**
> **but do not have love,**
> **I am nothing.**
> **If I give away everything I own,**
> **and if I hand my body over so that I may boast**
> **but do not have love,**
> **I gain nothing.**
> **Love is patient,**
> **love is kind.**
> **It is not jealous,**
> **[love] is not pompous,**
> **it is not inflated,**
> **it is not rude,**
> **it does not seek its own interests,**
> **it is not quick-tempered,**
> **it does not brood over injury,**
> **it does not rejoice over wrongdoing**
> **but rejoices with the truth.**
> **It bears all things,**
> **believes all things,**
> **hopes all things,**
> **endures all things.**
> **Love never fails.**
> **First Letter of St. Paul to the Corinthians 13:1-8**
> **[New American]**

Mary speaks of love in Medjugorje, in a motherly way, calling us her children:

I wish to tell you to open your hearts to the Lord of all hearts.
Give me all your feelings and all your problems.
   I wish to comfort you in all your trials.
   I wish to fill you with peace, joy, and the Love of God.
                                   June 20, 1985

Dear children:
Today my call to you is that in your life you live love
               toward God and neighbor.
Without love, dear children, you can do nothing.
Therefore, I am calling you to live in mutual love.
Only in that way will you be able to love and accept both me
          and all those around you who are coming into your parish.
Everyone will sense my love through you.
Therefore, I beseech you to start loving from today with an
ardent love, the love with which I love you.
                                   May 29, 1986

Mother Teresa, in *The Joy of Loving* (1997), makes a great observation:

The very fact that God
         has placed a certain soul in our way
                  is a sign that God wants us to do something for him or her.
It is not chance; it has been planned by God.
         We are bound by conscience to help him or her.
                                   Mother Teresa

Two great joys in life are family and friendship. A true friend is someone you can turn to and know they will listen no matter what you have done, and accept you as you are. And, in spite of all, they help you with good advice. The best way to have friends is to be a good friend. The Bible has some wonderful passages on friendship:

Your friend or your father's friend, do not forsake;
and do not go off to your brother's house
in the day of your calamity.
Better is a neighbor who is near than a brother far away.
Proverbs 27:10 [RSV]

Therefore encourage one another,
and build one another up,
just as you are doing.
1 St. Paul to the Thessalonians 5:11 [RSV]

A true friend sometimes has to tell you things you do not want to hear. But it is best to accept it in good grace, and you will be better off in the long run.

He whose ear heeds wholesome admonition
will abide among the wise.
Proverbs 15:31 [RSV]

Open rebuke is better than hidden love.
Better are the wounds of a friend
than the deceitful kisses of an enemy.
Proverbs 27:5-6 [Douay-Rheims]

The Book of Sirach has this to say about friendship:

A kind mouth multiplies friends,
and gracious lips prompt friendly greetings.
Let your acquaintances be many,
but one in a thousand your confidant...
A faithful friend is a sturdy shelter;
he who finds one finds a treasure.
A faithful friend is beyond price,
no sum can balance his worth.
Sirach 6:5-6, 14-15 [New American]

Love will bring happiness to you and those around you!

3   Keep the Ten Commandments of God

Keeping the Ten Commandments has never been easy. It is even harder today. The traditional family is suffering. Divorce, separation, remarriage, living together, or living alone are commonplace. Loneliness may lead one to seek out love and companionship, but it may be the wrong kind or the wrong setting.

Our movies, television, and books tell us America has become a land of widespread immorality,

So many of our young have never even heard of the Ten Commandments! This is a condensation of the original text:

I am the Lord thy God who have brought thee out of the house of bondage.   Thou shalt not have strange gods besides me.
Thou shalt not make for thyself any graven image.
Thou shalt not take the name of the Lord in vain.
Remember to keep holy the Lord's Day.
Honor thy Father and Mother.
Thou shalt not kill.
Thou shalt not commit adultery.
Thou shalt not steal.
Thou shalt not bear false witness against thy neighbor.
Thou shalt not covet thy neighbor's wife.
Thou shalt not covet thy neighbor's goods.

Jesus throughout the New Testament fulfills the Ten Commandments. Furthermore, Jesus frequently extends the original Ten Commandments, as with the Beautitudes on the Sermon on the Mount. He then gives an example.

"You have heard that it was said to the men of old,
'You shall not kill;
and whoever kills shall be liable to judgment.'
But I say to you that every one who is angry with his brother
shall be liable to judgment; whoever insults his brother
shall be liable to the council, and whoever says, 'You fool!'
shall be liable to the hell of fire.

218

> *So if you are offering your gift at the altar, and there remember that*
>> *your brother has something against you, leave your gift there*
>> *before the altar and go; first be reconciled to your brother, and*
>> *then come and offer your gift.*
> *Make friends quickly with your accuser, while you are going with him*
>> *to court, lest your accuser hand you over to the judge, and the*
>> *judge to the guard, and you be put in prison; truly, I say to*
>> *you, you will never get out till you have paid the last penny.*
>> *Matthew 5:21-26 [RSV]*

Jesus even goes further when he frowns on divorce, when he castigates the Pharisees in front of the great crowds for their "hardness of hearts."   He reminds them of the beginning at the time of creation, when man and woman are joined together and become one flesh:

> *They said to him,*
>> *'Why then did Moses command one to give a certificate of*
>> *divorce and to put her away? [Deuteronomy 24:1]"*
> *Jesus said to them,*
>> *For the hardness of your hearts*
>> *Moses allowed you to divorce your wives,*
>>> *but from the beginning it was not so.*
> *And I say to you,*
>> *that whoever divorces his wife, except for unchastity,*
>>> *and marries another commits adultery;*
>> *and he who marries a divorced woman, commits adultery.*
>>> *The Gospel of Matthew 19:8-9 [RSV]*

God gave the Ten Commandments in great ceremony to Moses:

> *On the morning of the third day*
>> *there were peals of thunder and lightning,*
> *and a heavy cloud over the mountain,*
>> *and a very loud trumpet blast,*
>>> *so that all of the people in the camp trembled.*
> *But Moses led the people out of the camp to meet God,*

and they stationed themselves at the foot of the mountain.
Mount Sinai was all wrapped in smoke,
>*for the LORD came down upon it in fire.*
The smoke rose from it as though from a furnace,
>*and the whole mountain trembled violently.*
The trumpet blast grew louder and louder,
>*while Moses was speaking*
>>*and God answering him with thunder.*
>>*Exodus 19:16-19 [New American]*

The Bible speaks of future revelations of its secrets.

But a very little while,
>*and Lebanon shall be changed into an orchard,*
>*and the orchard shall be regarded as a forest!*
On that day the deaf shall hear
>*the words of a book;*
And out of gloom and darkness,
>*the eyes of the blind shall see.*
>>*Isaiah 29:17-18 [New American]*

"Go, Daniel," he said, "because the words are
to be kept secret and sealed until the end time."
>>*Daniel 12:9 [New American]*

Are we beginning the end times? Are the secrets in Isaiah, Daniel, and Revelation in the Bible now being revealed?   Billy Graham has written a book *Storm Warnings* on this very subject.

The Ten Commandments of God is the code for our human race, our ancient covenant, given directly from God to Moses. Those who live the Ten Commandments may survive the prophecies read in Isaiah, Daniel and Revelation in the Bible and told in the messages of Mary in Medjugorje.

If we continue as we are, we will not survive the future.

You can break the Ten Commandments of God, but in time, if you persist, the Ten Commandments will break you.

4   Forgiveness is the key to peace.

It is common to build up anger, hurt and resentment in human relationships, at home, at work, or in friendships.   Once you have been disappointed over and over in a relationship, it is nearly impossible on a human level to open up to them, or to feel any warmth to them. If someone lies to you, or steals from you, or breaks your trust, it is hard to ever trust them again. If you give, but your gift or kindness is not appreciated, taken for granted, or greeted with contempt or even anger because it is "not enough," who wants to ever give again to that person!   Or if you have harmed someone, and they no longer trust you, it is very hard to continue in a relationship.

Everyone has family arguments. It may start off over something meaningless. Then some old arguments and old wounds come to mind, and someone remembers something that happened 10 years ago, and anger begins to well up. Then you're in a bad mood, and you speak sharply to someone else that just came home and wasn't even there when the argument began. Their feelings get hurt, and pretty soon the whole house is in an uproar. Hopefully, with time, everyone cools down, and love and forgiveness begin to flow, and everyone makes up.

People like to say they forgive, but some do not forget.   Some people like to get even. It is a natural thing to get even. One time I travelled with my parents on an Italian ship, and a man from Sicily told me when I was thirteen years old, "If someone is good to me, I take care of them. But if someone does me wrong, I get them." That is also what we learn in our movies, in our society. "Go ahead, make my day." The lesson we learn from Hollywood is you are cool if you get even when you have been wronged.

Once that natural wall of hurt, anger, and resentment gets built up, it is hard to continue in a marriage, in a business relationship, in a friendship.

Unless you forgive.

It has taken me sometime to learn that if you want forgiveness, you must forgive others. And all of us need forgiveness. It is all right there in the Lord's prayer:

> ***Our Father,***
> ***who art in heaven, hallowed by thy name,***
> ***thy kingdom come, thy will be done,***
> ***on earth as it is in heaven.***

Give us this day our daily bread,
   and forgive us our trespasses
   as we forgive those
      who trespass against us;
   and lead us not into temptation,
   but deliver us from evil.
If you forgive others their transgressions,
   your Heavenly Father will forgive you.
But if you do not forgive others,
   neither will your Father forgive your transgressions.
         Matthew 6:9-15

Forgiveness is found in the very first book of the Bible, in Genesis, when all the sons of Jacob, who once had sold their brother Joseph to the Ishmaelites for twenty pieces of silver, later approached their brother Joseph, who had become prominent in Egypt under Pharaoh during the famine:

"And now, we pray you,
   forgive the transgression
   of the servants of the God of your father."
Joseph wept when they spoke to him.
His brothers also came and fell down before him, and said,
   "Behold, we are your servants."
But Joseph said to them,
   "Fear not, for am I in the place of God?
   As for you, you meant evil against me;
      but God meant it for good,
      to bring it about that many people
      should be kept alive,
      as they are today.
   So do not fear;
      I will provide for you and your little ones."
Thus he reassured them and comforted them.
         Genesis 50:17-21 [RSV]

How many times must we forgive? One time? Two times? Three times? In our world today, if you are lucky, it is "three times and you're out!" Jesus gives us this answer:

> *Then Peter approaching asked him,*
> *"Lord, if my brother sins against me,*
> *how often must I forgive him?*
> *As many as seven times?"*
> *Jesus answered, "I say to you,*
> *not seven times but seventy times seven times.*
> *Matthew 18:21-22 [King James]*

How much suffering and disappointment can one of your own children bring you when(s)he is foolish! But Jesus gives us the Parable of the Lost Son as an example to us:

> *And he said, "There was a man who had two sons;*
> *and the younger of them said to his father,*
> *'Father, give me the share of property that falls to me.'*
> *And he divided his living between them.*
> *Not many days later, the younger son gathered all he had*
> *and took his journey into a far country, and*
> *there he squandered his property in loose living.*
> *And when he had spent everything, a great famine arose in that*
> *country, and he began to be in want.*
> *So he went and joined himself to one of the citizens of that*
> *country, who sent him into his fields to feed swine.*
> *And he would gladly have fed on the pods that the swine ate;*
> *and no one gave him anything.*
> *But when he came to himself he said,*
> *'How many of my father's hired servants have bread enough*
> *and to spare, but I perish here with hunger!*
> *I will arise and go to my father, and I will say to him,*
> *"Father, I have sinned against heaven and before you;*
> *I am no longer worthy to be called your son;*
> *treat me as one of your hired servants."'*
> *And he arose and came to his father.*

But while he was yet at a distance, his father saw him and had
compassion, and ran and embraced him and kissed him.
And the son said to him,
'Father, I have sinned against heaven and before you;
I am no longer worthy to be called your son.'
But the father said to his servants,
'Bring quickly the best robe, and put it on him;
and put a ring on his hand, and shoes on his feet;
and bring the fatted calf and kill it, and let us eat and make
merry; for this my son was dead, and is alive again;
he was lost, and is found.'
Luke 15:11-24 [RSV]

Sin and guilt weigh heavy on the human heart. Ask God to forgive your sins. Mother Teresa gives a wonderful example of our Father's forgiveness, to quote from her new 1997 book, *No Greater Love* :

"Your own child does something wrong.
What happens when your child comes to you and says,
"Daddy, I'm sorry."
What do you do?
You put both of your arms around her and kiss her (or him).
Why? Because that's your way of telling her that you love her.
God does the same thing.
He loves you tenderly...God is a forgiving father.
His mercy is greater than our sins. He will forgive us."
Mother Teresa

You are very fortunate if someone wants your forgiveness. Most people do not even bother. It is a great privilege to have the opportunity to forgive when you have been wronged, or to receive forgiveness when you have done wrong. Instead of an escalating war of getting even, you have the building of love and gratitude in a relationship.

Once you begin to forgive, it is a wonderful thing. If you truly forgive, and do not hold a grudge, often the other person actually is relieved and becomes grateful to you, and the relationship is actually strengthened.

5   Treasure Peace

There is a saying, "No news is good news." I used to think, how boring! I liked something going on all the time - something to stir the spirit, something to stir interest, something to stir passion.

It is the cool thing to live "on the edge" - living dangerously, a thrill a minute, a wild and crazy life. When you're young, you have so much energy, you think you are invincible! Be careful, and avoid trouble! It would be wise to heed this advice:

> *Can a man hide fire inside his bosom*
>   *and his garments not burn?*
> *Or can he walk upon hot coals*
>   *and his feet not be burnt?*
>   *Proverbs 6:27-28 [Douay-Rheims]*

The Wisdom of Solomon brings this dire warning:

> *But the wicked shall be punished according to their own devices:*
>   *who have neglected the just, and have revolted from the Lord.*
> *For he that rejected wisdom, and discipline, is unhappy:*
>   *and their hope is vain, and their labors without fruit,*
>   *and their works unprofitable*
> *Their wives are foolish and their children wicked,*
>   *Their offspring is accursed.*
>   *Wisdom of Solomon 3:10-12 [Douay-Rheims]*
> *But the children of adulterers will not come to maturity,*
>   *and the offspring of an unlawful union will perish.*
>   *Wisdom of Solomon 3:16 [RSV]*

What looks good today will bring misery tomorrow!
Jesus in the Gospel of St. Mark makes the important observation that what is within you is what you do.

> *And he said, "What comes out of a man*
>   *is what defiles a man. For from within,*

out of the heart of man, come evil thoughts, fornication,
theft, murder, adultery, coveting, wickedness, deceit,
licentiousness, envy, slander, pride, foolishness.
All these evil things come from within,
    and they defile a man."
    St. Mark 7:20-23 [RSV]

We are constantly being torn between the spirit and the desires of the flesh. St. Paul points out that Jesus helps us in this struggle:

For the law of the Spirit of life in Christ Jesus has set
    me free from the law of sin and death.
For God has done what the law, weakened by the flesh, could not do:
sending his own Son in the likeness of sinful flesh and for sin,
he condemned sin in the flesh,
    in order that the just requirement of the law
        might be fulfilled in us,
    who walk not according to the flesh
        but according to the Spirit.
For those who live according to the flesh
    set their minds on the things of the flesh,
but those who live according to the Spirit
    set their minds on the things of the Spirit.
To set the mind on the flesh is death,
    but to set the mind on the Spirit is life and peace.
    St. Paul to the Romans 8:2-6 [RSV]

St. Paul discusses the difference between the flesh, which places us under the "law" of sin and death, and the fruits of the Holy Spirit, which will give us life.

If I say, then: live by the Spirit
    and you will certainly not gratify the desire of the flesh.
For the flesh has desires against the Spirit,
    and the Spirit against the flesh;
    these are opposed to each other,
        so that you may not do what you want.

But if you are guided by the Spirit,
you are not under the law.
Now the works of the flesh are obvious:
immorality, impurity, licentiousness, idolatry,
sorcery, hatreds, rivalry, jealousy, outbursts of fury,
acts of selfishness, dissensions, factions,
occasions of envy, drinking bouts, orgies, and the like.
I warn you, as I warned you before, that those
who do such things will not inherit the kingdom of God.

In contrast, the fruit of the Spirit is
love, joy, peace, patience, kindness, generosity,
faithfulness, gentleness, self-control.
St. Paul to the Galatians 5:16-23 [New American]

The Book of Proverbs urges us to seek the Lord and his wisdom to enjoy a peaceful life and to avoid trouble.

For the Lord gives wisdom,
from his mouth come knowledge and understanding;
He has counsel in store for the upright;
he is the shield of those who walk honestly,
Guarding the paths of justice
and protecting the way of his pious ones.
Then you will understand rectitude and justice
honesty, every good path;
For wisdom will enter your heart,
knowledge will please your soul;
Discretion will watch over you,
understanding will guard you;
Saving you from the way of evil men,
from men of perverse speech,
Who leave the way of straight paths,
rejoice in perversity;
Whose ways are crooked,
and devious their paths;

Saving you from the wife of another,
from the adulteress with her smooth words,
Who forsakes the companion of her youth.
Proverbs 2:5-17[New American]

To develop a peaceful nature, we must **think** peaceful!

Finally, brothers,
whatever is true, whatever is honorable,
whatever is just, whatever is pure, whatever is lovely,
whatever is gracious, if there is any excellence
and if there is anything worthy of praise,
think about these things.
St. Paul to the Philippians 4:8 [New American]

Silence can help bring a peaceful life. One can think clearly in silence, and make wise and sensible decisions. And yes, one can receive spiritual guidance in silence. We gave up watching television and 4 television sets. It is amazing how free and productive life has become! Now there is time to think and pray, and live a thoughtful life. In case you haven't noticed, I am a great fan of Mother Teresa. Here is what Mother Teresa says about silence:

In the silence of the heart God speaks.
If you face God in prayer and silence, God will speak to you.
Then you will know that you are nothing. It is only when you
realize your nothingness, your emptiness, that God can fill you
with Himself. Souls of prayer are souls of great silence.
Silence gives us a new outlook on everything.
We need silence to touch souls. The essential thing is not what
we say but what God says to us and through us. In that silence,
He will listen to us; there He will speak to our soul, and there we
will hear His voice.
Listen in silence, because if your heart is full of other things,
you cannot hear the voice of God. But when you have listened to
the voice of God in the stillness of your heart, then your heart is
filled with God.
Mother Teresa

Serving others is an unpopular idea today. The life of Jesus was one of service. He even washed the feet of Peter and the disciples.

> *Whoever wishes to be great among you will be your servant;*
> *whoever wishes to be first among you*
> *will be the slave of all.*
> *For the Son of Man did not come to be served but to serve*
> *and to give his life as a ransom for many.*
> *St. Mark 10:43-45 [New American]*

The fruit of service is peace. No other modern life has exemplified this more than Mother Teresa.

> *Works of love are always works of peace. Whenever*
> *you share love with others, you'll notice the peace*
> *that comes to you and to them.*
> *Mother Teresa*

You will find happiness if you seek and treasure peace!

6   Show Mercy

It was William Shakespeare who spoke of mercy in his 1594 play, *The Merchant of Venice,* when Portia speaks to Shylock in Act IV, Scene I:

> *"The quality of mercy is not strained.*
> *It droppeth as the gentle rain from heaven*
> *Upon the place beneath. It is twice blest:*
> *It blesseth him that gives and him that takes.*
> *'Tis mightiest in the mightiest; it becomes*
> *The throned monarch better than his crown.*
> *His scepter shows the force of temporal power,*
> *The attribute to awe and majesty,*
> *Wherein doth sit the dread and fear of kings.*
> *But mercy is above this sceptered sway;*
> *It is enthroned in the hearts of kings;*
> *It is an attribute of God himself;*
> *And earthly power doth then show like God's*
> *When mercy seasons justice."*
> **William Shakespeare**

Hebrew Scripture, the Old Testament, which primarily portrays the God of justice, also speaks of a merciful God:

> **Out of the depths I call to you, LORD:**
> **Lord, hear my cry!**
> **May your ears be attentive**
> **to my cry for mercy.**
> **If you, LORD, mark our sins,**
> **Lord, who can stand?**
> **But with you is forgiveness**
> **and so you are revered.**
> **Psalm 130:1-4 [New American]**

> **Who is there like you, the God**
> **who removes guilt and pardons sin**

230

for the remnant of his inheritance;
Who does not persist in anger forever,
but delights rather in clemency,
And will again have compassion on us,
treading underfoot our guilt?
You will cast into the depths of the sea all our sins.
Micah 7:18-19 [New American]

Remember one of the Beatitudes Jesus gives in the Sermon on the Mount:

Blessed are the merciful, for they shall obtain mercy.
St. Matthew 5:7 [New American]

Jesus is very direct on the subject of mercy:

"When the Son of man comes in his glory,
and all the angels with him,
then he will sit on his glorious throne.
Before him will be gathered all the nations, and he will separate them
one from another as a shepherd separates the sheep from the goats,
and he will place the sheep at his right hand, but the goats at the left.
Then the King will say to those at his right hand,
'Come, O blessed of my Father,
inherit the kingdom prepared for you
from the foundation of the world;
for I was hungry and you gave me food,
I was thirsty and you gave me drink,
I was a stranger and you welcomed me,
I was naked and you clothed me,
I was sick and you visited me,
I was in prison and you came to me.'
Then the righteous will answer him,
'Lord, when did we see thee hungry and feed thee, or thirsty
and give thee drink? And when did we see thee a stranger
and welcome thee, or naked and clothe thee? And when did
we see thee sick or in prison and visit thee?'

And the King will answer them,
'Truly, I say to you,
    as you did it to one of the least of these my brethren,
        you did it to me.'
Then he will say to those at his left hand,
    'Depart from me, you cursed, into the eternal fire
        prepared for the devil and his angels;
    for I was hungry and you gave me no food,
    I was thirsty and you gave me no drink,
    I was a stranger and you did not welcome me,
    naked and you did not clothe me,
    sick and in prison and you did not visit me.'
Then they also will answer,
    'Lord, when did we see thee hungry or thirsty or a stranger or
    naked or sick or in prison, and did not minister to thee?'
Then he will answer them, "Truly, I say to you, as you did it not to
    one of the least of these, you did it not to me.'
And they will go away into eternal punishment,
    but the righteous into eternal life."
    Matthew 25:31-46 [RSV]

It is important for us to be merciful with our tongue. Remember the old saying, "If you can't say something nice about someone, don't say anything at all." This is an area all of us can improve upon!
The letter of James discusses the power and the need to control the tongue:

If anyone does not fall short in speech,
    he is a perfect man, able to bridle his whole body also.
If we put bits into the mouths of horses to make them obey us,
    we also guide their whole bodies.
It is the same with ships: even though they are so large and
    driven by fierce winds, they are steered by a very small
        rudder wherever the pilot's inclination wishes.
In the same way the tongue is a small member
    and yet has great pretensions.
Consider how small a fire can set a huge forest ablaze.

The tongue is also a fire.
It exists among our members as a world of malice,
defiling the whole body and setting the entire course
of our lives on fire, itself set on fire by Gehenna.
For every kind of beast and bird, or reptile and sea creature,
can be tamed and has been tamed by the human
species, but no human being can tame the tongue.
It is a restless evil, full of deadly poison.
James 3:2-8 [New American]

My grandfather taught me an old saying from Lebanon: "God gives us two ears and one tongue, so that we may listen twice as much as we speak." We must think peaceful thoughts and have love in our hearts if we are to have a merciful tongue. It is so important to speak kindly of others.

Grief in the heart of a man shall bring him low,
but with a good word he shall be made glad.
Proverbs 12:25 [Douay-Rheims]

Pleasing words are a honeycomb,
sweet to the taste and healthful to the body.
Proverbs 16:24 [New American]

Let anything you hear die within you;
be assured it will not make you burst.
Sirach 19:9 [New American]

So, before we speak unkindly of someone, or judge others, let us be merciful. After all, is there any one of us who is perfect? Remember the words of Jesus when the scribes and Pharisees wished to stone a woman who was caught in the very act of committing adultery:

"Let him among you who is without sin cast the first stone!"
John 8:7

Stricken by their consciences, they went away one by one, until no one was left!

Jesus has given us a gift of mercy through a great Catholic tradition, devotion to the **Sacred Heart of Jesus**.

Sister Margaret Mary Alocoque believed she had 4 apparitions of Jesus from 1673 to 1675 in Paral-le-Monial, France. Recalling Simon Peter and his Apostles who could not even spend one hour during his agony in the garden of Gethsemane, she said Jesus asked for humanity to pray one hour with him.

Sister Margaret Mary said Jesus made twelve promises of Mercy, the greatest being the grace of final repentance to those who receive Holy Communion on nine consecutive First Fridays, that one will die in the state of grace and be with Him in the end. Jesus promises peace in the family dedicated to his Sacred Heart. He promises a fountain and boundless ocean of mercy to sinners who seek forgiveness in devotion to his Sacred Heart.

Sister Margaret Mary was canonized a Saint by Pope Benedict XV in 1920, in which he also recognized the great promise of **Mercy** to those who attend the nine First Fridays.

Mary in Medjugorje calls us to perform acts of Mercy:

>**Today I invite you to do works of mercy with love,**
>>**out of love for me and for your brothers and sisters.**
>
>**All that you do for others,**
>>**do it with great joy and humility towards God.**
>
>**I am with you and day after day I offer your sacrifices and prayers to**
>>**God for the salvation of the world.** **November 25, 1990**

The Corporal Works of Mercy		The Spiritual Works of Mercy	
1	Feed the Hungry	1	Admonish sinners
2	Give drink to the thirsty	2	Instruct the uninformed
3	Clothe the naked	3	Counsel the doubtful
4	Shelter the homeless	4	Comfort the sorrowful
5	Comfort the imprisoned	5	Be patient with those in error
6	Visit the sick	6	Forgive offenses
7	Bury the dead	7	Pray for the living and the dead

This is the time of mercy. Will justice be kind to America when we are immersed in our selfish and materialistic pursuits, while millions in the world remain homeless and starving? We must begin to practice the Corporal and Spiritual Works of Mercy **now!**

7   Protect the Family

Thank God we have family!

The natural law puts man and woman together for mutual comfort and for the procreation of the human race. Religion has always protected the sanctity of marriage and the family. Marriage is God's blessing on the mutual and exclusive giving of a man and a woman to each other. Children are the fruit and the bond of a marriage. Love, marriage, children and family are what it's all about! While there has been heartache, so much joy and happiness have come from our family. We are all very blessed.

The Song of Songs, or the Song of Solomon, in Hebrew Scripture in the Old Testament, portrays in romantic fashion human love, a description of the sacredness and depth of married union. The following are brief passages from this beautiful Scripture:

> *Come from Lebanon, my bride,*
> *come from Lebanon, come!...*
> *You have ravished my heart, my sister,*
> *my bride;*
> *you have ravished my heart*
> *with one glance of your eyes,*
> *with one bead of your necklace.*
> *How beautiful is your love, my sister,*
> *my bride,*
> *how much more delightful is your love than wine...*
> *Song of Songs 4:8-10 [New American]*

> *Set me as a seal upon your heart,*
> *as a seal upon your arm.*
> *For love is as strong as death.*
> *Jealousy is cruel as the grave.*
> *Its flashes are flashes of fire,*
> *a most vehement flame.*
> *Many waters cannot quench love,*
> *Neither can floods drown it*
> *Song of Songs 8:6-7 [RSV]*

Jesus speaks on marriage in the Gospel of Mark:

> *"But from the beginning of creation,*
> *'God made them male and female.*
> *For this reason a man shall leave his father and mother*
> *and be joined to his wife,*
> *and the two shall become one flesh.'*
> *So they are no longer two but one flesh.*
> *Therefore, what God has joined together,*
> *let not man put asunder."*
> *St. Mark 10:6-10 [RSV]*

St. Paul continues in the New Testament a discussion of the marriage bond, such as the following:

> *The husband should fulfill his duty toward his wife,*
> *and likewise the wife toward her husband.*
> *A wife does not have authority over her own body,*
> *but rather her husband, and similarly*
> *a husband does not have authority over his own body,*
> *but rather his wife.*
> *First letter of St. Paul to the Corinthians 7:2-4 [New American]*

The Bible is most supportive of the natural family, and St. Paul eloquently speaks of relationships within the family unit, first husbands and wives:

> *Be subordinate to one another out of reverence for Christ.*
> *Wives should be subordinate to their husbands as to the Lord.*
> *For the husband is head of his wife*
> *just as Christ is head of the church,*
> *He himself the savior of the body.*
> *As the church is subordinate to Christ, so wives*
> *should be subordinate to their husbands in everything.*
> *Husbands, love your wives,*
> *even as Christ loved the church and handed himself*
> *over for her to sanctify her,*

> *cleansing her by the bath of water with the word,*
> *that he might present to himself the church in splendor,*
> > *without spot or wrinkle or any such thing,*
> > *that she might be holy and without blemish.*
> *So also husbands should love their wives as their own bodies.*
> *He who loves his wife loves himself.*
> *For no one hates his own flesh but rather nourishes and*
> *cherishes it, even as Christ does the church,*
> > *because we are members of his body.*
> *For this reason a man shall leave father and mother*
> > *and be joined to his wife,*
> > *and the two shall become one flesh.*
> *This is a great mystery,*
> > *but I speak in reference to Christ and the church.*
> *In any case, each one of you should love his wife as himself,*
> > *and the wife should respect her husband.*
> > > *St. Paul to the Ephesians 5:21-33 [New American]*

St. Paul gives excellent advice on choosing a wife:

> *This is the will of God, your holiness:*
> > *that you refrain from immorality,*
> > *that each of you know how to acquire a wife for himself*
> > > *in holiness and honor,*
> > > *not in lustful passion*
> > > *as do the Gentiles who do not know God.*
> > *First letter of St. Paul to the Thessalonians 4:3-5 [New American]*

Chastity is an old-fashioned virtue, but purity in dating allows friendship to grow. St. Paul speaks again on the Christian family:

> *Children, obey your parents [in the Lord], for this is right.*
> *"Honor your father and mother."*
> *This is the first commandment with a promise,*
> *"that it may go well with you and*
> > *that you may have a long life on earth."*

Fathers, do not provoke your children to anger,
but bring them up
with the training and instruction of the Lord.
St. Paul to the Ephesians 6:1-4 [New American]

There is much wisdom in the Bible on being a parent, which in this day and time is most helpful! The Book of Proverbs encourages discipline!

He who spares his rod hates his son,
but he who loves his son is diligent to discipline him.
Proverbs 13:24 [RSV]

Discipline your son while there is still hope;
Do not set your heart on his destruction.
Proverbs 19:18 [RSV]

The rod and reproof give wisdom;
but the child that is left to his own will
bring his mother to shame.
Proverbs 29:15 [RSV]

The Book of Sirach captures a father's care for his daughter:

A daughter keeps her father secretly wakeful,
and worry over her robs him of sleep;
when she is young, lest she do not marry,
or if married, lest she be hated;
while a virgin, lest she be defiled
or become pregnant in her father's house;
or having a husband, lest she prove unfaithful,
or, though married, lest she be barren.
Keep strict watch over a headstrong daughter,
lest she make you a laughingstock to your enemies,
a byword in the city and notorious among the people,
and put you to shame before the great multitude.
Sirach 42:9-11 [RSV]

See that there is no lattice in her room,
  no place that overlooks the approaches to the house.
Let her not parade her charms before men,
  or spend her time with married women;
For just as moths come from garments,
  so harm to women comes from women:
Better a man's harshness than a woman's indulgence,
  and a frightened daughter than any disgrace.
    Sirach 42:12-14 [New American]

St. Paul offers these words:

Children, obey your parents in everything,
  for this is pleasing to the Lord.
Fathers, do not provoke your children,
  so they may not become discouraged.
    St. Paul to the Colossians 3:18-21[New American]

One positive development in our society are the Promisekeepers, a group of men who intend to keep their promises to their family. One of their seven promises is a commitment to build strong marriages and families through love, protection, and Biblical values. Over a million Promisekeepers gathered peacefully at the Washington Monument in 1997 calling for reconciliation with God and commitment to their families.

I hope we all treasure our family!

8   Respect Life

We must respect life. Quoting from the New Jerusalem Bible, an English translation from the original *La Bible de Jerusalem* of France, the Lord speaks to Isaiah, saying he formed him and called him in the womb:

> *Thus says Yahweh, your redeemer,*
> *he who formed you in the womb.*
> *I, Yahweh, have made all things,*
> *I alone spread out the heavens.*
> > *Isaiah 44:24 [New Jerusalem Bible]*

> *Coasts and islands, listen to me,*
> > *pay attention, distant peoples.*
> *Yahweh called me when I was in the womb,*
> > *before my birth he had pronounced my name.*
> > *Isaiah 49:1 [New Jerusalem Bible]*

St. Luke speaks of life in the womb, when Elizabeth refers to Mary with child:

> *When Elizabeth heard Mary's greeting,*
> *the infant leaped in her womb,*
> *and Elizabeth, filled with the holy Spirit,*
> *cried out in a loud voice, and said,*
> *"Most blessed are you among women,*
> > *and blessed is the fruit of your womb.*
> > *Luke 1:41-44 [New American]*

The Bible tells us each one of us has been planned. How does God view the taking of innocent life?

> *Whosoever shall shed man's blood,*
> > *his blood shall be shed;*
> *For man was made to the image of God.*
> > *Genesis 9:6 [Douay-Rheims]*

There are six things the Lord hates,
  yes, seven are an abomination to him;
Haughty eyes, a lying tongue,
  and hands that shed innocent blood;
A heart that plans wicked schemes,
  feet that run swiftly to evil,
The false witness who utters lies,
  and he who sows discord among his brothers.
    Proverbs 6:16-19 [New American]

Judging by the Bible, it is not only important to respect life, but should this bloodshed continue, we will incur God's wrath.

You shall not desecrate the land where you live.
Since bloodshed desecrates the land,
  the land can have no atonement
  for the blood shed on it
  except through the blood of him who shed it.
    Numbers 35:33 [New American]

It is for us to intercede! We are doomed if we say nothing.

If you remain indifferent in time of adversity,
  your strength will depart from you.
Rescue those who are being dragged to death,
  and from those tottering to execution, withdraw not.
If you say, "I know not this man!"
  does not he who tests hearts perceive it?
He who guards your life knows it,
  and he will repay each one according to his deeds.
    Proverbs 24:10-12 [New American]

Ezekiel says we must stand up for what is right, or we are just as responsible! If we see someone do wrong, it is our responsibility to point it out to them, or we are just as culpable.

The word of the LORD came to me:

    "Son of man, speak to your people and say to them,
If I bring the sword upon a land,
    and the people of the land take a man from among them,
        and make him their watchman;
    and if he sees the sword coming upon the land
        and blows the trumpet and warns the people;
        then if any one who hears the sound of the trumpet
        does not take warning,
            and the sword comes and takes him away,
            his blood shall be upon his own head.
He heard the sound of the trumpet, and did not take warning;
    his blood shall be upon himself.
But if he had taken warning, he would have saved his life.
But if the watchman sees the sword coming
    and does not blow the trumpet,
    so that the people are not warned,
    and the sword comes, and takes any one of them;
    that man is taken away in his iniquity,
    but his blood I will require at the watchman's hand.
"So you, son of man, I have made a watchman
    for the house of Israel;
    whenever you hear a word from my mouth,
    you shall give them warning from me.
If I say to the wicked,
    O wicked man, you shall surely die,
    and you do not speak to warn
        the wicked to turn from his way,
        that wicked man shall die in his iniquity,
        but his blood I will require at your hand.
But if you warn the wicked to turn from his way,
    and he does not turn from his way;
    he shall die in his iniquity,
        but you will have saved your life.
        Ezekiel 33:1-9 [RSV]

In whatever way you have time, any effort on your part to stop this national tragedy of abortion can only serve all of us. It is for us to discuss adoption, to find a home, to save lives, and in the end, to save our nation!

9   Restore Leadership and Our National Tradition

First we need to develop a sense of peace within ourselves through the traditions of our Judeo-Christian heritage. For, as President Kennedy said, "peace lies in the hearts and minds of all people...let us strive to build peace, a desire for peace, a willingness to work for peace, in the hearts and minds of all the people."

Let us begin once again to respect and be thoughtful to others, our families, our neighbors, our women, our children, our elderly, our fellow citizens of different races, our homeless.

We need to respect the next person, respect his privacy, and judge him by his merits and be silent about his faults. Even if they are different or have different viewpoints, we are first and foremost all American.

United we stand, divided we fall.

It has taken the writing of this book for me to accept that there is nothing we can do about the deaths of President Kennedy, of Martin Luther King, of Robert Kennedy.

There is nothing we can do about the Vietnam War.

We have these words from President Kennedy: "We must deal with the world as it is, and not as it might have been had history of the past...been different."

There is nothing we can do about slavery.

Martin Luther King said on August 28, 1963 during his famous speech: "Let us not satisfy our thirst for freedom by drinking from the cup of bitterness and hatred."

There is nothing we can do about prejudice, or reverse prejudice.

There is nothing we can do about the wrongs our wife or husband, our parents or children, our neighbors or fellow workers have done.

Except that we can forgive. **Forgiveness is the key to peace.**

We can forgive and look ahead.

We can forgive and help others.

All we can do about our own mistakes is to change, to forgive ourselves and ask forgiveness.

We can speak up for what is right. America became strong because we stood up for what is right and fought what we saw as wrong. We have such a rich American tradition! Let us draw from the strength of our National heritage!

And we can **vote!**

We need to find a way to elect true, moral, and responsible leaders. We need to elect leaders in the White House and Congress that will respect God and lead America to live in peace with our Creator and each other. We must elect leaders who are men of moral integrity, who are truthful, respect the voters, and respect our democratic process. We need leaders who will once again respect right and wrong, and not what is politically correct or politically expedient. It appears more could be accomplished if all members of Congress would put aside party lines and work towards the betterment of our Nation.

The Supreme Court is composed of nine men. Let us pray they have the humility to respect the Constitution of the United States and the Natural Law!

We must save our environment!

We must balance the budget and we must pay off the National Debt! In 1960 the United States had a balanced budget! Now we have a 5.5 trillion national debt! The American economy is increasingly becoming dependent on foreign capital for its livelihood. Will it become impossible for us to support the Federal Government, to the point we must be supported by the International Monetary Fund, and thus become subserviant to the United Nations and a one-world order? Are we reaching a point where the Federal Government will have to represent the United Nations and foreign interests *before* the interests of the American people? Is this the beginning of a one-world order under the United Nations?

Or will just the opposite happen, will the debt become so burdensome that the Federal government will collapse, and we will end up like Russia, with each of the 50 states becoming a new country?

Until the debt is paid, we need to drastically reduce the size of the Federal bureaucracy, if necessary, to the same budget as 1960!

We need to encourage the media to once again become purveyors of goodness and morality. This is really up to the American people. If we become selective and moral in our choices, the media will get the message.

Let us return to our traditional American heritage and live in harmony with our Creator. We need to allow religious freedom in our schools once again, to allow our children to be raised in a Judeo-Christian environment, to learn to respect God, their parents and neighbors, and themselves. If 93% of Americans believe in God, and 80% belong to one of the three major religions, it is only democratic that school prayer be allowed four of five days every week!

10 Pray!

And to teach, by	Farewell, farewell! but this I tell
his own example,	To thee, thou Wedding Guest!
love and reverence	He prayeth well, who loveth well
to all things that	Both man and bird and beast.
God made and loveth.	He prayeth best, who lovest best
	All things both great and small;
	For the dear God who loveth us,
	He made and loveth all.

Samuel Taylor Coleridge
The Rime of the Ancient Mariner, 1798

This is the last message of the Ancient Mariner to the Wedding Guest.
It is for us to pray, to love, and to respect all around us. We must pray for peace.
We must pray for our families, for our leaders, for our Nation.

Mary in Medjugorje is said to continually urge us to prayer. She tells us that prayer can stop wars, and alter future events, and protect us from evil.

My children, you have forgotten.
Through prayer and fasting one can stop wars,
One can suspend the laws of nature.
July 21, 1982

Mary tells us that prayer will bring peace in your heart, then, like a ripple effect, peace in your family, peace in your nation, and world peace. We must change ourselves before we can change our country.

Dear children,
I , your Mother, love you and want to encourage you to prayer.
I am tireless, and keep calling you even when you are far from my
heart. I am a Mother, and although I feel pain for each who has gone
astray, I forgive easily and I am happy about each child that returns
to me.
November 14, 1985

Dear children,
I am praying for you and I intercede before God for each individual.
I am looking for your prayers, that you accept me and accept my
       messages as in the first days of the apparition.
And only then, when you open your hearts and pray,
    will miracles happen.

September 25, 1993

Mary uses the analogy of a flower to describe the effects of prayer:

I want to invite you again to prayer today.
When praying you are much more beautiful, like flowers
which after snow, show all their beauty and all their colors
become indescribable. Likewise, after prayer, you show to
better advantage before God, all your good points,
which makes you dear to Him. So, dear children, pray and
open your inner self to the Lord that He may make you a
harmonious and beautiful flower for heaven.

December 18, 1986

Mary urges us to pray in these recent messages:

Dear children,
Today I am with you and I, again, call all of you to come closer
    to me through your prayers. In a special way,
I call you to renunciation in this time of grace.
Meditate on and live, through your little sacrifices,
    the passion and death of Jesus for each of you.
Only if you come closer to Jesus will you comprehend
    the immeasurable love He has for each of you.
Through prayer and your renunciation you will become more
open to the gift of faith and love towards the Church
    and the people who are around you.
    I love you and bless you.
    Thank you for having responded to my call.

February 25, 1998

246

Dear children!
Today I call you, through prayer, to open yourselves to
God as a flower opens itself to the rays of the morning sun.
Little children, do not be afraid.
I am with you and I intercede before God for each of you so
that your heart receives the gift of conversion.
Only in this way, little children, will you comprehend the importance
of grace in these times and God will become nearer to you.

April 25, 1998

On July 13, 1917, Mary at Fatima said "In the end my Immaculate Heart will triumph." On October 25, 1998 Mary again referred to her Immaculate Heart:

Today I call you to come closer to my Immaculate Heart.
I call you to renew in your families the fervor of the first days
when I called you to fasting, prayer and conversion.
Little children, you accepted my messages with open hearts,
although you did not know what prayer was.
Today, I call you to open yourselves completely to me so that
I may transform you and lead you to the heart of my son
Jesus, so that he can fill you with his love. Only in this way
will you find true peace - the peace that only God gives you.

October 25, 1998

Mary in her message of November 25, 1998 speaks of the coming of Jesus:

Dear children!
Today I call you to prepare yourselves for the coming of Jesus.
In a special way, prepare your hearts. May holy Confession
be the first act of conversion for you and then, dear children,
decide for holiness. May your conversion and decision for
holiness begin today and not tomorrow. Little children, I call you all
to the way of salvation and I desire to show you the way to Heaven.
That is why, be mine and decide with me for holiness. Little
children, accept prayer with seriousness and pray, pray, pray.

November 25, 1998

Remember what Jesus said about prayer:

Ask and it will be given to you;
Seek and you will find;
knock and the door will be opened to you.
For everyone who asks, receives; and the one who seeks, finds,
    and to him who knocks, it will be opened.
Or what man of you if his son asks him for bread, will give him a
    stone? Or if he asks for a fish, will give him a serpent?
    If you then, who are evil,
        know how to give good gifts to your children,
    how much more will your Father who is in heaven
        give good things to those who ask him!
            St. Matthew 7:7-11 [RSV]

There is a convergence of thought noted in the Dead Sea Scrolls, the Bible, and now, the messages of Mary in Medjugorje.

In the Dead Sea Scrolls, we learned of the "War Scroll," probably written by the conservative Hebrew sect known as the Essenes. This speaks of the final battle between the Sons of Light and the Sons of Darkness. With God's help, the seventh battle is won by the Sons of Light.

The Bible speaks of the children of light:

Live as children of light,
    for light produces every kind of goodness
        and righteousness and truth.
 Try to learn what is pleasing to the Lord.
Take no part in the fruitless works of darkness;
    rather expose them, for it is shameful even
    to mention the things done by them in secret;
    but everything exposed by the light becomes visible,
    for everything that becomes visible is light.
Therefore, it says:
    "Awake, O sleeper, and arise from the dead,
        and Christ will give you light."
        St. Paul to the Ephesians 5:8-14 [New American]

With this in mind, the following message of Mary in Medjugorje becomes quite meaningful, as she echoes the Bible and the Dead Sea Scrolls:

Dear children, I want you to understand I am your mother.
That I want to help you and I call you to prayer.
Only by prayer can you understand
and accept my messages and practice them in your life.
Read Sacred Scripture,
live it, and pray to understand the signs of the time.
This is a special time.
Therefore I am with you to draw you
close to my heart and the heart of my son, Jesus.
Dear children,
I want you to be children of the light
and not of the darkness.
Therefore, live what I am telling you.
August 25, 1993

Revelation speaks of the new Jerusalem and peace for men of good will.

And I saw a new heaven and a new earth.
For the first heaven and the first earth had passed away,
and the sea is now no more.
And I John saw the holy city, the new Jerusalem,
coming down out of heaven from God,
prepared as a bride adorned for her husband.
And I heard a great voice from the throne, saying:
Behold the tabernacle of God with men,
and he shall dwell with them.
And they shall be his people;
and God himself with them shall be their God.
And God shall wipe away all tears from their eyes:
and death shall be no more,
nor mourning, nor crying, nor sorrow shall be any more,
for the former things are passed away.
Revelation of John 21:1-4 [Douay Rheims]

Christianity awaits the Second Coming of Jesus. The Hebrew people wait for the Messiah. The Dead Sea Scrolls speak of the great battle between the sons of light and the sons of darkness. The Gospel of John and St. Paul in the Bible speak on the sons or children of light. The Book of Revelation speaks of the battle between good and evil before the time of peace.
St. Paul tells us the children of the light must be vigilant for the Day of the Lord!

For you yourselves know very well that the
day of the Lord will come like a thief at night.
When people are saying, "Peace and security,"
then sudden disaster comes upon them,
like labor pains upon a pregnant woman,
and they will not escape.
But you, brothers, are not in darkness,
for that day to overtake you like a thief.
For all of you are children of the light
and children of the day.
We are not of the night or of darkness.
Therefore, let us not sleep as the rest do,
but let us stay alert and sober.
First letter of St. Paul to the Thessalonians 5:2-6 [New American]

St. John tells us so clearly an essential message of the Bible:

For God so loved the world that he gave his only Son,
that whoever believes in him should not perish
but have eternal life.
John 3:16 [RSV]

The Bible ends with a final call:

And the Spirit and the bride say "Come!"
And he that heareth let him say, "Come!"
And he that thirsteth, let him come;
And he that will, let him take the water of life freely.
Revelation 22:17 [Douay-Rheims]

250

After all, it was Jesus himself who said in the Gospels:

Come, follow me
Matthew 4:19 and Mark 1:17

This is what we must do to save our nation. I have faith that this will work.

We must live in harmony once again with God Our Creator and the Natural Law.

We must begin with ourselves and develop inner peace through prayer and acts of love, forgiveness, and mercy. It is up to all of us to change ourselves for the better. It is up to all of us to improve how we interact with our families, friends, and neighbors.

It is up to all of us to seek the truth and support what is right.

And, yes, it is up to you!

APPENDIX

The Appendix is the final Book of the New Testament of the Holy Bible, Revelation or the Apocalypse of John. This is the Revised Standard Version, the language being the exact same for all of Christianity.

The Book of Revelation from the Revised Standard Version of the Bible, copyright 1946, 1952, and 1971, is used by permission from the Division of Christian Education of the National Council of the Churches of Christ in the USA. It is reprinted via Harmony Media, Inc. of Gervais, Oregon.

The Book of Revelation is the only book of prophecy in the New Testament, written by the Apostle John on the island of Patmos in the Aegean Sea, while he was in exile, reportably in the year 95 or 96 A. D. Written in symbolism, the book has always been surrounded by mystery, and has fascinated mankind throughout the ages as to its meaning.

The Book of Revelation describes The Book of Life and gives a clear warning about the Final Day of Judgement.

The Book of Revelation is at once frightening, as it speaks of the rise of the antichrist and the end of the age, dramatic as it describes the final battle of good and evil, and, above all, optimistic, as it points to the triumph of Jesus Christ over evil and the dawn of a new creation.

Revelation or the Apocalypse of John

Chapter 1

1   The revelation of Jesus Christ, which God gave him to show to his servants what must soon take place; and he made it known by sending his angel to his servant John, 2 who bore witness to the word of God and to the testimony of Jesus Christ, even to all that he saw. 3 Blessed is he who reads aloud the words of the prophecy, and blessed are those who hear, and who keep what is written therein; for the time is near.

4   John to the seven churches that are in Asia:

Grace to you and peace from him who is and who was and who is to come, and from the seven spirits who are before his throne, 5 and from Jesus Christ the faithful witness, the first-born of the dead, and the ruler of kings on earth.

To him who loves us and has freed us from our sins by his blood 6 and made us a kingdom, priests to his God and Father, to him be glory and dominion for ever and ever. Amen.

7 Behold, he is coming with the clouds, and every eye will see him, every one who pierced him; and all tribes of the earth will wail on account of him. Even so. Amen.

8 "I am the Alpha and the Omega," says the Lord God, who is and who was and who is to come, the Almighty.

9 I John, your brother, who share with you in Jesus the tribulation and the kingdom and the patient endurance, was on the island called Patmos on account of the word of God and the testimony of Jesus. 10 I was in the Spirit on the Lord's day, and I heard behind me a loud voice like a trumpet 11 saying, "Write what you see in a book and send it to the seven churches, to Ephesus and to Smyrna and to Pergamum and to Thyatira and to Sardis and to Philadelphia and to Laodicea."

12 Then I turned to see the voice that was speaking to me, and on turning I saw seven golden lampstands, 13 and in the midst of the lampstands one like a son of man, clothed with a long robe and with a golden girdle round his breast; 14 his head and his hair were white as white wool, white as snow; his eyes were like a flame of fire, 15 his feet were like burnished bronze, refined as in a furnace, and his voice was like the sound of many waters; 16 in his right hand he held seven stars, from his mouth issued a sharp two-edged sword, and his face was like the sun shining in full strength.

17 When I saw him, I fell at his feet as though dead. But he laid his right hand upon me, saying, "Fear not, I am the first and the last, 18 and the living one; I died, and behold I am alive for evermore, and I have the keys of Death and Hades. 19 Now write what you see, what is and what is to take place hereafter.

20 As for the mystery of the seven stars which you saw in my right hand, and the seven golden lampstands, the seven stars are the angels of the seven churches and the seven lampstands are the seven churches.

Chapter 2

1 "To the angel of the church in Ephesus write: 'The words of him who holds the seven stars in his right hand, who walks among the seven golden

lampstands.

2   "'I know your works, your toil and your patient endurance, and how you cannot bear evil men but have tested those who call themselves apostles but are not, and found them to be false; 3 I know you are enduring patiently and bearing up for my name's sake, and you have not grown weary. 4 But I have this against you, that you have abandoned the love you had at first. 5 Remember then from what you have fallen, repent and do the works you did at first. If not, I will come to you and remove your lampstand from its place, unless you repent. 6 Yet this you have, you hate the works of the Nicolaitans, which I also hate. 7 He who has an ear, let him hear what the Spirit says to the churches. To him who conquers I will grant to eat of the tree of life, which is in the paradise of God.'

8   "And to the angel of the church in Smyrna write: 'The words of the first and the last, who died and came to life.

9   "'I know your tribulation and your poverty (but you are rich) and the slander of those who say that they are Jews and are not, but are a synagogue of Satan. 10 Do not fear what you are about to suffer. Behold, the devil is about to throw some of you into prison, that you may be tested, and for ten days you will have tribulation. Be faithful unto death, and I will give you the crown of life. 11 He who has an ear, let him hear what the Spirit says to the churches. He who conquers shall not be hurt by the second death.'

12   "And to the angel of the church in Pergamum write: 'The words of him who has the sharp two-edged sword.

13   "'I know where you dwell, where Satan's throne is; you hold fast my name and you did not deny my faith even in the days of Antipas my witness, my faithful one, who was killed among you, where Satan dwells. 14 But I have a few things against you: you have some there who hold the teaching of Balaam, who taught Balak to put a stumbling block before the sons of Israel, that they might eat food sacrificed to idols and practice immorality. 15 So you also have some who hold the teaching of the Nicolaitans. 16 Repent then. If not, I will come to you soon and war against them with the sword of my mouth. 17 He who has an ear, let him hear what the Spirit says to the churches. To him who conquers I will give some of the hidden manna, and I will give him a white stone, with a new name written on the stone which no one knows except him who receives it.'

18   "And to the angel of the church in Thyatira write: 'The words of the Son of God, who has eyes like a flame of fire, and whose feet are like burnished bronze.

19   "'I know your works, your love and faith and service and patient endurance, and that your latter works exceed the first. 20* But I have this against
you, that you tolerate the woman Jezebel, who calls herself a prophetess and
is teaching and beguiling my servants to practice immorality and to eat food
sacrificed to idols. 21 I gave her time to repent, but she refuses to repent of
her immorality. 22 Behold, I will throw her on a sickbed, and those who commit adultery with her I will throw into great tribulation, unless they repent of
her doings; 23 and I will strike her children dead. And all the churches shall
know that I am he who searches mind and heart, and I will give to each of you
as your works deserve. 24 But to the rest of you in Thyatira, who do not hold
this teaching, who have not learned what some call the deep things of Satan,
to you I say, I do not lay upon you any other burden; 25 only hold fast what
you have, until I come. 26 He who conquers and who keeps my works until
the end, I will give him power over the nations, 27 and he shall rule them with
a rod of iron, as when earthen pots are broken in pieces, even as I myself
have received power from my Father; 28 and I will give him the morning star.
29 He who has an ear, let him hear what the Spirit says to the churches.'

Chapter 3

1   "And to the angel of the church in Sardis write: 'The words of him who
has the seven spirits of God and the seven stars.
          "'I know your works; you have the name of being alive, and you are
dead. 2 Awake, and strengthen what remains and is on the point of death, for
I have not found your works perfect in the sight of my God. 3 Remember then
what you received and heard; keep that, and repent. If you will not awake, I
will come like a thief, and you will not know at what hour I will come upon you.
4 Yet you have still a few names in Sardis, people who have not soiled their
garments; and they shall walk with me in white, for they are worthy. 5 He who
conquers shall be clad thus in white garments, and I will not blot his name out
of the book of life; I will confess his name before my Father and before his
angels. 6 He who has an ear, let him hear what the Spirit says to the
churches.'
7   "And to the angel of the church in Philadelphia write: 'The words of the
holy one, the true one, who has the key of David, who opens and no one shall
shut, who shuts and no one opens.
8   "'I know your works. Behold, I have set before you an open door, which

no one is able to shut; I know that you have but little power, and yet you have kept my word and have not denied my name. 9 Behold, I will make those of the synagogue of Satan who say that they are Jews and are not, but lie-- behold, I will make them come and bow down before your feet, and learn that I have loved you. 10 Because you have kept my word of patient endurance, I will keep you from the hour of trial which is coming on the whole world, to try those who dwell upon the earth. 11 I am coming soon; hold fast what you have, so that no one may seize your crown. 12 He who conquers, I will make him a pillar in the temple of my God; never shall he go out of it, and I will write on him the name of my God, and the name of the city of my God, the new Jerusalem which comes down from my God out of heaven, and my own new name. 13 He who has an ear, let him hear what the Spirit says to the churches.'

14   "And to the angel of the church in Laodicea write: 'The words of the Amen, the faithful and true witness, the beginning of God's creation.

15   "'I know your works: you are neither cold nor hot. Would that you were cold or hot! 16 So, because you are lukewarm, and neither cold nor hot, I will spew you out of my mouth. 17 For you say, I am rich, I have prospered, and I need nothing; not knowing that you are wretched, pitiable, poor, blind, and naked. 18 Therefore I counsel you to buy from me gold refined by fire, that you may be rich, and white garments to clothe you and to keep the shame of your nakedness from being seen, and salve to anoint your eyes, that you may see. 19 Those whom I love, I reprove and chasten; so be zealous and re- pent. 20 Behold, I stand at the door and knock; if any one hears my voice and opens the door, I will come in to him and eat with him, and he with me. 21 He who conquers, I will grant him to sit with me on my throne, as I myself con- quered and sat down with my Father on his throne. 22 He who has an ear, let him hear what the Spirit says to the churches.'"

Chapter 4

1   After this I looked, and lo, in heaven an open door! And the first voice, which I had heard speaking to me like a trumpet, said, "Come up hither, and I will show you what must take place after this." 2 At once I was in the Spirit, and lo, a throne stood in heaven, with one seated on the throne! 3 And he who sat there appeared like jasper and carnelian, and round the throne was a rainbow that looked like an emerald. 4 Round the throne were twenty-four thrones, and seated on the thrones were twenty-four elders, clad in white

garments, with golden crowns upon their heads. 5 From the throne issue flashes of lightning, and voices and peals of thunder, and before the throne burn seven torches of fire, which are the seven spirits of God; 6 and before the throne there is as it were a sea of glass, like crystal.

And round the throne, on each side of the throne, are four living creatures, full of eyes in front and behind: 7 the first living creature like a lion, the second living creature like an ox, the third living creature with the face of a man, and the fourth living creature like a flying eagle. 8 And the four living creatures, each of them with six wings, are full of eyes all round and within, and day and night they never cease to sing, "Holy, holy, holy, is the Lord God Almighty, who was and is and is to come!" 9 And whenever the living creatures give glory and honor and thanks to him who is seated on the throne, who lives for ever and ever, 10 the twenty-four elders fall down before him who is seated on the throne and worship him who lives for ever and ever; they cast their crowns before the throne, singing, 11 "Worthy art thou, our Lord and God, to receive glory and honor and power, for thou didst create all things, and by thy will they existed and were created."

Chapter 5

1   And I saw in the right hand of him who was seated on the throne a scroll written within and on the back, sealed with seven seals; 2 and I saw a strong angel proclaiming with a loud voice, "Who is worthy to open the scroll and break its seals?" 3 And no one in heaven or on earth or under the earth was able to open the scroll or to look into it, 4 and I wept much that no one was found worthy to open the scroll or to look into it. 5 Then one of the elders said to me, "Weep not; lo, the Lion of the tribe of Judah, the Root of David, has conquered, so that he can open the scroll and its seven seals."

6   And between the throne and the four living creatures and among the elders, I saw a Lamb standing, as though it had been slain, with seven horns and with seven eyes, which are the seven spirits of God sent out into all the earth; 7 and he went and took the scroll from the right hand of him who was seated on the throne. 8 And when he had taken the scroll, the four living creatures and the twenty-four elders fell down before the Lamb, each holding a harp, and with golden bowls full of incense, which are the prayers of the saints; 9 and they sang a new song, saying, "Worthy art thou to take the scroll and to open its seals, for thou wast slain and by thy blood didst ransom men for God from every tribe and tongue and people and nation, 10 and hast

made them a kingdom and priests to our God, and they shall reign on earth."
11 Then I looked, and I heard around the throne and the living creatures and
the elders the voice of many angels, numbering myriads of myriads and
thousands of thousands, 12 saying with a loud voice, "Worthy is the Lamb
who was slain, to receive power and wealth and wisdom and might and honor
and glory and blessing!" 13 And I heard every creature in heaven and on
earth and under the earth and in the sea, and all therein, saying, "To him who
sits upon the throne and to the Lamb be blessing and honor and glory and
might for ever and ever!" 14 And the four living creatures said, "Amen!" and
the elders fell down and worshiped.

Chapter 6

1   Now I saw when the Lamb opened one of the **seven seals**, and I
heard one of the four living creatures say, as with a voice of thunder, "Come!"
2 And I saw, and behold, a white horse, and its rider had a bow; and a crown
was given to him, and he went out conquering and to conquer.
3   When he opened the second seal, I heard the second living creature
say, "Come!" 4 And out came another horse, bright red; its rider was permitted
to take peace from the earth, so that men should slay one another; and he
was given a great sword.
5   When he opened the third seal, I heard the third living creature say,
"Come!" And I saw, and behold, a black horse, and its rider had a balance in
his hand; 6 and I heard what seemed to be a voice in the midst of the four
living creatures saying, "A quart of wheat for a denarius, * and three quarts of
barley for a denarius; but do not harm oil and wine!"
7   When he opened the fourth seal, I heard the voice of the fourth living
creature say, "Come!" 8 And I saw, and **behold, a pale horse**, and its rider's
name was **Death**, and Hades followed him; and they were given power over a
fourth of the earth, to kill with sword and with famine and with pestilence and
by wild beasts of the earth.
9   When he opened the fifth seal, I saw under the altar the souls of those
who had been slain for the word of God and for the witness they had borne;
10 they cried out with a loud voice, "O Sovereign Lord, holy and true, how
long before thou wilt judge and avenge our blood on those who dwell upon
the earth?" 11 Then they were each given a white robe and told to rest a little
longer, until the number of their fellow servants and their brethren should be
complete, who were to be killed as they themselves had been.

12   When he opened the sixth seal, I looked, and behold, there was a great earthquake; and the sun became black as sackcloth, the full moon became like blood, 13 and the stars of the sky fell to the earth as the fig tree sheds its winter fruit when shaken by a gale; 14 the sky vanished like a scroll that is rolled up, and every mountain and island was removed from its place. 15 Then the kings of the earth and the great men and the generals and the rich and the strong, and every one, slave and free, hid in the caves and among the rocks of the mountains, 16 calling to the mountains and rocks, "Fall on us and hide us from the face of him who is seated on the throne, and from the wrath of the Lamb; 17 for the great day of their wrath has come, and who can stand before it?"

Chapter 7

1   After this I saw four angels standing at the four corners of the earth, holding back the four winds of the earth, that no wind might blow on earth or sea or against any tree. 2 Then I saw another angel ascend from the rising of the sun, with the seal of the living God, and he called with a loud voice to the four angels who had been given power to harm earth and sea, 3 saying, "Do not harm the earth or the sea or the trees, till we have sealed the servants of our God upon their foreheads." 4 And I heard the number of the sealed, a hundred and forty-four thousand sealed, out of every tribe of the sons of Israel, 5 twelve thousand sealed out of the tribe of Judah, twelve thousand of the tribe of Reuben, twelve thousand of the tribe of Gad, 6 twelve thousand of the tribe of Asher, twelve thousand of the tribe of Naphtali, twelve thousand of the tribe of Manasseh, 7 twelve thousand of the tribe of Simeon, twelve thousand of the tribe of Levi, twelve thousand of the tribe of Issachar, 8 twelve thousand of the tribe of Zebulun, twelve thousand of the tribe of Joseph, twelve thousand sealed out of the tribe of Benjamin.
9   After this I looked, and behold, a great multitude which no man could number, from every nation, from all tribes and peoples and tongues, standing before the throne and before the Lamb, clothed in white robes, with palm branches in their hands, 10 and crying out with a loud voice, "Salvation belongs to our God who sits upon the throne, and to the Lamb!" 11 And all the angels stood round the throne and round the elders and the four living creatures, and they fell on their faces before the throne and worshiped God, 12 saying, "Amen! Blessing and glory and wisdom and thanksgiving and honor and power and might be to our God for ever and ever! Amen."

13   Then one of the elders addressed me, saying, "Who are these, clothed in white robes, and whence have they come?" 14 I said to him, "Sir, you know." And he said to me, "These are they who have come out of the great tribulation; they have washed their robes and made them white in the blood of the Lamb.

15   Therefore are they before the throne of God, and serve him day and night within his temple; and he who sits upon the throne will shelter them with his presence. 16 They shall hunger no more, neither thirst any more; the sun shall not strike them, nor any scorching heat. 17 For the Lamb in the midst of the throne will be their shepherd, and he will guide them to springs of living water; and God will wipe away every tear from their eyes."

Chapter 8

1   When the Lamb opened the **seventh seal**, there was silence in heaven for about half an hour. 2 Then I saw the seven angels who stand before God, and **seven trumpets** were given to them. 3 And another angel came and stood at the altar with a golden censer; and he was given much incense to mingle with the prayers of all the saints upon the golden altar before the throne; 4 and the smoke of the incense rose with the prayers of the saints from the hand of the angel before God. 5 Then the angel took the censer and filled it with fire from the altar and threw it on the earth; and there were peals of thunder, voices, flashes of lightning, and an earthquake.

6   Now the seven angels who had the seven trumpets made ready to blow them.

7   The first angel blew his trumpet, and there followed hail and fire, mixed with blood, which fell on the earth; and a third of the earth was burnt up, and a third of the trees were burnt up, and all green grass was burnt up.

8   The second angel blew his trumpet, and something like a great mountain, burning with fire, was thrown into the sea; 9 and a third of the sea became blood, a third of the living creatures in the sea died, and a third of the ships were destroyed.

10   The third angel blew his trumpet, and a great star fell from heaven, blazing like a torch, and it fell on a third of the rivers and on the fountains of water. 11 The name of the star is Wormwood. A third of the waters became wormwood, and many men died of the water, because it was made bitter.

12   The fourth angel blew his trumpet, and a third of the sun was struck, and a third of the moon, and a third of the stars, so that a third of their light

was darkened; a third of the day was kept from shining, and likewise a third of the night.

13   Then I looked, and I heard an eagle crying with a loud voice, as it flew in midheaven, "Woe, woe, woe to those who dwell on the earth, at the blasts of the other trumpets which the three angels are about to blow!"

Chapter 9

1   And the fifth angel blew his trumpet, and I saw a star fallen from heaven to earth, and he was given the key of the shaft of the bottomless pit; 2 he opened the shaft of the bottomless pit, and from the shaft rose smoke like the smoke of a great furnace, and the sun and the air were darkened with the smoke from the shaft. 3 Then from the smoke came locusts on the earth, and they were given power like the power of scorpions of the earth; 4 they were told not to harm the grass of the earth or any green growth or any tree, but only those of mankind who have not the seal of God upon their foreheads; 5 they were allowed to torture them for five months, but not to kill them, and their torture was like the torture of a scorpion, when it stings a man. 6 And in those days men will seek death and will not find it; they will long to die, and death will fly from them.

7   In appearance the locusts were like horses arrayed for battle; on their heads were what looked like crowns of gold; their faces were like human faces, 8 their hair like women's hair, and their teeth like lions' teeth; 9 they had scales like iron breastplates, and the noise of their wings was like the noise of many chariots with horses rushing into battle. 10 They have tails like scorpions, and stings, and their power of hurting men for five months lies in their tails. 11 They have as king over them the angel of the bottomless pit; his name in Hebrew is Abaddon, and in Greek he is called Apollyon.

12   The first woe has passed; behold, two woes are still to come.

13   Then the sixth angel blew his trumpet, and I heard a voice from the four horns of the golden altar before God, 14 saying to the sixth angel who had the trumpet, "Release the four angels who are bound at the great river Euphrates." 15 So the four angels were released, who had been held ready for the hour, the day, the month, and the year, to kill a third of mankind. 16 The number of the troops of cavalry was twice ten thousand times ten thousand; I heard their number. 17 And this was how I saw the horses in my vision: the riders wore breastplates the color of fire and of sapphire and of sulphur, and the heads of the horses were like lions' heads, and fire and

smoke and sulphur issued from their mouths. 18 By these three plagues a third of mankind was killed, by the fire and smoke and sulphur issuing from their mouths. 19 For the power of the horses is in their mouths and in their tails; their tails are like serpents, with heads, and by means of them they wound.

20   The rest of mankind, who were not killed by these plagues, did not repent of the works of their hands nor give up worshiping demons and idols of gold and silver and bronze and stone and wood, which cannot either see or hear or walk; 21 nor did they repent of their murders or their sorceries or their immorality or their thefts.

Chapter 10

1   Then I saw another mighty angel coming down from heaven, wrapped in a cloud, with a rainbow over his head, and his face was like the sun, and his legs like pillars of fire. 2 He had a little scroll open in his hand. And he set his right foot on the sea, and his left foot on the land, 3 and called out with a loud voice, like a lion roaring; when he called out, the seven thunders sounded. 4 And when the seven thunders had sounded, I was about to write, but I heard a voice from heaven saying, "Seal up what the seven thunders have said, and do not write it down." 5 And the angel whom I saw standing on sea and land lifted up his right hand to heaven 6 and swore by him who lives for ever and ever, who created heaven and what is in it, the earth and what is in it, and the sea and what is in it, that there should be no more delay, 7 but that in the days of the trumpet call to be sounded by the seventh angel, the mystery of God, as he announced to his servants the prophets, should be fulfilled.

8   Then the voice which I had heard from heaven spoke to me again, saying, "Go, take the scroll which is open in the hand of the angel who is standing on the sea and on the land." 9 So I went to the angel and told him to give me the little scroll; and he said to me, "Take it and eat; it will be bitter to your stomach, but sweet as honey in your mouth." 10 And I took the little scroll from the hand of the angel and ate it; it was sweet as honey in my mouth, but when I had eaten it my stomach was made bitter. 11 And I was told, "You must again prophesy about many peoples and nations and tongues and kings."

Chapter 11

1   Then I was given a measuring rod like a staff, and I was told: "Rise and measure the temple of God and the altar and those who worship there, 2 but do not measure the court outside the temple; leave that out, for it is given over to the nations, and they will trample over the holy city for forty-two months. 3 And I will grant my two witnesses power to prophesy for one thousand two hundred and sixty days, clothed in sackcloth."

4   These are the two olive trees and the two lampstands which stand before the Lord of the earth. 5 And if any one would harm them, fire pours out from their mouth and consumes their foes; if any one would harm them, thus he is doomed to be killed. 6 They have power to shut the sky, that no rain may fall during the days of their prophesying, and they have power over the waters to turn them into blood, and to smite the earth with every plague, as often as they desire. 7 And when they have finished their testimony, the beast that ascends from the bottomless pit will make war upon them and conquer them and kill them, 8 and their dead bodies will lie in the street of the great city which is allegorically called Sodom and Egypt, where their Lord was crucified. 9 For three days and a half men from the peoples and tribes and tongues and nations gaze at their dead bodies and refuse to let them be placed in a tomb, 10 and those who dwell on the earth will rejoice over them and make merry and exchange presents, because these two prophets had been a torment to those who dwell on the earth. 11 But after the three and a half days a breath of life from God entered them, and they stood up on their feet, and great fear fell on those who saw them. 12 Then they heard a loud voice from heaven saying to them, "Come up hither!" And in the sight of their foes they went up to heaven in a cloud. 13 And at that hour there was a great earthquake, and a tenth of the city fell; seven thousand people were killed in the earthquake, and the rest were terrified and gave glory to the God of heaven.

14   The second woe has passed; behold, the third woe is soon to come.

15   Then the seventh angel blew his trumpet, and there were loud voices in heaven, saying, "The kingdom of the world has become the kingdom of our Lord and of his Christ, and he shall reign for ever and ever." 16 And the twenty-four elders who sit on their thrones before God fell on their faces and worshiped God, 17 saying,"We give thanks to thee, Lord God Almighty, who art and who wast, that thou hast taken thy great power and begun to reign. 18 The nations raged, but thy wrath came, and the time for the dead to be

judged, for rewarding thy servants, the prophets and saints, and those who fear thy name, both small and great, and for destroying the destroyers of the earth."

19   Then God's temple in heaven was opened, and the ark of his covenant was seen within his temple; and there were flashes of lightning, voices, peals of thunder, an earthquake, and heavy hail.

Chapter 12

1   And a great portent appeared in heaven, a woman clothed with the sun, with the moon under her feet, and on her head a crown of twelve stars;   2 she was with child and she cried out in her pangs of birth, in anguish for delivery. 3 And another portent appeared in heaven; behold, a great red dragon, with seven heads and ten horns, and seven diadems upon his heads. 4 His tail swept down a third of the stars of heaven, and cast them to the earth. And the dragon stood before the woman who was about to bear a child, that he might devour her child when she brought it forth; 5 she brought forth a male child, one who is to rule all the nations with a rod of iron, but her child was caught up to God and to his throne, 6 and the woman fled into the wilderness, where she has a place prepared by God, in which to be nourished for one thousand two hundred and sixty days.

7   Now war arose in heaven, Michael and his angels fighting against the dragon; and the dragon and his angels fought, 8 but they were defeated and there was no longer any place for them in heaven. 9 And the great dragon was thrown down, that ancient serpent, who is called the Devil and Satan, the deceiver of the whole world--he was thrown down to the earth, and his angels were thrown down with him. 10 And I heard a loud voice in heaven, saying, "Now the salvation and the power and the kingdom of our God and the authority of his Christ have come, for the accuser of our brethren has been thrown down, who accuses them day and night before our God. 11 And they have conquered him by the blood of the Lamb and by the word of their testimony, for they loved not their lives even unto death. 12 Rejoice then, O heaven and you that dwell therein! But woe to you, O earth and sea, for the devil has come down to you in great wrath, because he knows that his time is short!"

13   And when the dragon saw that he had been thrown down to the earth, he pursued the woman who had borne the male child. 14 But the woman was given the two wings of the great eagle that she might fly from the serpent into

the wilderness, to the place where she is to be nourished for a time, and times, and half a time. 15 The serpent poured water like a river out of his mouth after the woman, to sweep her away with the flood. 16 But the earth came to the help of the woman, and the earth opened its mouth and swallowed the river which the dragon had poured from his mouth. 17 Then the dragon was angry with the woman, and went off to make war on the rest of her offspring, on those who keep the commandments of God and bear testimony to Jesus. And he stood on the sand of the sea.

Chapter 13

1   And I saw a beast rising out of the sea, with ten horns and seven heads, with ten diadems upon its horns and a blasphemous name upon its heads. 2 And the beast that I saw was like a leopard, its feet were like a bear's, and its mouth was like a lion's mouth. And to it the dragon gave his power and his throne and great authority. 3 One of its heads seemed to have a mortal wound, but its mortal wound was healed, and the whole earth followed the beast with wonder. 4 Men worshiped the dragon, for he had given his authority to the beast, and they worshiped the beast, saying, "Who is like the beast, and who can fight against it?"
5   And the beast was given a mouth uttering haughty and blasphemous words, and it was allowed to exercise authority for forty-two months; 6 it opened its mouth to utter blasphemies against God, blaspheming his name and his dwelling, that is, those who dwell in heaven. 7 Also it was allowed to make war on the saints and to conquer them. And authority was given it over every tribe and people and tongue and nation, 8 and all who dwell on earth will worship it, every one whose name has not been written before the foundation of the world in the book of life of the Lamb that was slain. 9 If any one has an ear, let him hear: 10 If any one is to be taken captive, to captivity he goes; if any one slays with the sword, with the sword must he be slain. Here is a call for the endurance and faith of the saints.
11   Then I saw another beast which rose out of the earth; it had two horns like a lamb and it spoke like a dragon. 12 It exercises all the authority of the first beast in its presence, and makes the earth and its inhabitants worship the first beast, whose mortal wound was healed. 13 It works great signs, even making fire come down from heaven to earth in the sight of men; 14 and by the signs which it is allowed to work in the presence of the beast, it deceives those who dwell on earth, bidding them make an image for the beast which

was wounded by the sword and yet lived; 15 and it was allowed to give breath to the image of the beast so that the image of the beast should even speak, and to cause those who would not worship the image of the beast to be slain. 16 Also it causes all, both small and great, both rich and poor, both free and slave, to be marked on the right hand or the forehead, 17 so that no one can buy or sell unless he has the mark, that is, the name of the beast or the number of its name. 18 This calls for wisdom: let him who has understanding reckon the number of the beast, for it is a human number, its number is six hundred and sixty-six.

Chapter 14

1 Then I looked, and lo, on Mount Zion stood the Lamb, and with him a hundred and forty-four thousand who had his name and his Father's name written on their foreheads. 2 And I heard a voice from heaven like the sound of many waters and like the sound of loud thunder; the voice I heard was like the sound of harpers playing on their harps, 3 and they sing a new song before the throne and before the four living creatures and before the elders. No one could learn that song except the hundred and forty-four thousand who had been redeemed from the earth. 4 It is these who have not defiled themselves with women, for they are chaste; it is these who follow the Lamb wherever he goes; these have been redeemed from mankind as first fruits for God and the Lamb, 5 and in their mouth no lie was found, for they are spotless.

6 Then I saw another angel flying in midheaven, with an eternal gospel to proclaim to those who dwell on earth, to every nation and tribe and tongue and people; 7 and he said with a loud voice, "Fear God and give him glory, for the hour of his judgment has come; and worship him who made heaven and earth, the sea and the fountains of water."

8 Another angel, a second, followed, saying, "Fallen, fallen is Babylon the great, she who made all nations drink the wine of her impure passion."

9 And another angel, a third, followed them, saying with a loud voice, "If any one worships the beast and its image, and receives a mark on his forehead or on his hand, 10 he also shall drink the wine of God's wrath, poured unmixed into the cup of his anger, and he shall be tormented with fire and sulphur in the presence of the holy angels and in the presence of the Lamb. 11 And the smoke of their torment goes up for ever and ever; and they have no rest, day or night, these worshipers of the beast and its image, and who-

ever receives the mark of its name."

12   Here is a call for the endurance of the saints, those who keep the commandments of God and the faith of Jesus.

13   And I heard a voice from heaven saying, "Write this: Blessed are the dead who die in the Lord henceforth." "Blessed indeed," says the Spirit, "that they may rest from their labors, for their deeds follow them!"

14   Then I looked, and lo, a white cloud, and seated on the cloud one like a son of man, with a golden crown on his head, and a sharp sickle in his hand. 15 And another angel came out of the temple, calling with a loud voice to him who sat upon the cloud, "Put in your sickle, and reap, for the hour to reap has come, for the harvest of the earth is fully ripe." 16 So he who sat upon the cloud swung his sickle on the earth, and the earth was reaped.

17   And another angel came out of the temple in heaven, and he too had a sharp sickle. 18 Then another angel came out from the altar, the angel who has power over fire, and he called with a loud voice to him who had the sharp sickle, "Put in your sickle, and gather the clusters of the vine of the earth, for its grapes are ripe." 19 So the angel swung his sickle on the earth and gathered the vintage of the earth, and threw it into the great wine press of the wrath of God; 20 and the wine press was trodden outside the city, and blood flowed from the wine press, as high as a horse's bridle, for one thousand six hundred stadia.

Chapter 15

1   Then I saw another portent in heaven, great and wonderful, seven angels with seven plagues, which are the last, for with them the wrath of God is ended.

2   And I saw what appeared to be a sea of glass mingled with fire, and those who had conquered the beast and its image and the number of its name, standing beside the sea of glass with harps of God in their hands. 3 And they sing the song of Moses, the servant of God, and the song of the Lamb, saying,

"Great and wonderful are thy deeds, O Lord God the Almighty! Just and true are thy ways, O King of the ages! 4 Who shall not fear and glorify thy name, O Lord? For thou alone art holy. All nations shall come and worship thee, for thy judgments have been revealed."

5   After this I looked, and the temple of the tent of witness in heaven was opened, 6 and out of the temple came the seven angels with the seven

plagues, robed in pure bright linen, and their breasts girded with golden girdles. 7 And one of the four living creatures gave the seven angels seven golden bowls full of the wrath of God who lives for ever and ever; 8 and the temple was filled with smoke from the glory of God and from his power, and no one could enter the temple until the seven plagues of the seven angels were ended.

Chapter 16

1   Then I heard a loud voice from the temple telling the seven angels, "Go and pour out on the earth the **seven bowls** of the wrath of God."
2   So the first angel went and poured his bowl on the earth, and foul and evil sores came upon the men who bore the mark of the beast and worshiped its image.
3   The second angel poured his bowl into the sea, and it became like the blood of a dead man, and every living thing died that was in the sea.
4   The third angel poured his bowl into the rivers and the fountains of water, and they became blood. 5 And I heard the angel of water say,
    "Just art thou in these thy judgments, thou who art and wast, O Holy One. 6 For men have shed the blood of saints and prophets, and thou hast given them blood to drink. It is their due!" 7 And I heard the altar cry, "Yea, Lord God the Almighty, true and just are thy judgments!"
8   The fourth angel poured his bowl on the sun, and it was allowed to scorch men with fire; 9 men were scorched by the fierce heat, and they cursed the name of God who had power over these plagues, and they did not repent and give him glory.
10   The fifth angel poured his bowl on the throne of the beast, and its kingdom was in darkness; men gnawed their tongues in anguish 11 and cursed the God of heaven for their pain and sores, and did not repent of their deeds.
12   The sixth angel poured his bowl on the great river Euphrates, and its water was dried up, to prepare the way for the kings from the east. 13 And I saw, issuing from the mouth of the dragon and from the mouth of the beast and from the mouth of the false prophet, three foul spirits like frogs; 14 for they are demonic spirits, performing signs, who go abroad to the kings of the whole world, to assemble them for battle on the great day of God the Almighty. 15 ("Lo, I am coming like a thief! Blessed is he who is awake, keeping his garments that he may not go naked and be seen exposed!") 16 And

they assembled them at the place which is called in Hebrew Armageddon.
17   The seventh angel poured his bowl into the air, and a loud voice came out of the temple, from the throne, saying, "It is done!" 18 And there were flashes of lightning, voices, peals of thunder, and a great earthquake such as had never been since men were on the earth, so great was that earthquake. 19 The great city was split into three parts, and the cities of the nations fell, and God remembered great Babylon, to make her drain the cup of the fury of his wrath. 20 And every island fled away, and no mountains were to be found; 21 and great hailstones, heavy as a hundred-weight, dropped on men from heaven, till men cursed God for the plague of the hail, so fearful was that plague.

Chapter 17

1   Then one of the seven angels who had the seven bowls came and said to me, "Come, I will show you the judgment of the great harlot who is seated upon many waters, 2 with whom the kings of the earth have committed fornication, and with the wine of whose fornication the dwellers on earth have become drunk." 3 And he carried me away in the Spirit into a wilderness, and I saw a woman sitting on a scarlet beast which was full of blasphemous names, and it had seven heads and ten horns. 4 The woman was arrayed in purple and scarlet, and bedecked with gold and jewels and pearls, holding in her hand a golden cup full of abominations and the impurities of her fornica-tion; 5 and on her forehead was written a name of mystery: "Babylon the great, mother of harlots and of earth's abominations." 6 And I saw the woman, drunk with the blood of the saints and the blood of the martyrs of Jesus.

When I saw her I marveled greatly. 7 But the angel said to me, "Why marvel? I will tell you the mystery of the woman, and of the beast with seven heads and ten horns that carries her. 8 The beast that you saw was, and is not, and is to ascend from the bottomless pit and go to perdition; and the dwellers on earth whose names have not been written in the book of life from the foundation of the world, will marvel to behold the beast, because it was and is not and is to come. 9 This calls for a mind with wisdom: the seven heads are seven mountains on which the woman is seated; 10 they are also seven kings, five of whom have fallen, one is, the other has not yet come, and when he comes he must remain only a little while. 11 As for the beast that was and is not, it is an eighth but it belongs to the seven, and it goes to perdi-tion. 12 And the ten horns that you saw are ten kings who have not yet received royal power, but they are to receive authority as kings for one hour, together with the beast. 13 These are of one mind and give over their power and authority to the beast; 14 they will make war on the Lamb, and the Lamb will conquer them, for he is Lord of lords and King of kings, and those with him are called and chosen and faithful."

15　　And he said to me, "The waters that you saw, where the harlot is seated, are peoples and multitudes and nations and tongues. 16 And the ten horns that you saw, they and the beast will hate the harlot; they will make her desolate and naked, and devour her flesh and burn her up with fire, 17 for God has put it into their hearts to carry out his purpose by being of one mind and giving over their royal power to the beast, until the words of God shall be fulfilled. 18 And the woman that you saw is the great city which has dominion over the kings of the earth."

Chapter 18

1　　After this I saw another angel coming down from heaven, having great authority; and the earth was made bright with his splendor. 2 And he called out with a mighty voice,

　　"Fallen, fallen is Babylon the great! It has become a dwelling place of demons, a haunt of every foul spirit, a haunt of every foul and hateful bird; 3 for all nations have drunk the wine of her impure passion, and the kings of the earth have committed fornication with her, and the merchants of the earth have grown rich with the wealth of her wantonness."

4　　Then I heard another voice from heaven saying,

　　"Come out of her, my people, lest you take part in her sins, lest you share in her plagues; 5 for her sins are heaped high as heaven, and God has remembered her iniquities. 6 Render to her as she herself has rendered, and repay her double for her deeds; mix a double draught for her in the cup she mixed. 7 As she glorified herself and played the wanton, so give her a like measure of torment and mourning. Since in her heart she says, 'A queen I sit, I am no widow, mourning I shall never see,' 8 so shall her plagues come in a single day, pestilence and mourning and famine, and she shall be burned with fire; for mighty is the Lord God who judges her."

9　　And the kings of the earth, who committed fornication and were wanton with her, will weep and wail over her when they see the smoke of her burning; 10 they will stand far off, in fear of her torment, and say, "Alas! alas! thou great city, thou mighty city, Babylon! In one hour has thy judgment come."

11   And the merchants of the earth weep and mourn for her, since no one buys their cargo any more, 12 cargo of gold, silver, jewels and pearls, fine linen, purple, silk and scarlet, all kinds of scented wood, all articles of ivory, all articles of costly wood, bronze, iron and marble, 13 cinnamon, spice, incense, myrrh, frankincense, wine, oil, fine flour and wheat, cattle and sheep, horses and chariots, and slaves, that is, human souls.

14   "The fruit for which thy soul longed has gone from thee, and all thy dainties and thy splendor are lost to thee, never to be found again!"

15   The merchants of these wares, who gained wealth from her, will stand far off, in fear of her torment, weeping and mourning aloud,

16   "Alas, alas, for the great city that was clothed in fine linen, in purple and scarlet, bedecked with gold, with jewels, and with pearls! 17 In one hour all this wealth has been laid waste."

        And all shipmasters and seafaring men, sailors and all whose trade is on the sea, stood far off 18 and cried out as they saw the smoke of her burning, "What city was like the great city?" 19 And they threw dust on their heads, as they wept and mourned, crying out, "Alas, alas, for the great city where all who had ships at sea grew rich by her wealth! In one hour she has been laid waste. 20 Rejoice over her, O heaven, O saints and apostles and prophets, for God has given judgment for you against her!"

21   Then a mighty angel took up a stone like a great millstone and threw it into the sea, saying, "So shall Babylon the great city be thrown down with violence, and shall be found no more; 22 and the sound of harpers and minstrels, of flute players and trumpeters, shall be heard in thee no more; and a craftsman of any craft shall be found in thee no more; and the sound of the millstone shall be heard in thee no more; 23 and the light of a lamp shall shine in thee no more; and the voice of bridegroom and bride shall be heard in thee no more; for thy merchants were the great men of the earth, and all nations were deceived by thy sorcery. 24 And in her was found the blood of prophets and of saints, and of all who have been slain on earth."

Chapter 19

1   After this I heard what seemed to be the loud voice of a great multitude in heaven, crying, "Hallelujah! Salvation and glory and power belong to our God, 2 for his judgments are true and just; he has judged the great harlot who corrupted the earth with her fornication, and he has avenged on her the blood of his servants." 3 Once more they cried, "Hallelujah! The smoke from

her goes up for ever and ever." 4 And the twenty-four elders and the four living creatures fell down and worshiped God who is seated on the throne, saying, "Amen. Hallelujah!" 5 And from the throne came a voice crying, "Praise our God, all you his servants, you who fear him, small and great." 6 Then I heard what seemed to be the voice of a great multitude, like the sound of many waters and like the sound of mighty thunderpeals, crying, "Hallelujah! For the Lord our God the Almighty reigns. 7 Let us rejoice and exult and give him the glory, for the marriage of the Lamb has come, and his Bride has made herself ready; 8 it was granted her to be clothed with fine linen, bright and pure"-- for the fine linen is the righteous deeds of the saints.

9   And the angel said to me, "Write this: Blessed are those who are invited to the marriage supper of the Lamb." And he said to me, "These are true words of God." 10 Then I fell down at his feet to worship him, but he said to me, "You must not do that! I am a fellow servant with you and your brethren who hold the testimony of Jesus. Worship God." For the testimony of Jesus is the spirit of prophecy.

11   Then I saw heaven opened, and behold, a white horse! He who sat upon it is called Faithful and True, and in righteousness he judges and makes war.   12 His eyes are like a flame of fire, and on his head are many diadems; and he has a name inscribed which no one knows but himself. 13 He is clad in a robe dipped in blood, and the name by which he is called is The Word of God. 14 And the armies of heaven, arrayed in fine linen, white and pure, followed him on white horses. 15 From his mouth issues a sharp sword with which to smite the nations, and he will rule them with a rod of iron; he will tread the wine press of the fury of the wrath of God the Almighty. 16 On his robe and on his thigh he has a name inscribed, King of kings and Lord of lords.

17   Then I saw an angel standing in the sun, and with a loud voice he called to all the birds that fly in midheaven, "Come, gather for the great supper of God, 18 to eat the flesh of kings, the flesh of captains, the flesh of mighty men, the flesh of horses and their riders, and the flesh of all men, both free and slave, both small and great." 19 And I saw the beast and the kings of the earth with their armies gathered to make war against him who sits upon the horse and against his army. 20 And the beast was captured, and with it the false prophet who in its presence had worked the signs by which he deceived those who had received the mark of the beast and those who worshiped its image. These two were thrown alive into the lake of fire that burns with sulphur. 21 And the rest were slain by the sword of him who sits upon the

horse, the sword that issues from his mouth; and all the birds were gorged with their flesh.

Chapter 20

1   Then I saw an angel coming down from heaven, holding in his hand the key of the bottomless pit and a great chain. 2 And he seized the dragon, that ancient serpent, who is the Devil and Satan, and bound him for a thousand years, 3 and threw him into the pit, and shut it and sealed it over him, that he should deceive the nations no more, till the thousand years were ended. After that he must be loosed for a little while.
4   Then I saw thrones, and seated on them were those to whom judgment was committed. Also I saw the souls of those who had been beheaded for their testimony to Jesus and for the word of God, and who had not worshipped the beast or its image and had not received its mark on their foreheads or their hands. They came to life, and reigned with Christ a thousand years. 5 The rest of the dead did not come to life until the thousand years were ended. This is the first resurrection. 6 Blessed and holy is he who shares in the first resurrection! Over such the second death has no power, but they shall be priests of God and of Christ, and they shall reign with him a thousand years.
7   And when the thousand years are ended, Satan will be loosed from his prison 8 and will come out to deceive the nations which are at the four corners of the earth, that is, Gog and Magog, to gather them for battle; their number is like the sand of the sea. 9 And they marched up over the broad earth and surrounded the camp of the saints and the beloved city; but fire came down from heaven and consumed them, 10 and the devil who had deceived them was thrown into the lake of fire and brimstone where the beast and the false prophet were, and they will be tormented day and night for ever and ever.
11   Then I saw a great white throne and him who sat upon it; from his presence earth and sky fled away, and no place was found for them.
12   And I saw the dead, great and small, standing before the throne, and books were opened. Also another book was opened, which is the **Book of life**. And the dead were judged by what was written in the books, by what they had done. 13 And the sea gave up the dead in it, Death and Hades gave up the dead in them, and all were judged by what they had done. 14 Then Death and Hades were thrown into the lake of fire. This is the second death, the lake

of fire; 15 and if any one's name was not found written in the book of life, he was thrown into the lake of fire.

Chapter 21

1   Then I saw a new heaven and a new earth; for the first heaven and the first earth had passed away, and the sea was no more. 2 And I saw the holy city, new Jerusalem, coming down out of heaven from God, prepared as a bride adorned for her husband; 3 and I heard a loud voice from the throne saying, "Behold, the dwelling of God is with men. He will dwell with them, and they shall be his people, and God himself will be with them; 4 he will wipe away every tear from their eyes, and death shall be no more, neither shall there be mourning nor crying nor pain any more, for the former things have passed away."

5   And **he** who sat upon the throne said, "**Behold**, I make all things new." Also he said, "Write this, for these words are trustworthy and true." 6 And he said to me, "It is done! I am the Alpha and the Omega, the beginning and the end. To the thirsty I will give from the fountain of the water of life without payment. 7 He who conquers shall have this heritage, and I will be his God and he shall be my son. 8 But as for the cowardly, the faithless, the polluted, as for murderers, fornicators, sorcerers, idolaters, and all liars, their lot shall be in the lake that burns with fire and brimstone, which is the second death."

9   Then came one of the seven angels who had the seven bowls full of the seven last plagues, and spoke to me, saying, "Come, I will show you the Bride, the wife of the Lamb." 10 And in the Spirit he carried me away to a great, high mountain, and showed me the holy city Jerusalem coming down out of heaven from God, 11 having the glory of God, its radiance like a most rare jewel, like a jasper, clear as crystal. 12 It had a great, high wall, with twelve gates, and at the gates twelve angels, and on the gates the names of the twelve tribes of the sons of Israel were inscribed; 13 on the east three gates, on the north three gates, on the south three gates, and on the west three gates. 14 And the wall of the city had twelve foundations, and on them the twelve names of the twelve apostles of the Lamb.

15   And he who talked to me had a measuring rod of gold to measure the city and its gates and walls. 16 The city lies foursquare, its length the same as its breadth; and he measured the city with his rod, twelve thousand stadia; its length and breadth and height are equal. 17 He also measured its wall, a

hundred and forty-four cubits by a man's measure, that is, an angel's. 18 The wall was built of jasper, while the city was pure gold, clear as glass. 19 The foundations of the wall of the city were adorned with every jewel; the first was jasper, the second sapphire, the third agate, the fourth emerald, 20 the fifth onyx, the sixth carnelian, the seventh chrysolite, the eighth beryl, the ninth topaz, the tenth chrysoprase, the eleventh jacinth, the twelfth amethyst. 21 And the twelve gates were twelve pearls, each of the gates made of a single pearl, and the street of the city was pure gold, transparent as glass.

22   And I saw no temple in the city, for its temple is the Lord God the Almighty and the Lamb. 23 And the city has no need of sun or moon to shine upon it, for the glory of God is its light, and its lamp is the Lamb. 24 By its light shall the nations walk; and the kings of the earth shall bring their glory into it, 25 and its gates shall never be shut by day--and there shall be no night thoro; 26 they shall bring into it the glory and the honor of the nations. 27 But nothing unclean shall enter it, nor any one who practices abomination or falsehood, but only those who are written in the Lamb's book of life.

Chapter 22

1   Then he showed me the river of the water of life, bright as crystal, flowing from the throne of God and of the Lamb 2 through the middle of the street of the city; also, on either side of the river, the tree of life with its twelve kinds of fruit, yielding its fruit each month; and the leaves of the tree were for the healing of the nations. 3 There shall no more be anything accursed, but the throne of God and of the Lamb shall be in it, and his servants shall worship him; 4 they shall see his face, and his name shall be on their foreheads. 5 And night shall be no more; they need no light of lamp or sun, for the Lord God will be their light, and they shall reign for ever and ever.

6   And he said to me, "These words are trustworthy and true. And the Lord, the God of the spirits of the prophets, has sent his angel to show his servants what must soon take place. 7 And behold, I am coming soon."

Blessed is he who keeps the words of the prophecy of this book.

8   I John am he who heard and saw these things. And when I heard and saw them, I fell down to worship at the feet of the angel who showed them to me; 9 but he said to me, "You must not do that! I am a fellow servant with you and your brethren the prophets, and with those who keep the words of this book. Worship God."

10   And he said to me, "Do not seal up the words of the prophecy of this

book, for the time is near. 11 Let the evildoer still do evil, and the filthy still be filthy, and the righteous still do right, and the holy still be holy."

12   "Behold, I am coming soon, bringing my recompense, to repay every one for what he has done. 13 I am the Alpha and the Omega, the first and the last, the beginning and the end."

14   Blessed are those who wash their robes, that they may have the right to the tree of life and that they may enter the city by the gates. 15 Outside are the dogs and sorcerers and fornicators and murderers and idolaters, and every one who loves and practices falsehood.

16   "I **Jesus** have sent my angel to you with this testimony for the churches. I am the root and the offspring of David, the bright morning star."

17   The Spirit and the Bride say, "**Come**." And let him who hears say, "Come." And let him who is thirsty come, let him who desires take the water of life without price.

18   I warn every one who hears the words of the prophecy of this book: if any one adds to them, God will add to him the plagues described in this book, 19 and if any one takes away from the words of the book of this prophecy, God will take away his share in the tree of life and in the holy city, which are described in this book.

20   He who testifies to these things says, "Surely I am coming soon." Amen. Come, Lord Jesus!

21   The grace of the Lord Jesus be with all the saints. Amen.

REFERENCES
Chapter 1
1963

Kennedy John F. *Profiles in Courage.* Harper & Brothers, New York, 1956.

Time Magazine, Election Extra Edition, November 16, 1960.

Kennedy John F. Inaugural Address, The Washington Post, January 21, 1961.

*Kennedy John F. Televised address on the Cuban Missile Crisis, October 22, 1962, courtesy of the John Fitzgerald Kennedy Library, Columbia Point, Boston, Massachusetts 02125.

*Kennedy John F. Commencement address at American University, June 10, 1963 (on world peace), courtesy of the John Fitzgerald Kennedy Library, Boston, Massachusetts.

*Kennedy John F. Televised address, the Civil Rights speech, June 11, 1963, courtesy of the John Fitzgerald Kennedy Library, Boston, Mass.

Clark TC. Supreme Court of the United States. *School District of Abington Township, Pennsylvania v. Schempp* (374 US 203), Decision June 17, 1963.

Black HL. Supreme Court of the United States. *Engel v. Vitale* (370 US 421), Decision June 25, 1962.

*King, Martin Luther. *I Have A Dream* speech, The Lincoln Memorial, August 28, 1963.Washington, D. C. (live, and multiple sources).

*Mansfield, M. Eulogy for JFK. The original daily edition of the Washington Post, November 25, 1963.

The original daily edition of the Washington Sunday Star, November 24, 1963.

The original daily editions of the Washington Post, November 23 and 25, 1963.

Time Magazine, November 29, 1963 weekly issue.

Time Magazine, January 3, 1964, Martin Luther King, 1963 Time's Man of the Year.

Schlesinger AM, Jr. *A Thousand Days - John F. Kennedy in the White House.* Houghton Mifflin Company, Boston, 1965.

Sorensen TC. *Kennedy.* Harper & Row, New York, 1965.

Kennedy, Robert F. *Thirteen Days - A Memoir of the Cuban Missile Crisis.* WW Norton, New York, 1968.

Kunhardt, PB (ed). LIFE *in Camelot - The Kennedy Years* , Time-Life, New York, 1988.

Daniel C (ed): Chronicle of the 20th Century. Dorling Kindersley, London, 1995

Ravitch D., editor. *The American Reader - Words that Moved a Nation.* Harper Perennial, New York, 1990.

MacSiccar I. *John F. Kennedy.* JG Press, publisher, copyright Brompton Books Corporation, Greenwich, Connecticut, 1995.

Warner, J. *Billboard's American Rock 'n' Roll in Review.* Schirmer Books, New York,1997.

Whitburn J. *Joel Whitburn's Billboard Top Pop Albums 1955-1996.* Record Research, Menomonee Falls, Wisconsin, 1996.

Brooks T, Marsh E. Complete Directory to Prime Time TV Shows. Ballantine Books, New York, First Edition, 1979, Sixth Edition, 1985

*original text

Chapter 2
Life in America

Haddad LM, Shannon MW, Winchester JF (eds): *Clinical Management of Poisoning and Drug Overdose,* Third Edition. WB Saunders, Philadelphia, 1998, particularly these chapters: Schwartz M. Opiates and Narcotics; Martin B, Szara S. Marijuana; Albertson TE, Marelich GP, Tharratt RS. Cocaine; Kleinschmidt KC, Delaney KA. Ethanol.

Fauci AS, Lane HC. HIV Disease and AIDS, in Fauci AS et al (Eds): *Harrison's Principles of Internal Medicine*, 14th Edition, McGraw-Hill, New York, 1998.

Bartlett JG, Fauci AS, Feinberg MB et al. Report of the NIH Panel to define Principles of Therapy of HIV infection and Guidelines for the Use of Antiretroviral Agents in HIV-infected Adults and Adolescents. Annals of Internal Medicine 128:1057-1100, 15 June 1998.

Miller KD, Polis MA. Approach to the Patient with HIV infection and AIDS, in Howell JM et al (eds): *Emergency Medicine.* WB Saunders Company, Philadelphia, 1998.

AIDS 12 suppl (1): S_1-S_2, 1998.

Communicable Disease Center. Morbidity and Mortality Weekly Review (MMWR) 47: April 24, 1998.

HIV/AIDS Rx Information Service Website June 17, 1998 (http://www.hivatis.org).

Warren E, Russell RB, Cooper JS, Boggs H, Ford GR, Dulles AW, McCloy JJ. The Warren Commission Report: Report of the President's Commission on the Assassination of President John F. Kennedy - original release, September 24, 1964. Reprint of Official & Complete Unabridged edition, St. Martin's Press, New York.

Lane, Mark. *Rush to Judgement. A Critique of the Warren Commission Inquiry.* Holt, Rinehart and Winston, New York, 1966.

Garrison J. *On the Trail of the Assassins.* Sheridan Square Press, New York, 1988.

Marrs J. *Crossfire.* Carroll & Graf Publishers, New York, 1989.

Prouty LF. *JFK. The CIA, Vietnam and the Plot to Assassinate John F. Kennedy.* Birch Lane Press, Carol Publishing Group, New York, 1992.
Scheim DE. *Contract on America.* Shapolsky, New York, 1988.

Emery F. *Watergate.* Touchstone, Simon & Schuster, New York, 1995.

The original daily edition of the Savannah Morning News, December 2, 1997.
The original daily edition of the Savannah Morning News, March 25-26, 1998
The internet edition of the Denver Post, April 20-27, 1999

Chapter 3
Selected References on Near-Death Experiences

Moody, Raymond A., Jr., M. D.
Life After Life - The Investigation of a Phenomenon -Survival of Bodily Death. Mockingbird Books, Marietta, Georgia, 1975.
Reflections on Life After Life. Bantam Books, New York, 1977.

James, William. *The Varieties of Religious Experience - a Study in Human Nature.* MacMillan, New York, 1902.

Plato. *The Republic.* Harvard Classics, P. F. Collier& Sons, New York, 1909.

New American Bible, St. Joseph's Edition- Catholic Publishing, New York, 1975. The Authorized King James Version of the Holy Bible - Mid America Bible Society, Gordonsville, Tennessee, 1993. The Holy Scripture - Jewish Publication Society of America, Philadelphia, 1993.

Dante A. *The Divine Comedy.* Italy, 1608-1620. Modern translation by John Ciardi, Penguin, New York, 1970.

Morse, Melvin, MD
A Near-Death Experience in a 7-year-old child. Am J Dis Child 137:959-961, 1983.
Closer to the Light.. Ivy Books, Random House, New York, 1990.

Owens JE, Cook EW, Stevenson I. Features of "near-death experience" in relation to whether or not patients were near-death. Lancet 336:1175-1177, 1990.

Greyson, Bruce MD
    Distressing Near-Death Experiences. Psychiatry 55:95-110, 1992.
    Varieties of Near-Death Experiences. Psychiatry 56:390-99, 1993.
Sabom, M. *Recollections of Death.* Harper & Row, New York, 1982.

Penfield W. *The Mystery of the Mind: A Critical Study of Consciousness and the Human Brain.* Princeton University Press, Princeton, NJ, 1975

Personal Interviews.

Chapter 4
The Bible

The Holy Bible. Old Testamont in the Douay Challoner Text, New Testament and Psalms in the Confraternity Text. Catholic Press, Chicago, Illinols, 1950.

New American Bible, St.Joseph Edition. Catholic Publishing, New York, 1975

The Revised Standard Version of the Holy Bible, St. Ignatius Catholic Edition, Ignatius Press, San Francisco, 1966.

The Douay-Rheims Holy Bible. Old Testament, English College of Douai, 1609; New Testament, English College of Rheims, France, 1582. Revision, Bishop Challoner, 1749-1752, England. John Murphy Co., Baltimore, Maryland, 1914

The Authorized King James Version of the Holy Bible. England, 1611 Mid America Bible Society, Gordonsville, Tennessee, 1993.

The Holy Scripture. Jewish Publication Society of America, Philadelphia, 1993.

The Navarre Bible - St. Mark. Four Courts Press, Dublin, Ireland, 1988.

The New Jerusalem Bible. Doubleday, New York, 1985.

Minto Andrew L. *Introduction to Scripture, Principles of Biblical Study I.*
Miletec, Stephen F. *St. Mark as Catechist, Principles of Biblical Study II.*
Franciscan University, Steubenville, Ohio,
Course lecture texts and notes, 1998 and 1999.

Clifford RJ, Murphy RE, in Brown RE, Fitzmeyer JA, Murphy RE (eds)
The New Jerome Biblical Commentary. Prentice Hall, Englewood
Cliffs, New Jersey, 1990.

Jensen J. *God's Word to Israel.* Liturgical Press, Collegeville, Minnesota,
1988.

Johnson LT. *The Writings of the New Testament.* Fortress Press,
Philadelphia, pages 512-548, 1986.

Rappaport U. *Dead Sea Scrolls.* Israeli Publishing Institute, Jerusalem, 1967.
Reprint. Harvey House, Irvington-on-Hudson, New York.

Vanderkam JC. *The Dead Sea Scrolls Today.* WB Eerdmans Publishing Co.
Grand Rapids, Michigan, 1994.

Vermes G. *The Dead Sea Scrolls in English, 4th Ed.* Penguin, London, 1995.

Josephus Flavius. *Antiquities of the Jews.* Translation by William Whiston,
London, 1733. JC Winston, Philadelphia.

Pope John Paul II. *The Catechism of the Catholic Church.* Catholic Book
Publishing Company, New York, 1992.

Goodspeed EJ. *The Apocrypha.* University of Chicago Press, 1938.
Reprint. Vintage/Random House, New York, 1959.

Meeks WA (ed) and the Society of Biblical Literature: *The Harper Collins
New Revised Standard Version Study Bible, with Apocrypha/
Deuterocanonical books.* Harper Collins Publishers, London, 1993.

Ware T. *The Orthodox Church.* Penguin Books, New York, 1978.

Chapter 5
The Rosary and the Apparitions of Mary

Anonymous. *Words from Heaven.* St. James Publishing, Sterrett, Alabama 35147.

Barbaric, S   *In the School of Love.* Faith Publishing, Milford, Ohio, 1993.

Connell JT   *Visions of the Children.* St. Martin's Press, New York, 1992
Meetings with Mary. Random House, New York, 1995.

Delaney JJ   *A Woman Clothed with the Sun..* Doubleday, New York, 1960 and 1990.

Flynn T, M.   *Thunder of Justice.* MaxKol Comm. Sterling, Virginia, 1993.

Foley, Fr. R   *Drama of Medjugorje.* Veritas, Dublin, Ireland, 1992.

Johnston F.   *The Wonder of Guadalupe.* Tan Books & Publishers, Rockford, Illinois, 1981

LeBlanc, F   *Cause of our Joy.*   Pauline Books & Media, Boston, 1991.

Petrisko TW   *Call of the Ages.* Queenship Publishing, Santa Barbara, California, 1995.

Walsh, WT.   *Our Lady of Fatima.* Image, Doubleday, 1947 and 1990.

Weible W.   *Medjugorje, the Message.* Paraclete Press, Massachusetts, 1989.

Clark AC.   *Bosnia - what every American should know.* Berkley Books, New York, 1996.

Karahasan D. *Sarajevo, Exodus of a City.* Kodansha International, New York, 1994.

Drakulic S.   *The Balkan Express.* Harper Perennial, New York, 1994.

Chapter 6
The Culture of Life

Thomas Jefferson et al. *The Declaration of Independence.* World Book
    Encyclopedia, Chicago, 1990.

James Madison et al. *The Constitution of the United States.* World Book
    Encyclopedia, Chicago, 1990.

Anonymous. American History You Never Learned. St. James Publishing,
    Sterrett, Alabama, 1993.

Reich WT. *Encyclopedia of Bioethics,* Revised Edition. Simon & Schuster
    MacMIllan,New York, 1995.

John Paul II. *Evangelium Vitae (The Gospel of Life).* Times Books,
    Random House, New York, 1995

Beauchamp TL, Childress JF. *Principles of Biomedical Ethics*, 4th Edition.
    Oxford University Press, 1994.

Milton, John. *Paradise Lost.* London, 1667. Reprint, The Harvard Classics,
    P. F. Collier & Sons, New York, 1909.

Shelley, Mary. *Frankenstein or, The Modern Prometheus.* Lackington,
    Hughes,Harding, Mavor, and Jones, London, 1818. Reprint, New
    American Library, New York, 1963.

Marvell, Andrew. *A Dialogue Between the Soul and Body.* Notes from
    English Literature Class, Holy Cross College, Massachusetts, 1960.

Cover story, *The Pope's Plea .* Society: Life, Death, and the Pope.
    Newsweek, April 10, 1995.

News Release. Vatican calls for global ban on human cloning. February 26,
    1997.

Time Magazine. *Will There Ever Be Another You - A Special Report on Cloning.* March 10, 1997.

Land RD. Statement on Human Cloning of the Southern Baptist Convention. Light, July-August, 1997.

Headline story, *Supreme Court's rejection of assisted suicide leaves door ajar.* American Medical News 40:26, July 14, 1997

Foley KM. Competent Care for the Dying instead of physician-assisted suicide. New Engl J Med 336:54-58, 1997.

Gates TJ. Euthanasia and Assisted Suicide. Amer Family Phys 55:2437-2444, 1997.

Hanauske-Abel HM. Not a slippery slope or sudden subversion: German medicine. National socialism in 1933. BMJ 313:1453-1462, 1996.

Rehnquist WH. Supreme Court of the United States, State of *Washington v. H. Gluckberg* (96-110) on writ of certiorari to US court of appeals for the Ninth Circuit, Argument January 8, 1997, Decision June 26, 1997.

Rehnquist WH. Supreme Court, *Vacco,* Attorney General, State of New York *v. Quill* (95-1858), certiorari to the US Court of Appeals for the Second Circuit, Argument January 8, 1997, Decision June 26, 1997.

Kubler-Ross E. *On Death and Dying.* MacMillan, New York, 1969.

Blackmun J. Supreme Court of the United States. *Roe v. Wade,* District Attorney of Dallas (410 US 113), Decision and Dissenting opinions, January 22, 1973.

Blackmun J. Supreme Court of the United States. *Doe v. Bolton,* Attorney General of Georgia (410 US 179), Decision and Dissenting Opinions, January 22, 1973.

Wilmut I, Schnieke AE, McWhir J, Kind AJ, Campbell KHS. Viable offspring derived from fetal and adult mammalian cells. Nature 385:810-813, 1997.

Chapter 7
Save Our Nation

Mother Teresa. *A Simple Path*. Ballantine Books, New York, 1995.
Mother Teresa. *The Joy in Loving.* Penguin, New York, 1996.
Mother Teresa. *No Greater Love.* New World Library, Novato, Calif, 1997.

Gibran K. *The Prophet.* Albert A. Knopf, New York, 1970.

Untermeyer L. *Treasury of Great Poems.* Galahad Books, New York, 1993.

Shakespeare W. *The Merchant of Venice.* Stratford-upon-Avon, written and
    produced, 1597; published, 1600. Bantam, New York, 1980.

Coleridge ST. *The Rime of the Ancient Mariner.* Published, 1798.
            in *Coleridge.* Everyman's Library, AA Knopf, New York, 1997.

Miller JM (ed). *The Encyclicals of John Paul II.* Our Sunday Visitor,
    Huntingdon, Indiana, 1996.
Martinez LM. *The Sanctifier, The Holy Spirit.* Pauline Books, Boston, 1982.

Graham, Billy. *Angels.* Word Publishing, Dallas, 1975 and 1994.
Graham, Billy. *Storm Warning.* Word Publishing, Dallas, Texas 1992.
Graham, Billy. *The Holy Spirit.* Word Publishing, 1997.

O'Sullivan P. *All About the Angels.* St. Martin de Porres Apostolate, Dublin,
    1945. Reprint. Tan Publishers, Rockford, Ill., 1990.
Harvey G. *On the Wings of Angels.* Gramercy, Random House, New York,
    1993
Bunson, M. *The Angelic Doctor* Our Sunday Visitor, Huntingdon,
    Indiana, 1994

Aquinas, St. Thomas. *Summa Theologica.* Christian Classics, 1982.

St. Augustine. *The City of God.* Image Doubleday, New York, 1954.

Paul VI. *Humanae Vitae (Of Human Life).* Pauline Books, Boston, 1968.
Lewis CS. *The Four Loves.* Harcourt-Brace, Orlando, Florida, 1960
Maugham WS. *The Razor's Edge.* Doubleday, New York, 1944.

GOD BLESS AMERICA

This patriotic song was composed by Irving Berlin, and was first sung by Kate Smith on November 11, 1938. Irving Berlin was a generous man, and donated the royalties of this song to the Boy Scouts and Girl Scouts of America. It has become our unofficial national anthem.

God Bless America,
Land that I love.
Stand beside her,
And guide her,
Through the night
With the Light from above,
From the mountains,
To the prairies,
To the ocean,
White with foam,
God bless America,
My home sweet home.
God bless America,
My home sweet home.